GERMAN MINORITIES
AND THE THIRD REICH

GERMAN MINORITIES AND THE THIRD REICH

Ethnic Germans
of East Central Europe
between the Wars

Anthony Komjathy
and
Rebecca Stockwell

HM
HOLMES & MEIER PUBLISHERS, INC.
NEW YORK ● LONDON

First published in the United States of America 1980 by
Holmes & Meier Publishers, Inc.
30 Irving Place
New York, N.Y. 10003

Great Britain:
Holmes & Meier Publishers, Ltd.
131 Trafalgar Road
Greenwich, London SE10 9TX

Library of Congress Cataloging in Publication Data

Komjathy, Anthony Tihamer.
  German minorities and the Third Reich.

  Bibliography: p.
  Includes index.
  1. Germans in Eastern Europe—History. 2. Germans
in Central Europe—History. 3. Europe, Eastern—Politics
and government. 4. Central Europe—Politics and government.
5. National socialism. I. Stockwell, Rebecca,
joint author. II. Title.
DJK28.G4K65   943'.00431   79-26520

ISBN 0-8419-0540-1

Manufactured in the United States of America

Contents

Acknowledgments

In order to re-create thoroughly and realistically the conditions and circumstances of our subject, it was necessary to review in detail not only the published documents of the period, but also the unpublished documents, notes, and correspondence of the different ethnic German groups. This tremendous job could not have been completed without the help of others. It is our pleasure here to express gratitude for their help.

We would like to mention first of all Professor Hans Booms, president of the Bundesarchiv in Koblenz. His unconditional support of our work, as well as his permission to read through all the confidential sources, helped us greatly to understand the problems. Archivrat R. Hofmann, by calling our attention to many files of archive material, saved us considerable time and energy and made it possible for us to arrive at more objective interpretations.

We received similar wholehearted cooperation from the director of the Politisches Archiv des Auswärtigen Amtes, Professor Klaus Weinandy. We would like to express here our gratitude to him, as well as to Dr. Maria Keipert, who patiently fulfilled our requests for sources.

Professor Stephen Fischer-Galati read our manuscript. Thanks to his suggestions and comments, we eliminated some of the shortcomings of our study.

Professor Walter Gray of Loyola University of Chicago read large portions of our manuscript and helped us greatly with his remarks and positive criticism.

Because of the tremendous quantity of sources, it is possible that we overlooked some data, which could create an impression of bias and a lack of objectivity. If that happened, it was entirely accidental and unintentional.

Introduction

One of the topics of recent European history that has received great attention here and abroad is the role of German minority groups in East Central Europe before and during World War II. Generalizations made under the influence of wartime propaganda created a stereotype of German minority behavior according to which all ethnic Germans were fanatical supporters of Hitler, promoters of Nazism, obedient servants of the Third Reich's imperialistic foreign policy, and, during the war, a fifth column of the advancing German armies. These accusations of the German minorities, which had lived in East Central Europe for centuries, were used to justify their mass expulsion after the war.[1]

The ethnic Germans defended themselves with countercharges. They stated that they were the victims of prejudicial generalizations, that they had only fought against the forced assimilation attempts of their respective governments, and that they had, in the majority, remained loyal to the state in which they lived. Thus their mass expulsion was vengeful rather than just.

An interesting phenomenon in scholarly treatment of that controversy is that, with few exceptions, the studies describe only the conditions of the different ethnic German groups, treat their leaders' relationships with their respective governments, or review the relationship of these governments to the Third Reich.[2] The crucial question—what was the relationship between the German minority groups and the Third Reich?—is usually omitted. If raised, it is not really answered. Yet the crux of the matter is this: Did the Germans of East Central Europe really work against the interests of their respective countries, or were they actually concerned with not harming them? In other words, did they commit treason, or did they remain loyal citizens?

To answer these questions one must leave the field of history and enter that of philosophy. From the point of view of the governments, it was perhaps desirable to assimilate the ethnic groups in order to create a single, homogeneous nation-state. If assimilation of ethnic groups is acceptable from the moral point of view, what methods may a government use to promote it? On the other hand, does an ethnic group have the right to resist assimilation and in defense of its ethnicity to organize itself into a recognizable cultural entity, into a separate political group or even territory? Furthermore, is the preservation of ethnicity in perpetuity really in the interest of an ethnic group?

It is impossible to answer these questions to everyone's satisfaction, nor do we intend to try. Rather, we would like to point out the depth and complexity of the problem with the help of a short historical review.

When during World War I both sides began to feel the effects of attrition, they sought additional allies not only outside Europe (the United States) but also within the enemy camp. The Allies found support among the bitter, oppressed national minority groups of East Central Europe. To gain their active participation the British and French governments promised them autonomy or even independence. These far-reaching promises, made under the stress of war without any deep study of the situation, received a moral justification from the principle of national self-determination announced by President Woodrow Wilson in his Fourteen Points, January 8, 1918. Once the promises were given a moral basis, they had to be redeemed even if circumstances did not seem to warrant such action. In order to honor their moral commitments and prevent the oppression of the different minority groups in postwar Europe, the peacemakers created minority treaties to protect the rights of these groups.[3]

The moral principles of the minority treaties were these: Minority citizens had equality before the law, the right to use their own language in addressing administrative and judicial authorities, and the right to establish charitable, religious, and educational institutions that used the minority language exclusively. If the number of minority students reached a certain level in the public primary schools, they were entitled to receive instruction in their mother tongue. The minority also had the right to share a proportionate amount of any subvention granted by the state to educational and charitable institutions.

A frequently overlooked, but very important, aspect of these privileges is that they were intended to protect the rights of ethnic *individuals*. It was the right of the individual to decide whether he wanted to keep his ethnic identity by using the privileges described or to assimilate to the majority. In other words, the minority resolutions of the League of Nations were intended to prevent the oppression of minorities, not the assimilation of ethnic groups. Supporters of the League of Nations foresaw the solution of ethnic problems by unavoidable assimilation. "Many groups, such as the German groups of Yugoslavia, will disappear. This will take place more or less rapidly. Also many groups which still exist in Romania, Czechoslovakia, and Hungary will probably be assimilated....There should never be anything but natural assimilation."[4]

There were three serious problems with these minority rights and their interpretation. The first was that the minority treaties were incorporated into clauses of the respective peace treaties. Since the Versailles and related treaties were signed by the defeated nations under pressure, their governments and populaces rejected them *in toto*, and revisionist movements[5] sprang up in Bulgaria, Germany, Hungary, and Poland almost simultaneously with the ratification of the treaties. These revisionist movements naturally rejected the idea that minority status was an individual choice. They demanded the return of the lost territories with their populations. Assimilation woud mean the loss of these territories forever, so the revisionist forces used every available means (legal and illegal) to prevent it.

The second problem was created by the governments of some of the Successor States.[6] They interpreted the incorporation into the treaties of clauses for the protection of minorities as unlawful intrusion into their sovereign rights. As a result, while they accepted on paper the principle of "natural assimilation," in reality they used every available method to force and speed up assimilation and so eliminate as soon as possible the threat of revision. The minority leaders' natural reaction to this policy was a fanatical effort to preserve the ethnicity of their groups, to interpret ethnicity not as an individual concern but as a group interest, and to seek outside aid and support, political and financial, legal and illegal, for the preservation of the ethnic group.

An interesting aspect of the German minority problem is the composition of the groups. They were not racially pure Germans at all, as they claimed to be during the Nazi era. In Silesia, for example, a great number of "ethnic Germans" were germanized Poles. In Czechoslovakia, because of inter-marriage, Czech blood circulated in the veins of a great number of Sudeten Germans. A separate study would be necessary for the examination of the German Jews living outside Germany. Before the Nazi takeover, and even after it, many Jews regarded themselves as Germans of the Jewish religious faith.[7] The governments in eastern Europe knew that, but registered the Jews as a separate nationality group, no matter to what nationality they professed to belong,[8] in order to reduce the number of Germans living in their countries, at least on paper. But the assimilated Jews continued to regard themselves as Germans and many of them played an eminent role in the German ethnic organizations.[9] This attitude of the Jews proves the thesis that nationality is the choice of an individual, as the minority treaties interpreted it. Of course, the German Jews were condemned as aliens by the Nazis, as enemies by the Successor States, and were criticized by the leaders of the Zionist movement.

The third problem was created by the different governments, which disregarded some resolutions of the minority treaties. For various reasons they granted more privileges than they were required to. Romania, for example, allowed the *Deutsche Partei*; the Czechs allowed three different parties organized on the basis of nationality rather than political interest. The governments also allowed neighboring states to give their co-national minorities cultural and economic aid. The *Winterhilfe* for Silesian German coal miners—although illegal according to the minority treaties—was tolerated and so "legalized" by the Polish government. In practice, then, the minority groups were able to maintain close contact with their patron states, contrary to the spirit of the minority treaties. Such contacts naturally strengthened their national consciousness, undermined or prevented develop-ment of unconditional loyalty to the state government, and made them available as an instrument for the pursuit or realization of a revisionist or imperialistic policy. None of the minority groups living in the territory of other states had such a strong patron country as the Germans. Thus the behavior and treatment of the German minority groups became crucial problems in each of the Successor States.

The principles of the minority treaties were so differently interpreted by the parties involved that their actions cannot be judged strictly from a moral, legal, or ideological point of view. At any rate, our purpose in this study is not to pass final judgment. Our intentions are to view, analyze, and investigate the events and their causes; to explore the possible alternative solutions; and to evaluate the activities of the German minority groups in different countries from two utilitarian points of view: (1) How did the policies of the respective governments advance the assimilation of the minority groups, and what was the minority groups' reaction to these policies? (2) How did German policy promote the interest of the ethnic groups living outside Germany? Was the German government really concerned with the interest of German minorities, or did the Third Reich only use the German minority groups as an instrument in its struggle for the conquest of Europe?

CHAPTER I

Germany's Concern for Germans Abroad

Before 1933

German settlements in the different regions of East Central Europe were very numerous, and their history reached back to the fourteenth century. From that time on Germans migrated in large groups toward the east to escape the often miserable living conditions at home and to enjoy the special economic and political privileges offered them by the kings of Hungary and Poland. Then in the seventeenth century, after the end of the long Turkish occupation of Hungary, the Habsburgs resettled many of their German subjects in the liberated areas[1] simply to repopulate them.

These German settlers "maintained but few contacts with Germany itself: and on the whole, Germans living in Germany did not have any strong interest in the fate of their sons and daughters who migrated abroad."[2] These "sons and daughters" displayed an equal indifference toward their kinsmen in Germany. During the 1848 Hungarian revolution many of these German settlers, as well as volunteers from Germany proper, fought against Habsburg absolutism on the side of the Hungarian people.[3]

After the defeat of the 1848 revolutions in Germany, "German nationalism lost much of its original liberalism."[4] Intolerant, romantic nationalism soon gave birth to the movement of pan-Germanism. During the era of Emperor Wilhelm II German official policy displayed only a negative attitude toward the east and the Balkans, that is, the goal was to keep the Russians out. Private societies such as the *Alldeutscher Verband* (better known as the Pan-German League) aimed at the creation of a great Germany, which would include all Germans and German-inhabited territories "regardless of geographies and sovereignties."[5] The League succeeded in creating some interest in Germany concerning the *Auslandsdeutsche*, who were Germans who lived elsewhere, whether as citizens of Germany or the other country.

After World War I, because of the decision of the peacemakers to abandon the idea of plebiscites, numerous German groups were incorporated into France, Czechoslovakia, and Poland.[6] These Germans were *Reichsdeutsche*, citizens of Germany. They did not have any chance to express their will freely. Overnight—by decision of the peacemakers—they became citizens of a foreign state. What was even more shocking to them, they became a minority. Many of them chose to leave their homes and migrate to Germany. Others stayed and continued their lives as citizens of new states, hoping that the minority treaties would protect their rights.

Under the influence of popular nationalism the new governments of the Successor States tried to convince the minorities to give up their native identity, customs, and culture and to assimilate to the state nationality group. These assimilation attempts created different reactions within the German minorities. The most uncompromising ones left their homes and migrated to Germany,[7] where they joined their compatriots who had escaped to Germany before the Successor States occupied the territories. These new immigrants joined the revisionist forces and became supporters of the dying pan-German associations. Those who remained in the Successor States split into two groups. The militants began to organize themselves against the "degermanizing" policy of the state, while the others tried to work out a *modus vivendi* with the new state authorities.

This division of the Germans formerly enjoying a privileged status within the German and Habsburg empires produced far-reaching consequences both at home and abroad. Now for the first time there were Germans living in Germany who had a strong interest in the fate of the minorities living in the Successor States. They hoped to realize their dream: revision of the peace treaties in cooperation with the German minorities. Numerous members of the German minority groups had personal contact with Germans living in Germany. Many of them sought their help and expected their deliverance through close cooperation with these *Reichsdeutsche*.

Nineteenth-century pan-German ideas were revived and the old organizations, such as the *Verein für das Deutschtum im Ausland* (VDA, Association for Germans Abroad, founded in 1881) and the *Alldeutscher Verband* (General German Associations, founded in 1890), became active again. New organizations, such as the *Deutsche Schutzbund* (German Defense League, founded in 1919), and the *Deutsche Auslandinstitut* (DAI, German Foreign Institute, founded in 1917), extended the fields of concern of the *Reichsdeutsche*. They wanted to serve the interest not only of those Germans who lived in territories formerly belonging to the German and Habsburg empires, but also of those Germans whose ancestors had migrated abroad centuries before and who lived in different sovereign countries. The DAI wanted to prevent the degermanization of these *Volksdeutsche* (Germans who were citizens of other countries), to reawaken and strengthen their German self-consciousness, and thus to save them for Germandom. Besides these associations, close to a hundred, less influential social, political, and religious organizations competed for the support of the "patriotic" *Reichsdeutsche* in order to help the *Auslandsdeutsche*. Before the end of World War I almost all of these organizations had enjoyed the moral and financial support of the Imperial government.

The minority treaties, however, made the support of the openly pan-German and revisionist organizations a sensitive and risky undertaking for the new Republican government. The protection and representation of ethnic Germans living outside of Germany were forbidden by the peace treaty, and thus only cultural, religious, and charitable contacts were permitted. These restrictions narrowed the number of organizations that could be supported by the government without taking political risks, and the DAI and the VDA became predominant.

The DAI had its headquarters in Stuttgart in the Haus des Deutschtums and published a scholarly journal entitled *Der Auslandsdeutsche*. The DAI organized lectures and exchanges of scholars with the German organizations of East Central Europe, led trips to foreign countries, and invited student groups to visit Germany. Since it had no goals other than the preservation of Germandom (that is, of German citizens living abroad), it did not take part in politics—it did not attempt to undermine the loyalty of ethnic Germans toward the state in which they lived. Its activities were tolerated but carefully watched by the foreign governments.

The VDA also declared in its constitution that "the Association does not pursue political, sociopolitical, or confessional goals."[8] Faithful to its original aims, it supported the schools, libraries, cultural associations, choirs, and other organizations of German minority groups. It also organized trips abroad and held lectures.

Meanwhile, the old pan-German associations began to lose public support and membership. Membership in the Pan-German League, for example, declined from 40,000 in 1922 to 8,000 in 1933.[9] Some of the more radical members joined the Nazi movement; others swelled the membership of the VDA, which increased from 100,000 in 1914 to 2,000,000 in 1926.[10] Although Gustav Stresemann, who started out as a pan-Germanist,[11] left the movement, he continued to believe in a strong, imperialistic German foreign policy and became a staunch supporter of the DAI and VDA. In December 1928, at the VDA's annual meeting, the membership expressed gratitude to Stresemann "for his foreign policy, which strengthened the confidence of the *Auslandsdeutsche* in the German motherland."[12] The VDA should have thanked Stresemann for much more. He had secured secret funds from his government and organized the OSSA *Vermittelungs und Handelsgesellschaft m.b.h.*, a cover-up limited company, to make financial transactions and "donations" to ethnic German groups.[13]

The income of the VDA grew from the relatively small amount of RM 451,000 in 1923 to the significant sum of RM 1,501,920 in 1925, RM 2,216,765 in 1927, and RM 2,726,825 in 1929.[14] This income was secured from membership fees, commercial transactions, street collections, and various grants and donations. Since the membership fee, RM 1 per year per person, covered only about 12 percent of the total expenses,[15] the VDA had to use different methods to raise money for its purposes. In its fund-raising campaigns it appealed to the patriotism of Germans and painted a grim picture of the sinister forces (foreign governments) that waged a continuous war against Germandom. "One for All and All for One or All of Us Will Go to the Dogs" is the revealing title of one of the VDA's fund-raising pamphlets.[16] No wonder foreign governments—in this case, the Czech ministry of justice—launched counterattacks, investigated VDA activities, and declared that the VDA was a hostile organization that worked "against the independence and constitutional unity of our state" by making pan-German propaganda.[17]

The Czech accusations, generally accepted and believed by other East Central European governments,[18] were only partially true. The "apolitical" VDA did try to strengthen ethnic Germans' consciousness and help the population of Germandom in foreign countries, and thus it directly sought to neutralize the assimilation efforts of the respective governments. With these activities, it violated the minority treaties. But the minority treaties also prohibited the "forceful assimilation" of ethnic minorities, so every East Central European government also violated the principles of the treaties. An awkward situation developed in which the DAI and VDA, while doing cultural work, actually fulfilled a political mission, and the East Central European governments, while accusing the DAI and VDA of violating international law, tolerated the activities of these associations.

Stresemann and his government had tried to undermine the Pan-German League by restricting financial support mainly to the DAI and VDA, but this method did not prove entirely successful. The pan-Germanists still enjoyed respectability and admiration in high industrial and military circles. Furthermore, since many of them became members of the VDA, they made that organization a forum for pan-German expansionist ideas. A very close cooperation existed between the DAI and VDA on the one hand, and the Pan-German League, *Deutsche Flottenverein*, *Deutschmänner Schwarzweissrot*, *Deutsche Hochschulring*, and *Deutsche Adelgenossenschaft* on the other.[19] The VDA's most important branches were the school groups, women's groups, and the local academic branches. These groups, simply because of the general folkish spirit dominating academic life,[20] were advocates of revisionist and pan-German propaganda. The main theme of their lectures, meetings, and presentations always centered on revisionism and the need to maintain contact with and financially aid the *Auslandsdeutsche*.[21] Illustrious professors such as Heinrich Ritter von Srbik ended their historical lectures with such remarks as "The Reich is preserved and the *Alldeutsche* conviction lives in our hearts stronger than ever."[22] More and more VDA meetings were chaired by high-ranking retired army and navy officers.[23] Clearly the activities even of the two government-supported organizations dealing with the *Auslandsdeutsche* contradicted Germany's foreign political aims by providing arguments and facts for those states that wanted to see Germany remain powerless and excommunicated from the community of democratic nations as long as possible. But did these activities really contradict the government's foreign policy? Was even Stresemann himself a convinced internationalist, or did he secretly remain, as he was in his younger years, a true pan-Germanist? The question is still unanswered, but some historians argue that he was at least a German nationalist.[24]

The whole concept of preserving Germandom in foreign lands and the desire to prevent assimilation to other nations makes no sense unless the mother country, that is, Germany, wanted to use these groups for some economic, political, or in the case of war, military advantage. The romantic, sentimental nationalist argument that Germandom should be preserved because of the cultural mission of the German people becomes suspect when we take account of the money involved in promoting these groups at a time when the German Republic was struggling against inflation, and then depression. The German government subsidized the VDA with RM 2,000,000 in 1926, when the VDA's income from private sources already exceeded RM 2,000,000.[25] The government gave other organizations another RM 2,000,000 that same year. Why did the government choose to invest RM 4,000,000 in "sentimental nationalism" in a year when the number of unemployed persons was close to 5,000,000?[26]

If the German government had revisionism in mind as a foreign political goal, then the investment certainly would pay off: in case of a plebiscite in the lost territories the vote of every single *Auslandsdeutsche* would count. An interesting point in connection with the government cooperation with these organizations is that both the DAI and the VDA placed less and less emphasis on work directed toward the territories lost to France and Belgium. At the time of the Locarno treaties and afterward the attention of both organizations was turned more and more to the Germans living in East Central Europe. Their expenses for work with the *Auslandsdeutsche* took 54.7 percent of their income.[27] This was supplemented with a donation of RM 3,000,000 by the German foreign ministry. This "donation" for cultural support and financial aid to ethnic Germans was greater than the entire annual budget of the VDA. No wonder the VDA and other organizations "complied loyally" with the requests and general directions of official "contributors," that is, the ministry of finance, the foreign ministry, and the intelligence service.[28] This "loyal compliance" made the VDA a useful instrument of German foreign policy, which pursued—for the time being secretly—revisionist aims.

A review of the Weimar Republic's concern for the Germans living outside Germany leads to the conclusion that the Weimar Republic did not seek to destroy the pan-German concern for the *Auslandsdeutsche*. On the contrary, after the elimination of the many competing groups it centralized the movement in the DAI and VDA. Through large donations and subsidies to these two organizations the republican government gave them semiofficial status, and at the same time made them dependent on the goodwill of the government. Accepting and promoting revisionism itself, the Weimar Republic tried to prevent the assimilation of ethnic Germans to their respective nation-states and thus successfully prepared the way for the use of these ethnic groups by successive German governments. These developments fulfilled the romantic, idealistic dreams of the pan-Germanists.

Through cultural work, material support, and financial aid the German government and the different patriotic and nationalist organizations helped the *Auslandsdeutsche* to keep their German self-consciousness as individuals and as a group. This help enabled them to slow down, if not completely stop, the process of assimilation and preserve the preconditions for a foreign policy that openly embraced revisionism and even imperialism. Important changes in the attitudes, aims, and activities of these associations, as well as of the ethnic German organizations, occurred with the Nazi *Gleichschaltung* (coordination) of the entire system. With this step, the party openly took over the care of the *Auslandsdeutsche*.

The Hitler Era

Hitler was appointed chancellor of Germany on January 30, 1933. His appointment seemed to represent a victory for all the revolutionary forces. "For 1933, like other revolutionary years, produced great hopes, a sense of new possibilities, the end of frustration, the beginning of action, a feeling of exhilaration, and anticipation after years of hopelessness."[29] There were good reasons for this revolutionary mood in Germany. The economic crisis was so bad that nobody could imagine its getting worse. The unemployment figure passed the six million mark in 1933.[30] The wounds caused by the loss of war and the humiliating Versailles Treaty were still not healed. The republican governments that succeeded Stresemann's seemed to have no control over either the worsening economic crisis or the political divisions of the nation, which were growing sharper every day. The young generation of Germans who had fought in the trenches were thirty-five to forty-five years old in 1933. They were mature enough to take up leadership positions in every field, were eager to assume control, and were ready for action. Yet all the leadership positions were occupied by the older generation, who were well into their fifties, frequently even sixty or seventy. The majority of Germans believed that they had reached the bottom of their misery and that conditions could not become worse. Germany had suffered enough. Now a new era should begin under the direction of the younger generation.

"Hitler recognized this mood when he told the German people to hold up their heads and rediscover their old pride and self-confidence. Germany, united and strong, would end crippling divisions which had held her back, and recover the place that was her due in the world."[31] Striving for just such a future, the younger generation of Germans launched a general offensive to take over the leadership positions of the older men. The organizations concerned with the Germans living abroad were not immune to the general mood, and they also experienced a power struggle within their ranks. At the same time a sharp competition developed between the DAI and the VDA.

The DAI, under the leadership of its energetic general secretary, Dr. Fritz Wertheimer (of Jewish ancestry), by 1933 had extended its activities into new fields.[32] Its original aims, taking care of the cultural and other needs of German citizens living abroad and helping German citizens in their emigration to foreign countries, were expanded to include concern for *all* Germans living outside of Germany, that is, the ethnic Germans. With this new interest, the

DAI was clearly invading an area that up to now had been under the sole jurisdiction of the VDA. With the help of Dr. Wilhelm Frick, minister of interior,[33] the VDA repelled this DAI invasion in June 1933. Fortunately for the VDA, Frick entrusted its newly elected president, Hans Steinacher, with putting the DAI in order. The DAI was reorganized according to Steinacher's suggestions and restricted again to matters dealing with German citizens living abroad. This restriction made Foreign Minister Constantin von Neurath unhappy: He regarded the DAI representatives as "men who had either gone bankrupt or had not any kind of work or had no success in their business and so on."[34]

On August 3, 1933, the doorman of the DAI, a Nazi party member, on his own initiative blocked the entry of General Secretary Wertheimer to the Haus des Deutschtums. Minister of the Interior Frick again asked Steinacher to form a committee and end this ridiculous situation by choosing new leadership for the DAI.[35] After considerable negotiations and consultations with the ministry of the interior as well as the foreign ministry, the committee agreed on Karl Strölin, the Nazi lord mayor of Stuttgart, as the next president of the DAI. For the position of general secretary the committee picked another Nazi, the Transylvanian Saxon Richard Csáki.[36] With these two appointments Nazi control over the DAI was firmly secured. At the same time the leadership was rejuvenated; both Strölin and Csáki were under fifty years of age.

The VDA also felt the pressure of political developments, as well as the pressure of the young generation. Its leaders, retired Minister of Defense Otto Gessler[37] and retired Admiral Seebohm, were over sixty years old. The young generation was represented in the leadership by Hans Steinacher, at that time forty years of age, who was elected as referent of student affairs in September 1932. In 1933, after Hitler's appointment as chancellor, the younger members of the VDA demanded new elections in order to revitalize the VDA leadership. This demand was against the desire of President Hindenburg and the foreign ministry. They hoped to prevent the nazification of all the institutions by keeping the old leadership in control. Nevertheless, the VDA began preparations for the elections of April 1933. Among the contenders for leadership were Hans Schemm, representing the NSDAP (National Socialist German Workers Party), and Alfred Rosenberg, who was already the leader of the foreign political bureau of the Nazi party (*Aussenpolitisches Amt der NSDAP*, organized in 1931).[38] The candidate of the VDA was Hans Steinacher, who, although not from among the old leaders, was looked upon by many as the man who would be able to prevent the *Gleichschaltung* of the VDA.[39]

At the April 30, 1933, meeting of the VDA, Steinacher was elected the new *Reichsführer*. No objections were raised against his election, either by the party or by Rosenberg.

Did the NSDAP tolerate Steinacher's election because Hitler had grown impatient with the ambitions as well as the philosophy of Rosenberg and wanted to prevent him from assuming new power?[40] Or did Hitler consider the

VDA one of the less important targets for *Gleichschaltung*?[41] Or was Steinacher tolerated because in NSDAP circles his views were well known and the Nazis looked on him as a trustworthy man, a prospective convert to Nazism?[42] This last idea did not occur to Steinacher. He believed in the possibility of coexistence with the Hitler regime.

Steinacher took charge of the VDA at once. Besides securing the support of the new foreign minister, Neurath (on May 27, 1933), for a VDA that would resist NSDAP influence and control, he reorganized the staff of the VDA[43] and announced the implementation of the *Führerprinzip* (leadership principle), thus unifying and strengthening the organization.[44] He consulted and gained the support of Hitler's deputy, Rudolf Hess, against any future takeover attempts by the NSDAP or Alfred Rosenberg. He also prepared the annual "Whitsun days" meeting of the VDA in Passau for June 2, 1933. After the Passau meeting he helped to find a more "able" leadership for the DAI at the request of Frick and accompanied Hans Otto Roth, representative of the German party in the Romanian parliament, to an audience with Hitler on June 15, 1933.[45] Hitler's "strong personality" impressed Steinacher,[46] and perhaps because of this audience he wrote an article in the July 7, 1933, issue of the *Freie Stimmen* in which he described the "new road" that the VDA would have to follow in order to be able to participate fully in the "reordering of Europe."[47]

Since Steinacher wanted to save the VDA from *Gleichschaltung*, there is reason to assume that the changing of the guard (that is, the struggle for leadership) ended with the victory of the young generation without the submission of the VDA to NSDAP control. At the same time, Steinacher's role in the nazification of the DAI, unless it is interpreted as instigated by jealousy toward a competitor, suggests that Nazi influences would prevail in the VDA without installing a Nazi party member at the helm. Steinacher's "new roads" article seemed to point in that direction.

During this period membership in the Pan-German League had dwindled from 40,000 in 1923 to about 8,000 by 1933.[48] The 1933 presidential elections of the League, while securing the leadership for old fighters such as Heinrich Class (who was sixty-five in 1933) and Alfred Hugenberg (sixty-eight), caused the alienation of the young generation.

Hitler, whose relations with Class began in 1920 and who was grateful to Hugenberg for the support he received from the League in the days preceding his appointment as chancellor,[49] at the beginning shared the conviction of many pan-Germanists that "national socialism is the child of the Pan-German League."[50] He appointed Hugenberg to the post of minister of commerce in his cabinet, hoping with that gesture to secure the League's continued cooperation. However, the old leadership of the League was not ready to deny its basic principles for the sake of Hitler's goodwill. Class criticized the Nazi *Gleichschaltung* and stated that it would work only if it interpreted the "greatest good" as the "absolute and uniform solidarity of all the Germans

with their *Volk*." And besides, there must be complete freedom of views. Class
emphasized that the League would work for the realization of its goals in the
old spirit and would advocate the doctrine "that the people's state will become
a reality when it reaches its coronation by the return of the German
Kaisertum."[51] The "old spirit" Class referred to was conservatism: the return
of leadership to the old ruling class, the restoration of the monarchy, the
rebuilding of Germany's military power, and the liquidation of the Versailles
Treaty, which would restore Germany to a dominant position in Europe.[52]
Except for "old spirit" conservatism and belief in freedom of opinion, Hitler
professed the same doctrines as the League. It is hardly surprising, therefore,
that a great many young middle-class people deserted the League and joined
the Nazi movement. It is also understandable that their conservatism,
preaching of freedom of opinion, and monarchist convictions antagonized
Hitler.

The League's membership doubled in 1933, but it never regained the mass
support it had enjoyed in the early 1920s. Hitler probably looked upon the
League as more of a nuisance than a threat. Since it had the support of the
ruling class and the financial backing of rich industrialists, the League was able
to continue to function without falling victim to the *Gleichschaltung*. Because
of its relative security, it became the reservoir of anti-Nazi elements from
widely varying points of the political spectrum: freemasons, war veterans,
churchmen, government officials, professionals, army officers. Those
assembled in it "not only waited for Hitler's downfall, but wanted to bring it
about themselves."[53] The League was finally dissolved on March 13, 1939, at
the orders of Reinhard Heydrich, the SS Obergruppenführer. Its leaders, Class
and Hugenberg, were respectively 71 and 74 years old at the time.

The centralization attempts of the regime and the competition for control
among high Nazi officials brought changes to the organizations dealing with
the *Auslandsdeutsche* in the early years of the Nazi government. This
reorganization produced the structure described below.

The *Aussenpolitisches Amt der NSDAP* (APA) was established on April 1,
1933, under the control of Alfred Rosenberg, who hoped to make it a foreign
service that would eventually replace the foreign ministry.[54] Despite this
ambition, Rosenberg's office remained a kind of information service providing
foreign visitors with data concerning the Nazi movement,[55] trying to gain their
cooperation and support by arranging visits for them to Germany, and
collecting industrial, scientific, and other intelligence data from these (mostly
unsuspecting and naive) visitors. The APA also promoted Nazi ideas abroad,
sometimes by illegal means.[56]

The *Auslandabteilung der Reichsleitung der NSDAP*, in existence since
1931, was led by Dr. Hans Nisland, and upon his retirement on May 8, 1933,
by Ernst Wilhelm Bohle. It was renamed the *Ausland Organisation der
NSDAP* (AO) in 1935, but its aim remained unchanged: the spread of Nazi
ideology among German citizens living abroad.[57] Its membership was

restricted to German citizens, who both provided information about ethnic German organizations for the Reich authorities and spread Nazi ideas among the ethnic Germans.[58]

The *Deutsche Ausland Institut,* after its nazification under the leadership of Karl Strölin, became a clearinghouse for matters concerning the relationship of Germans living in the Reich to those living abroad. This new assignment secured for the DAI predominance among the *Volksdeutsche* organizations. Its duties were preparation of documentation for *"Volksdeutsche* work" in the Reich, care for the cultural and economic needs of Germans in the border zones and abroad, and participation in the education of all Germans to strengthen their national consciousness.[59] In this last aspect the DAI cooperated closely with the AO, helping to prepare the curriculum for training camps where the AO educated Germans from Germany as well as abroad in the Nazi spirit.[60]

After the *Verein für das Deutschtum im Ausland* received its "Magna Carta," as Steinacher called it, from Hess on June 2, 1933, it tried to assert its jurisdiction over all matters dealing with the *Auslandsdeutsche.*[61] With this intention in mind, Steinacher organized the *Volksdeutscher Rat* (VR) in October 1933 as a higher administrative body, almost a ministry of ethnic German affairs, directly subordinated to the staff of the Führer, Hess.[62] This meant that the VR, and through it the VDA, was voluntarily subordinating itself to a party official instead of a government official. In light of this fact, Steinacher's preclusion of party members from the VR seems meaningless. He placed unconditional trust in Hess, though Hess was obviously more a devoted follower of Hitler than a protector of the VDA.[63] Furthermore, Steinacher's public statements did not promote the idea of independence for the VR.[64]

In the spring of 1934, in order to bring the VDA closer to Nazi ideology and the terminology of Hitler, Steinacher even changed the name of his organization from *Verein für das Deutschtum im Ausland* to *Volksbund für das Deutschtum im Ausland* (the abbreviation remained VDA). The alternative interpretation of Steinacher's motives is that this name change was part of his plan to accomplish the step-by-step nazification of the VDA. Any attempts at appeasement he may have made were wiped out by his new interpretation of the word *Auslandsdeutsche.* According to this new definition, only German citizens abroad were *Auslandsdeutsche.* In contrast, the *Volksdeutsche* were ethnic Germans, whose care was made the duty of the AO.[65]

From 1934 on, the history of the VDA is a continuous struggle for a certain degree of independence[66] in order to support the ethnic Germans, especially those in Europe. However, the VDA had many competitors in this field, and by giving its support to Nazi-led ethnic German groups it became a mere instrument of Nazi foreign policy.[67]

The *Volksdeutsche Mittelstelle* (VoMi) was established on January 27, 1937, by SS *Reichsführer* Heinrich Himmler, as the successor to the secret "von Kursell Büro."[68] Publicly it was subordinated to the foreign ministry, but in reality it was directly controlled by Hess and led by SS Colonel Werner

Lorenz. His deputy, Hermann Behrends, had earned his position in the Gestapo.[69] VoMi coordinated the relations of the different organizations and institutions within the Reich with the *Volksdeutsche* organizations abroad, in order to secure the loyalty of the ethnic Germans to the Nazi party. It even acted on occasion as representative of the *Volksdeutsche*.[70] It advised their leaders how to conduct campaigns for the nazification of ethnic Germans. The secret of VoMi's great influence was its right to hand out subsidies to the *Volksdeutsche*.

The Pan-German League, with its shrinking membership and lessening influence, no longer played an important role. The remainder of the organizations that existed before 1933 were either dissolved or absorbed by the institutions just described. *Gleichschaltung* was completely successful. The organizations dealing with the *Auslandsdeutsche* and *Volksdeutsche* became obedient instruments of Hitler, even though the competition for survival or for more authority continued among them until 1938. By this time the leadership of all these associations had passed into the hands of the younger generation. Since the struggle between the generations had begun in 1930, one wonders what would have been the outcome of Hitler's fight for power if this changing of the guard had occurred in 1930. In that case the younger men, who by 1933 were in Hitler's camp, would have represented the establishment against Hitler, rather than Hindenburg and his generation.

Hitler's Ideas about the Volksdeutsche

Germany's foreign political situation did not change with Hitler's rise to power. Stresemann had already reached the immediate goals.

Hitler's foreign policy was simple. He wanted not only to restore the old boundaries of imperial Germany, but also to secure land and space (*Lebensraum*) for the German people, if necessary by conquest.[71] A more forceful diplomacy, especially the waging of war, required a united Germany, restored to its economic and military strength. Hitler consciously worked to realize these preconditions from the very beginning of his rule.

What were the tasks of the ethnic Germans in this grand strategic plan? In theory, they were most obviously to keep their German nationality, to unite in a strong nationwide organization, to promote the aims of the Reich's foreign policy in their respective countries, and, in case of war, to serve as a fifth column for the German army. The role of the Reich organizations dealing with the ethnic Germans was to do their best to prepare them for their future duties.

The situation was not quite so clear in reality. Hitler had no definite ideas about the role of the *Volksdeutsche*. Should they be prepared to help the German army in war, or simply wait for their "liberation" by the army? In December 1933 Hitler declared that the rebuilt German army would enable him to defend the minority rights of the ethnic Germans, and if these ethnic Germans would like to join the Reich, the army would march in to bring freedom to them.[72] This statement seems to indicate that he did not intend to assign any role to the ethnic Germans other than to preserve their German identity. If they wanted to join the Reich, they were simply to ask him for their deliverance. Furthermore, Hitler believed in the case of South Tyrol that "it would be a crime to stake [German blood] for two hundred thousand Germans."[73] He seemed to mean that he intended to use the minority question and the ethnic German groups only as instruments to promote Germany's interests. Characteristically, it never occurred to him to ask the ethnic Germans what they expected from their mother country.

Still other factors made Hitler even more undecided concerning the future of ethnic Germans. Should he annex all territories in which ethnic Germans lived? In the case of the borderlands and Austria, annexation was feasible. But what about the *Volksdeutsche* in Yugoslavia, Romania, and the Soviet Union? The annexation of these territories could be achieved only at the price of a new world war, and besides, they would make Germany a multinational empire! This solution contradicted Hitler's philosophy, which, following Bismarck, advocated the creation of a great German nation-state.[74]

Hitler's confusion and indecisiveness were magnified by the very different ideas of his lieutenants concerning the role of the ethnic Germans. The result was complete confusion in the policy of the organizations that cared for them. If we add to this the great rivalry among these organizations, it becomes clear why their actions were contradictory and frequently illogical. With the exception of the Pan-German League, they all wanted their activities among the ethnic Germans to serve the interests of Germany—a natural desire on the part of good patriots. This desire did not mean, however, that the DAI, VDA, AO, VoMi, or even the German foreign ministry regarded the ethnic Germans as pawns who could be exploited and if necessary sacrificed to the interests of the Reich.

The leaders of the Reich German organizations, thinking in nationalist, pan-German, or even National Socialist ideological terms, simply could not imagine that the aims and goals of the ethnic Germans could differ from those of the Reich. After all, didn't all ethnic Germans in East Central Europe desire to return to their mother country? Of course, this goal was a clear violation of the minority treaties. Thus the Successor States considered the aims of these organizations, as well as of the ethnic Germans who accepted their help, to be illegal and immoral.

But did the ethnic Germans, the *Volksdeutsche*, really accept the imperialistic goals of the Reich? Or did they have their own goals, some of which opposed these imperialistic aims? The simple fact that the ethnic Germans, with the exception of sometimes very numerous groups of young people, had to be convinced and "educated," sometimes bribed, into accepting these imperialistic ideas, proves that the majority of *Volksdeutsche* were concerned more with their own local interests than with the interests of Germany.[75]

The most effective method of influencing the ethnic Germans and gaining their loyalty seemed to be good propaganda work combined with financial support. Propaganda and education—or, as they were nicely called, "cultural work"—had two targets: the Reich Germans who were to be made aware of their responsibilities toward their brethren living abroad; and the ethnic Germans, who were to be imbued with a sense of loyalty toward the Reich.

To educate the Reich Germans the DAI, VDA, and other organizations were active in every field of life. The VDA assigned to its local groups the different ethnic German groups as areas of concern (*Betreuungsgebiete*), thus making the local groups individually responsible for *Volksdeutsche*.[76]

It organized "Days of the German Nation" (*Tage des deutschen Volkstums*), which aimed "to win more German citizens to the folk German idea and work."[77] The ethnic Germans of East Central Europe were always represented at these celebrations by a (sometimes very numerous) delegation.[78] To make these celebrations a sure success the VDA closely cooperated in their organization with the local NSDAP, the *Hitlerjugend*, (Hitler Youth), the *Bund der deutschen Mädchen* (Federation of German Girls), the SA (*Sturmabteilung*), and the SS (*Schutzstaffel*). The entire population of a city and vicinity "had to participate in some way."[79]

Academic groups invited to their meetings ethnic German lecturers, mostly from East Central Europe, and organized trips for businessmen, scholars, and students designed to make them admirers of the Reich.[80] The DAI usually organized a reception for the visiting groups and devoted the entire occasion to pan-German and folk propaganda.[81] Trips to see the ethnic Germans of East Central Europe, the so-called *Volkstumfahrten*, were also frequently organized with the aim of making Reich Germans familiar with and interested in the life of the ethnic Germans. The expenses involved were minimal since local families hosted the travelers.[82]

A pamphlet entitled *What Every German Should Know about the Germans Abroad* was widely distributed throughout Germany, again with the purpose of strengthening interest in the affairs of the *Volksdeutsche*.[83] The VDA published *Der Volksdeutsche* at a cost of RM 150,000 in 1936, but distributed it free in Germany as well as abroad.[84] The German papers readily published stories about the folk Germans. For example, the visit of two fliers from Danzig to Germany in 1933 was a recurring news item for four months, giving the fliers as well as their sponsoring organization (VDA) the opportunity to popularize revisionism in connection with Danzig.[85] With the help of cooperating industrialists the organizations even used chocolate bar wrappers to create interest in the ethnic Germans. The *Gebroder Stollwerk AG* in Cologne contributed part of the profits from the sale of candy bars wrapped in paper featuring *Volksdeutsche* custom from all over Europe and bearing the slogan *Deutsch überall* (German everywhere).

Similar propaganda was aimed at the ethnic Germans to "awaken their feelings that they belonged to the Reich."[86] The travels of Reich Germans abroad and of the ethnic Germans in Germany reinforced each other. The returning *Volksdeutsche* were impressed by the progress of the Reich and shocked by the contrasting primitive conditions of ethnic Germans living in

East Central Europe. They praised Germany and attempted to make fellow *Volksdeutsche* more conscious of their German identity and nationality and win their sympathy and loyalty for the Reich. If nationalist arguments did not work, the propagandists switched their emphasis to the socialistic aspects of Nazi doctrine.[87] Reich organizations sent papers, books, and occasionally entire libraries to ethnic German associations. In addition, the Reich and its organizations frequently provided secret, and sometimes even open, financial aid to poor, unemployed Germans or struggling German businessmen abroad to help them survive economic crises or natural disasters.[88]

All these activities required money—great sums of it. Already in 1932 the amount spent "for the preservation of Germandom" by the foreign ministry was RM 8,059,000.[89] The bulk of this money was spent in Silesia, Pomerania, Posen, and Danzig. The ministry of finance also reserved each year a certain sum to be used for the strengthening of Germandom abroad. In 1936 this amount exceeded RM 7,708,000.[90]

The VoMi's budget cannot be determined with certainty because many of its documents were lost in the war. But it clearly had a great amount of money at its disposal. It subsidized the DAI with RM 480,000 annually,[91] helped to organize the *Deutsche Stiftung* (German Foundation)[92] with contributions amounting to RM 150,000, and gave occasional financial assistance to the VDA.[93] The VDA, in theory a self-supporting institution, had an income from membership fees, public collections, and business transactions of RM 6,019,062.[94] It also received occasional aid from the foreign, propaganda, and finance ministries.[95]

The money spent by NSDAP organizations and the Hitler Youth on work with the *Volksdeutsche* cannot be determined. It is almost impossible to pinpoint the use of amounts under vague entries in their budgets.[96]

OSSA provided financial aid to the *Volksdeutsche* in large amounts,[97] and openly, but most of its transactions were made through its affiliated companies.[98] Thus the exact amounts it gave to the ethnic Germans are not known. It is difficult even to estimate the total amount spent for the "preservation of Germandom abroad." It must have run to tens of millions of marks annually, but it is impossible to determine how much of this money actually reached *Volksdeutsche* organizations in the different East Central European countries. But one thing is clear: this huge investment on the part of the Reich produced only very small benefits.

The great inefficiency of the work among the *Volksdeutsche* and the rather inept use of money to buy the sympathies and loyalty of the ethnic Germans can be traced to conditions in the Reich. Hitler's indecisiveness concerning the usefulness of the ethnic Germans to Reich foreign policy, the great number of competing organizations dealing with them, and the power struggle for leadership within, and for predominance and exclusivity among, these different organizations were all contributing factors. Without a central idea and a centralized organization, or even well-defined fields of interest, these organizations pursued separate goals with their own methods.

The chaos of the situation is reflected in the behavior of ethnic Germans during the foreign political crises that concerned the countries in which they lived. These crises were: for Poland the recurring Danzig question, for Czechoslovakia the Munich crisis, for Hungary the First Vienna Decision, for Romania the Second Vienna Decision, and for Yugoslavia the *coup d'état* of March 27, 1941. These events represented the greatest tests for the Reich government, for the organizations concerned with the *Volksdeutsche*, and for the *Volksdeutsche* themselves.

A review of the conditions of the German minorities in the different East Central European countries will reveal how effective the Reich German organizations were in influencing them. Furthermore, it will give us a picture of the degree of loyalty or disloyalty of the ethnic Germans and will help to answer the question: Were they a fifth column?

CHAPTER II

Sudeten German Dilemma

Conditions to 1935

According to the Austrian census of 1910 there were 3,747,000 Germans living in the Historic Provinces of Bohemia, Moravia, and Silesia. They lived in solid blocks near Germany and Austria where their families had lived, in some cases, for centuries. The blocks formed "language islands" separated by areas in which Czechs were the majority. In the newly created Czechoslovakia the Germans were the largest minority group, 23.4 percent of the whole population according to the 1921 census.[1] Obviously it was important to the Czechoslovak government to gain their cooperation, but there were serious obstacles. The Germans were oriented culturally toward Austria and Germany, while the Czechs traditionally favored Russia and, more recently, France. The majority of the Germans lived in cities and were industrialized, while the Czechs were for the most part country folk. The Germans were usually better educated, but seldom spoke Czech. Furthermore, the Czech "program for a democratic national settlement lay more in individual convictions than in a well-prepared government plan."[2]

The Germans could not agree on a plan either. Those who nurtured pan-German sentiments wanted to join with Germany, and they would win over many adherents after 1933. Many others, still loyal to the old monarchical idea, worked for the inclusion of their territory in Austria. Still others, mostly the industrialists and tradesmen who feared competition from the more modern German industry and wanted to keep their traditional markets in Bohemia,[3] were willing to join the new Czechoslovak state under certain conditions, which varied from complete territorial to limited cultural autonomy. The Germans in Czechoslovakia were in agreement on only one point—they wanted to preserve their German identity. The majority thought that the best form for the preservation of their distinct German nationality was an "independent collective entity," that is, complete autonomy.[4] They found justification for their demand in the fact that the peacemakers had violated the principle of self-determination by denying plebiscites to the Sudeten Germans.[5]

The Czech leaders, foremost among them Tomáš Masaryk and Eduard Beneš,[6] after securing the cooperation of the Slovaks and Ruthenes,[7] made great efforts to keep the Historic Provinces intact and integrated into Czechoslovakia. Thus the "Czechs who had wrestled with their German-Bohemian neighbors so relentlessly under the Hapsburg regime . . . reversed their policy the moment they themselves became the ruling element in the country."[8] Their arguments, based on economic necessity, strategic interests, and political considerations, were accepted by the peacemakers.[9] Both the Czech leaders and the peacemakers hoped that the Czechoslovak republic would be able to solve the problems created by the inclusion of different nationality groups by following the example of Switzerland. Until 1933 they were successful. "The new relations which they had cultivated with the *Deutschböhmen* since the foundation of the Czechoslovak Republic were almost up to the Swiss or Canadian standard of inter-communal fraternity: a light shining in the darkness of East European national oppressions and vendettas."[10]

Still, it was in the interest of the Czechoslovak state to encourage assimilation. The Czechs tried to achieve it with a liberal approach, awarding more privileges to the German minorities than the minority treaties had proposed. The ethnic Germans had the right, according to the new Czecho-slovak constitution, to organize their own political parties.[11] The German Social Democratic, German Agrarian, and German Christian Socialist parties commanded the votes of the great majority of the ethnic group.[12] Although these three parties regarded the Versailles Treaty as unjust and wanted to secure autonomous status for the ethnic Germans, they accepted the reality of the Czechoslovak state and were willing to cooperate with the government. However, some of the other German parties misused the privileges granted by the Czech government and with their activities, which threatened the dissolution of the state, forced the Czech government to make exceptions to its general liberal policy. For example, the German National Socialist party (DSNAP), along with some other smaller rightist parties, remained staunchly anti-Czechoslovak. It was influenced by strong revisionist and pan-German ideas, and its barely concealed goal was the complete separation of the German territories from the Czechoslovak state. The Czech government, referring to the 1923 Law for the Protection of the Republic, suspended the activities of these parties on October 4, 1933. This was only one day after the parties had decided to dissolve themselves and join the new Sudeten German Home Front under the leadership of Konrad Henlein.

Although Hitler's domestic and foreign successes made National Socialist ideas more attractive to the ethnic Germans, their change of attitude was not sudden and was not caused solely by the victory of the Hitler movement.[13] More important was the activity of the different ethnic German associations and clubs, whose tenacious work among youths since 1920 began to bear fruit in 1935.[14] What were these associations?

The most universally accepted association among the ethnic Germans of

Czechoslovakia was the *Deutscher Kulturverband* (German Cultural Association), popularly called the Bund. Already in 1926 the Bund had 2,050 local branches; its income from membership fees and donations exceeded 45 million Czechoslovak crowns in 1925. It maintained twenty-two private schools and eighty-seven kindergartens.[15] Up to 1935 the Bund concentrated its efforts on preserving Germandom and emphasized the loyalty of its members to the Czechoslovak state.[16] Its loyalty was praised by the Czechoslovak cultural minister, Franz Spina.[17]

The Bohemian Movement was organized in 1919, and its goal was "the inner liberation of our people through the renewal of public life."[18] It professed the conviction that in public life not political parties but personalities should lead the German minority group, emphasized the importance of participation by the young in the "renewal" of public life, and wanted to create a summit organization to secure "cooperation and unity" within the minority. Its organization was hierarchic; its first president was Karl Metzner. It published yearly the *Böhmerlandblätter*, the *Böhmerland Jahrbuch*, and the *Böhmerland Flugschriften*. Although the movement dissolved itself voluntarily in 1925 because of the "constant harassment of the Czech police," its principles, ideas, and goals were carried on by other associations.

The successor of the Bohemian Movement was the *Bereitschaft* (Readiness). This was another youth movement, which drew its membership from the Sudeten-German Youth Movement, as did the *Kameradschaftsbund* (Comrade's Band), the *Aufbruchkreis* (Outset Circle), and the *Wandervögel* (Ramblers; its older members were organized in a *Männerbund*, Men's Band).[19] While the Sudeten-German Youth Movement had cultural goals, and the aim of the *Wandervögel* was to teach ethnic German city youths about peasant life through trips to the countryside,[20] the *Kameradschaftsbund* and the *Aufbruchkreis* had political goals. The *Kameradschaftsbund* was revisionist and pan-German, "advocating the establishment of a dictatorship"; the *Aufbruchkreis* was Nazi-oriented and extremely radical.[21] Members of these two associations and of the dissolved National Socialist party formed the Sudeten German Home Front (later Sudeten German party, SDP). The Outset Circle caused some concern for Konrad Henlein, who thought that their radicalism might endanger the existence of the whole party.[22]

Competing with all these organizations for the support of the Czechoslovakian *Volksdeutsche* were some Catholic Church groups, unorganized and with small membership, therefore insignificant, and the *Socialistischer Jugendverband* (Socialist Youth Association), which also influenced only a small minority of Sudeten Germans. In 1931, after ten years of organizational work, the Socialist Youth Association's membership was only 10,000.[23] The reason for its relative ineffectiveness was that there were too many organizations competing for youthful membership. The best known competitors were the *Bereitschaft*, whose goal was to renew political and *völkish* nationalist life among Sudeten German youth; the old organization of the *Wandervögel*; the *Sudetendeutsche Jugendbewegung Böhmerland*, which wanted to further the leadership principle while uniting all Germans regardless of parties. In addition to these rightist organizations the Communist youth organization also cut into potential Socialist membership. Since radical movements are generally more attractive than moderate ones to young people, all these extremist organizations tended to lure members from the socialist camp.

Although this short review does not include all the ethnic German associations, social and sport clubs, church groups and other organizations, it does illustrate one important point: the Germans used their rights, secured for them in the Czechoslovak constitution and in the minority treaties, to organize their own ethnic affairs according to what they perceived as their interests.

Economic Conditions

The main points of the Czechoslovak government's financial policy in the 1920s were the liquidation of war bonds and a tax on capital, especially war profits. The government's first impulse was to repudiate the bonds; after all, the war had been waged by Austria-Hungary against the convictions and interests of the nationalist Czechs. But during the war the population of Austria-Hungary had been pressured to buy war bonds and the defeat had impoverished these bond buyers. The capital levy assessed by the Czech government was tied to currency reform, and in the case of landowners, was balanced against compensation due them for confiscated land.[24]

These measures affected all the nationalities of Czechoslovakia, but the Germans appeared to be hardest hit—perhaps because they had more to lose. They had been the heaviest war bond buyers,[25] they were the industrialists most hurt by the fall in exports, and they were the largest landowners whose lands were expropriated and were only moderately compensated by the laws of 1919 and 1920.[26] Since most of the landless agricultural workers who benefited from the expropriations were Czechs and Slovaks, the hard feelings of German landowners were entirely predictable. On the whole, however, despite some local incidents of harassment of German landowners by Czech officials, the land reform was moderately and peacefully enforced. Nevertheless, the upper limit was enforced more leniently in the case of Czech landowners.[27]

Tension began to rise over minor, sometimes imagined, violations of rights as the economic problems of the 1930s increased German animosity toward the Czechs. The Depression that affected all of Europe was felt somewhat later in Czechoslovakia; but when it came, it settled with particular severity in the Sudetenland. This circumstance caused suffering Germans to blame the government for having caused their ills and for doing nothing to remedy them. Since most of the light industry was in the Sudetenland, this area was the hardest hit by unemployment.[28] While the government in Prague certainly did not cause the Depression or turn it against the Germans in particular, it was probably biased on some counts of delaying aid or giving it inequitably or withholding it altogether from the German minority. In the distribution of available jobs the Czechs certainly practiced discrimination in favor of their own nationality workers.[29] On the other hand the state provided a proportionally just amount of unemployment benefits to the Sudeten-German Workers Union to help their membership. This fairness in aid, however, did not change the fact that the unemployment rate was three times as high in the German areas as in the Czech areas.[30]

The Sudeten Germans fared no better in the field of civil service where their number declined from 24.08 percent in 1921 to 12.9 percent in 1935.[31] The reason for the decrease was the obligatory language examinations, since relatively few Germans spoke the Czech language satisfactorily. The administrators of Sudeten German origin who spoke only German were restricted in job opportunities to the German-inhabited areas. Those who spoke Czech fluently, however, were eligible for positions in the entire state administration and bureaucracy of the republic. Since the language examinations were made stricter in the early 1930s, it is not unreasonable to suppose that the Czech local authorities desired to open up positions to their own nationality group during the Great Depression. Thus unemployment among the Sudeten Germans grew steadily. Under such trying economic conditions, any people may become susceptible to extremist ideas and propaganda, especially if the political leadership is unwilling or unable to find a way out of the crisis. That is what happened in Czechoslovakia. The Sudeten German population, which up to 1935 had generally supported leftist parties, shifted its allegiance to the right.[32]

Political Conditions

The constitution of the Czechoslovak republic did not limit the number of political parties and twenty-three parties competed in the April 1920 elections. The reasons for the large number of parties were "great diversity in social background and culture, unequal political experience, and considerations of religion,"[33] as well as permission to organize parties on the basis of nationality. These many parties split the electoral vote so that no clear majority emerged from the successive elections. Thus the governments formed on the basis of these elections were always coalition governments with decision-making power shared by five parties. The coalition governments were usually controlled by the Czech Agrarian party, which united with the Slovak Agrarians to form the Czechoslovak Republican Party. The other members of the coalition were supplied by the National Democrat, the Social Democrat, the (Czech) National Socialist,[34] and the Populist parties. This coalition ruled until the 1925 elections, when striking gains made by the Communists influenced the Agrarian prime minister, Frantisek Švehla, to invite the German Agrarians and Clericals into the coalition. This invitation did not represent any danger to the Czechoslovak republic since the German Social Democrat party, which was the strongest German party and second only to the Czechoslovak Social Democrats nationwide, was prepared to support the republic.[35] This willingness to cooperate was approved by the German voters, who in 1929 gave 1,252,281 votes to the activist parties and only 393,297 to the negativists (parties unwilling to cooperate with the republic).[36] The government decided to try to eliminate the negativists from public life, with the tacit approval of the German majority.[37]

The government went further than condemning the negativists for their real or alleged cooperation with the German Reich. As the Nazi movement gained ground in Germany in the early 1930s, some of the youth groups in Czechoslovakia began to imitate Nazis in their uniforms, flags, and salutes. The Czechoslovak government had largely ignored the German youth organizations in the first postwar decade, but it now began to pay closer attention to their obvious fascination with German nationalism. In 1931 the government prohibited *Volkssport* (People's Sports) and Nazi uniforms; by 1932 it felt strongly enough about the matter "to indulge in the dangerous luxury of a great indictment, and launched the famous *Volkssport* trial." In September 1932 seven young men were tried for treason in Brno; three were convicted and sentenced to three years.[38] Since the evidence was too flimsy to support such a serious conviction, there was great interest in the appeal, which was due to come up in September 1933.

Meanwhile the nation's attention centered on the German election in March 1933. Not everyone in Czechoslovakia was content just to watch the election; forty-two Nazis from Asch, including ten Reich Germans, were arrested and tried in June for having crossed the border to Germany and participated in a Nazi meeting during the election period.[39] The atmosphere had become altogether unfavorable for anyone suspected of connections with Nazi Germany.[40] The German minister in Prague reported in June 1933 that there were nearly seven hundred persons in prison awaiting trial, and pressure was increasing on German university students in Prague.

It was in this atmosphere that the *Volkssport* case was appealed. Among the most interested observers of the case were the members of the DSNAP.[41] When it became obvious that the appellate court would not overturn the lower court's decision (although it did drop the most serious charge and lighten the sentences), the DSNAP knew its days were numbered. It forestalled government action by dissolving itself on October 3, 1933. The next day the government officially prohibited the DSNAP and any association with it, which, in theory at least, would have kept even Reich party members from having any dealings with Czechoslovak citizens. There were some 30,000 Reich Germans living in Czechoslovakia at the time. The German National party was prohibited along with the Nazis. Several prominent party members were arrested, while others fled to Germany[42] or went underground. Thus the right-wing Sudeten German parties were smashed, and they would not revive in the old form. There were many, even among the Sudeten Germans, who were relieved at this. The Social Democrats, for example, supported German anti-Nazi activity and propaganda[43] in Czechoslovakia.

These political developments, coupled with the economic conditions, confused the Sudeten German population more and more. Those thinking along nationality lines exclusively lost faith in their old leftist parties for cooperating with the Czech government, which was seemingly determined to destroy the Sudeten German minority economically as well as politically. Therefore they became more and more receptive to Reich German propaganda, which increased concerning educational and cultural matters.

Educational and Cultural Life

The educational task that faced the new state of Czechoslovakia was varied and challenging. The statistics of 1918 show that illiteracy was a serious problem inherited from Austria-Hungary. While illiterates above the age of ten made up only 2.12 percent of the population in Bohemia, as one proceeded eastward they increased from 2.9 percent in Moravia, 3.65 percent in Silesia, and 26.8 percent in Slovakia (of those over the age of six), to a staggering 57.6 percent in Ruthenia.[44]

The distribution of schools employing the different languages was also inequitable, with an overall deficiency of Czech, Slovak, and Ruthenian schools, and in the eastern provinces a lack of German ones. The government had immediately begun to try to remedy this problem and had made significant progress by 1930.[45] The number of German schools in Czechoslovakia compared favorably with that in Prussia: Czechoslovakia had one German school for every 862 Germans, Prussia only one for every 1,112.[46] The number of German schools in the Habsburg era had been disproportionately high compared to the number of Czech schools. In the school year 1913–14 the Czechs, who made up 62.54 percent of the total population of the Historic Provinces, had 60.1 percent of the elementary schools, 58.1 percent of the higher elementary schools, and 52.68 percent of the secondary and normal schools. In comparison, the Germans (34.92 percent of the population) had 37.8 percent, 41.5 percent, and 46.3 percent, respectively.[47] Because of this imbalance it is not surprising that the new government closed some German schools, at least temporarily. However, by 1936 the Germans had a number of elementary schools very nearly proportional to their share of the population.[48] The average number of children in the classes was somewhat favorable to the Germans, and in 1937 the situation was as follows:[49]

	Lower Elementary Level	*Higher Elementary Level*
Total number of schools	2,855	2,105
Total number of students	1,728,950	459,975
Percentage of Czech schools	65.5	75.4
Percentage of German Schools	27.3	21.7
Teacher-student ratio, Czech	1:37	1:38
Teacher-student ratio, German	1:34	1:37

From the professional educational point of view, perhaps the most important factor that influences teaching and learning effectiveness is the teacher-student ratio. This ratio was better in the German schools than in the Czech schools, and it could be considered excellent compared with that in most East European countries. Sudeten Germans had relatively few complaints about secondary and higher education.[50] But a controversy did develop around the German university in Prague, which with the demonstrations, arguments, and emotionalism that followed, greatly contributed to the deterioration of the relationship between Sudeten German intellectuals and the Czechoslovak authorities.

The German university in Prague had been declared Czechoslovak state property in 1920. This law, however, was not implemented up to 1934. On November 20, 1934, the rector of the Czech university, Professor Dom, demanded that certain spaces in the buildings (classrooms), the library, and the German university insignia be relinquished to him. The reaction of the German students was immediate. There were demonstrations and even fights with Czech students, during which the police remained passive. Finally, the ministry of culture forced compliance with the 1920 regulations, but for long afterward the German faculty and students commemorated the events of November 1934, finding reason to criticize the Czechs more sharply every year.[51]

In education, as in other matters affecting minority rights, the Czechoslovak laws were fair. The problem was implementation, especially by the local authorities, who on many occasions executed the laws in outright opposition to the policy of enlightened Czechoslovak leaders. The Sudeten German population experienced only the practical effects of the implementation of Czechoslovak laws. Thus they interpreted them as a direct attack on their ethnicity and looked for allies in their struggle to combat attempts to curtail if not eradicate their "Germanness."

Henlein and the 1935 Election

After the dissolution of the DSNAP and the National party, their members were left in a state of despair, leaderless, often jobless, and at the mercy of the Czechoslovak authorities. Hitler had denied any connection between the Nazi party and *Volkssport*,[52] and the tendency of Sudeten Germans to turn to the Reich for protection now seemed to be viewed with embarrassment, rather than as an opportunity for German expansion.[53] The German foreign ministry did, however, respond to Sudeten German National Socialist distress with secret financial aid distributed through the Prague legation.[54] The danger to the legation of bringing in illegal funds by diplomatic courier was acute, but no other way was available because of the alertness of the Czechoslovak authorities and the strict foreign exchange regulations. Germany was also most anxious to avoid being linked overtly with the Sudeten problem at this time. The Führer's deputy, Rudolf Hess, issued a directive forbidding the admission of Sudeten Germans into the SS, SA, *Hitlerjugend*, or any other Reich organization in January 1934.[55]

Still, money poured into the elections through other channels—that is, the Reich German organizations.[56] Although it is difficult to trace all the money that was sent into Czechoslovakia to help the Sudeten German candidates, it can be safely stated that it was around RM 330,000.[57] The Germans received a very good return on their investment. The Sudeten German party (SDP) captured 1.2 million of the 1.8 million Sudeten German votes, representing forty-two seats in the chamber of deputies, while all the other German parties combined had only twenty-two places.[58] Walter Koch, the German minister in Prague, found the result gratifying. According to him, the most important outcome was the two-thirds unity of Sudeten Germans. He added a cautionary reminder in his report that the SDP deputies would still be a minority and thus unable to "exert a decisive influence on Government policy," and he urged that the Reich press be restrained from showing too great enthusiasm over the victory. The German minister was correct to be so cautious in his evaluation of the election results. It was true that the SDP had captured two-thirds of the votes and increased its number of seats in parliament, but not without considerable Reich German financial support. Since the elections were held in the midst of the Depression, it is probable that many voters supported the SDP not from genuine conviction but from hope of economic gain. Possibly Koch feared that too great emphasis on the victory by the German press would discredit the SDP with the Sudeten Germans, who had first-hand knowledge of how the voters had been influenced. He also stated some doubts about the ideological trustworthiness of Henlein and his party, saying the SDP was perhaps not so "close to our political ideas as it is assumed to be in some Reich German circles."[59]

Koch's assessment of Henlein was realistic. In 1932 the SDP leader had made his first contact with a Reich German organization—the VDA rather than the Nazi party. This contact was strengthened through a personal meeting with Hans Steinacher on German soil in late 1934. After that date Henlein sought contact with other Reich German organizations not connected with the Nazi party.[60] Henlein's orientation was strongly supported by Admiral Wilhelm Canaris, who believed that "Hitler's way may lead to an effective catastrophe."[61] Henlein and the majority of his party had the same goal after their election victory as they had before: autonomy for the Sudeten territories through parliamentary action within the Czechoslovak republic. They were not willing to accept orders from the Reich, only money.

This independent policy of Henlein embittered the pro-Nazi membership within the party as well as the Nazi authorities of the Reich. As the Austrian ambassador to Prague correctly noted, it led to "misunderstanding and power struggles," which haunted the Sudeten German party up to 1938.[62] The attacks on Henlein came from different directions: from the Nazis of his own party, people like K. H. Frank, Rudolf Kasper, Heinz Rutha, and Rudolf Haider; from Nazis in the Reich, like Himmler, Krebs, and Ribbentrop; even from old pan-German circles, whose press organ, the *Rumburger Zeitung*, published bitter tirades against him.[63]

The year 1935 was lucky politically for the SDP—the party won the second largest number of seats in the Czechoslovak parliament.[64] Still, in a parliament made up of 300 deputies, the 72 German deputies were a distinct minority, and a divided one at that since the SDP had captured only two-thirds of the German electorate.[65] What made the SDP victory important was that the bitter election campaign had destroyed the formerly dominant national coalition of Czech parties. The resulting power struggle ended favorably for all the minorities when President Masaryk appointed Milan Hodža as prime minister on November 5, 1935.[66]

The resignation of Masaryk (November 21, 1935) opened a new political struggle. The SDP could have played a decisive role in this struggle, but instead the party decided to abstain from voting. This abstention gave the decisive role to the Slovak parties, which elected Eduard Beneš to the presidency.

Choices for the Ethnic Germans

Sudeten Germans' aims regarding their role, present and future, within Czechoslovakia differed according to their party affiliation. These aims are summarized in the following three courses proposed by various factions: cooperation with the Czechoslovakian government as equal citizens within the framework of a democratic republic (activists);[67] cooperation conditional upon receiving cultural autonomy (Henlein's group); and finally, separation of the Sudetenland from Czechoslovakia (Sudeten radical nationalists). The last group was divided about whether to join Germany or Austria.[68] Because of economic conditions such as unemployment, which was especially high among Sudeten German youth, the group that rejected the idea of cooperation, followed the new Nazi ideology, and enjoyed the moral and practical support of the German Reich grew the most rapidly.

The deepening economic crisis undermined support for the activist parties, which had begun to cooperate with the government in 1925. As the government attempted to solve economic problems for the country as a whole, support for heavy industry and agriculture took priority over saving Sudeten German light industry. Thus unemployment was higher among the Germans than the Czechs, and the Germans suffered proportionately more.[69] The Sudeten Germans believed their suffering resulted from a Czechoslovak nationalistic policy, which made them more nationalistic.[70] The activists could have improved their image with the voters only by changing the government's economic policy, but since they were in the minority, it was impossible for them to do this.

Activist policy suffered a setback in the political arena in 1933. At the end of 1932 the goal of cultural autonomy seemed within reach when the minister of education, Ivan Derer, submitted a draft law for this purpose. The law missed its favorable chance of passing when a few days after its submission, Hitler gained control in Germany. "The repercussions were immediately felt in Czechoslovakia."[71] The rightist Sudeten parties immediately interpreted this failure to pass the cultural autonomy law as a "mere trick of the government and the 'Activist' leaders were pilloried as traitors."[72] This event presented the activists with a dilemma. If they continued to cooperate with the government, they would lose even more support. If they became German nationalists, they would betray their own principles.

By 1934 both Czechs and Germans were ignoring the spirit of the minority treaties. The Sudeten Germans turned more and more to extreme nationalism, rejecting the idea of cooperation, let alone assimilation. The moderates in the Czech government also lost influence and control, and though Masaryk still advocated a tolerant policy in order to win the minorities' confidence, his "well-meant advice was not always heeded by the far too powerful bureaucracy of the state."[73] By the time Hodža was appointed prime minister and offered cooperation to the activist parties, these parties represented only a minority of the Sudeten Germans. Thus activist policy did not offer any hope and was rejected in the 1935 election.

The former members of the dissolved DSNAP, who now made up the radical right wing of the SDP, advocated a policy that would result in annexation of the Sudetenland by Germany. This plan, of course, was totally unacceptable to any Czechoslovak government since it meant the destruction of the state. Since the German group could not hope to implement this plan on its own, it needed outside help. But openly seeking such help would have given the Czechoslovak government more reason to regard the German minority as a subversive element, and so would have led to a worsening of their conditions. Ultimately, the goal could be reached only by war, but that would mean great losses for the Sudeten Germans. Their territory would be transformed into a theater of war, which would cause a deterioration of their economy and a heavy loss of life. Not too many Sudeten Germans were willing to make such great sacrifices in light of the fact that Sudeten German industry, even if incorporated into Germany peaceably, would be confronted with almost insurmountable competition from the much better developed Reich industry. Thus striving for this goal was not really in the interest of the Sudeten Germans.

After the failure of the activists to realize German minority ambitions and the rejection of the alternative offered by the Nazis, a third course was proposed by the newly created Sudeten German Homefront (SHF). The official program of the SHF advocated complete autonomy for the Sudeten German regions. It was a radical version of the activists' aim, which was only cultural autonomy.[74] The international situation in 1935 offered no hope for a peaceful, legal revision of the peace treaties by League of Nations resolution.

Their experiences as an opposition group for fifteen years had proved to the Sudeten Germans that lack of cooperation with the Czech government would gain them nothing. At the same time, the failure of the activist policy had shown that an ethnic group divided into different political parties could not expect to realize its ambitions. Now they hoped to succeed by uniting the ethnic group in one great mass organization that, by sheer numbers, would force the Czechoslovak government to grant its goals. This mass organization was the SHF.

In early 1935 the SHF was transformed into a political party in order to be able to represent the Sudeten Germans in the national elections. The new *Sudeten Deutsche Partei* (SDP) united all shades of the political spectrum. Its leadership, headed by Konrad Henlein, who was considered by the Germans as well as the Czechs to be a moderate nationalist, also reflected the views of the different groups that made up the SDP. But just before the 1935 elections the former members of the DSNAP, who had created within the SDP a radical nationalistic faction, began to grow more influential because they were able to secure the financial support of the Reich organizations for the forthcoming elections.[75] It amounted to the considerable sum of RM 330,000, and unquestionably played an important role in the election victory of the SDP.[76] After the victory the radical alternative seemed to be the most realistic platform.

In the prevailing conditions the SDP seemed to represent the best interests of the ethnic Germans of Czechoslovakia. With its aims of autonomy and the transformation of Czechoslovakia into a federalist state, the party was acceptable within the political and constitutional life of the Czech republic. Undeniably, the Reich government, the organizations dealing with the *Auslandsdeutsche*, and the Nazi party tried to direct the SDP according to their own interests. It was also clear that the Nazis within the SDP leadership would do their best to influence the party's policy according to their own ideology and, if possible, to take over its leadership. But for the time being, the moderate SDP leaders seemed to be firmly in control. What direction the SDP would take in the future depended on their actions, and even more on the actions and reactions of the new Czechoslovak government.

Policy of the Czechoslovak Government

What made Hitler's coming to power so significant for Czechoslovakia was the ethnic composition of the state. The spread of strong nationalist or separatist ideas among the different ethnic groups would mean a formidable new obstacle to the strengthening of the state's central authority and the more or less successful assimilation efforts, and might even endanger national security. The growing popularity of autonomist demands in Slovakia and Ruthenia proved how dangerous the effects of Nazi victory were.[77] The propagandizing of Sudeten Germans for German Nazism, winning their allegiance from the Czechoslovak state to the German Reich, would cripple

Czechoslovakia, possibly trigger a civil war, and create international complications.

It is not surprising then that Czech reaction to the upsurge of nationalism among the ethnic groups was strong. The Czechs were determined to stop any activity that might endanger the security of the state. But the election successes of the SDP and the losses of the German activists created a new situation: the German population, judging by these signs, wanted some new basis for future cooperation. Thus the Czechoslovak government had to review its policy and find an alternative that would further the realization of its own aims.

Up to 1935 the Czech government's Sudeten policy had been to cooperate with the activist parties while cracking down on the enemies of the state. In order to maintain the activist parties' popularity with the ethnic German electorate it would have been in the interest of the Czech government to grant them little successes; for example, cultural autonomy. However, this opportunity was missed when the draft bill of 1932 failed to pass. The upsurge of nationalism among the Slovak and Ruthenian autonomist parties made the revival of the bill now, in 1935, seemingly impossible. It would have led to the fragmentation of the state, and very few Czech patriots would have been willing to accept this. Thus, autonomy was too high a price to pay for the cooperation of the German ethnic group. To continue the present policy of ignoring the SDP and cooperating with the activist parties only would lead to the complete alienation of the ethnic Germans.

Since the German Nazis in Czechoslovakia denied their loyalty to the state and gave it instead to the Hitler regime, it was undoubtedly in the interest of Czechoslovakia to suppress them. Such a policy would be wholeheartedly supported by the Czech nationalists in the government bureaucracy as well as in private life. However, it was also in the interest of the Czechoslovak government not to alienate the loyal ethnic German majority during this operation. Dissolving the Nazi group had been only a legal solution. It was now necessary to limit the Nazis' influence, separate them from the Sudeten German masses, and most of all prevent them from becoming martyrs of Germandom. For the success of this policy, the government had to find a group of moderate Sudeten Germans who could unite the ethnic Germans behind their own goals while remaining loyal and cooperative.

In short, the government's policy required the substitution of SDP support for that of the activists. It hoped with this policy to promote political cooperation, and at the same time to serve primarily Czech national and state interests in every area. The success of the policy depended on the ability of the government to turn the attention of the ethnic Germans from their crucial demand, autonomy, and pacify them with concessions that would improve their conditions without weakening basic state interests. The task was difficult. But for the time being the conditions seemed favorable for the government. One year after the dissolution of the DSNAP the *Deutscher Kulturverband* and its chairman, Dr. Funke (representing the largest German organization), emphasized the loyalty of the members to the state and also sent a telegram declaring their loyalty to the president of the republic.[78] The election successes of the SDP—it became the second largest party in the parliament—also suggested to the government that rapprochement might be possible. Since the leaders of the new party were relatively unknown, it seemed to be good policy to make contact with them and learn about their views. But the growing, vehement anti-Nazi attitude of the Czech parties, press, and public opinion made rapprochement a very dangerous task for the new government; concessions to the ethnic Germans would threaten the loss of Czech support. Still, this alternative looked promising enough to pursue.

An attempt to transform Czechoslovakia into a federalist republic seemed to be the most dangerous possibility from the point of view of national security. Giving autonomy to the ethnic regions would weaken the authority of the central government, might very well strengthen the separatist forces, and would mean the abandonment of the idea of a unified nation-state. It would meet with bitter opposition from the Czech nationalists and probably disapproval by the Little Entente states, thereby creating an international political problem. But if a federal transformation of the state could be implemented smoothly, then the great majority of the different ethnic groups would be pacified and the radical elements among them would lose support. This course of action was risky even if successful because of German, Hungarian, and Polish revisionism. It would have to be pursued slowly and carefully.

The best plan for the Czechoslovak government seemed to be a rapprochement with the newly formed Sudeten German majority, granting them concessions that would raise their leaders' popularity without endangering the security of the state, at the same time cracking down on those elements among both Sudeten Germans and Czechs who wanted to prevent the mutual understanding of government and minorities. With the appointment of Milan Hodža as prime minister and foreign minister in 1935 the Czechoslovak government was led by a man who well understood minority grievances. He also foresaw the dangers of Hitler's foreign policy and chose as a basic aim of his own foreign policy the formation of a "bloc of Danubian nations to thwart Hitler's *Drang nach Osten* (push toward the east)."[79] Unfortunately, his plans were opposed not only by the radical Czech nationalists, but also by the newly elected president, Eduard Beneš. Thus rapprochement had a very slight chance or no chance at all.

Alternatives of the Reich

Hitler professed traditional pan-German ideas and wanted to gain control of all the German-inhabited territories in Europe. This distant goal was to be reached by achieving first the revision of the peace treaties, and then the annexation of ethnic German territories to the Reich. The first months of 1935 did not seem to bring Germany closer to these goals. Although the outcome of the Saar plebiscite (January 13) boosted German morale and gained some respect for revisionist demands in Europe, the Laval-Mussolini agreement (January 7),[80] Polish reassurances given to France (March),[81] the reintroduction of conscription in Germany (March 14), which created an anti-German mood in Europe, and the French-Soviet mutual assistance treaty (May 2), which isolated Germany from the rest of Europe, all demanded caution in the pursuit of revisionist and pan-German aims.

The landslide victory of the SDP in Czechoslovakian elections did not change Germany's international position. Yet the German government had to assess this new situation, explore the possible alternatives, and select the one that would best promote Germany's foreign political aims. In 1935 the aim of Germany's foreign policy was the peaceful revision of the Versailles Treaty, which meant cooperation with the League of Nations in order to obtain its consent for plebiscites. Although Germany had withdrawn from the League on October 14, 1933, Hitler was not in a position to defy the treaty openly. If plebiscites were to be held in the disputed territories, it was in Germany's interest to ensure a favorable outcome for herself by preserving the Germandom of the *Auslandsdeutsche*. How to do this was a question that strongly divided Reich German authorities as well as public opinion.

The Nazi party wanted to accomplish this goal by nazification of the ethnic Germans. This approach proved unsuccessful in the Sudeten territories because of the alertness of the Czechoslovak government and the less than unanimous support of the Nazis among the Sudeten Germans. The *Auswärtiges Amt* (AA; Foreign Ministry) promoted the traditional policy toward the ethnic Germans, that is, preserving their Germandom through satisfying their cultural needs, keeping them conscious of their Germandom, and nurturing their sentiments and desires to join the Great German Reich. In implementing this policy—which seemed to be successful in light of the 1935 Czechoslovak elections—the organizations caring for the *Auslandsdeutsche* seemed to be doing a very good job, since their activities did not compromise the Reich government. At the same time, it was in the interest of both the Sudeten Germans and the Reich, to further the unification of the ethnic group into a great mass movement. The SDP was the plausible choice for this purpose. Thus the continuation of present policy of the *Auswärtiges Amt* offered the most promising approach.

To go to war to annex the lost and German-inhabited territories was Hitler's first choice. But for Germany to start a war under present economic, military, domestic, and foreign political conditions would have been insane.[82] War could be taken into consideration as a future solution (and was). In case of war with Czechoslovakia, the Sudeten Germans could play a vital role. But opinions were divided on what this role should be. Hitler never designed any active role for the ethnic Germans in case of an armed conflict. The *Auswärtiges Amt*, following the advice of the VDA and other organizations, never worked out such plans either to avoid endangering the lives of the ethnic German population. The army did plan to use ethnic Germans, but only specially trained volunteers from among the Sudeten refugees who were residing in the Reich. Curiously enough, the possibility of a Sudeten German national uprising was never even discussed. Perhaps this omission reflected a realistic evaluation of existing conditions among the Sudeten Germans. Some minor and local party officials did, on their own initiative, attempt to organize the more militant members of the ethnic group into small fighting forces, but their effectiveness was doubtful and most of them were neutralized owning to the good work of Czech counterintelligence.[83]

Course of Events after 1935

After the elections Henlein wanted to learn whether or not Hitler agreed with his policy, but Hitler refused to see him.[84] Not receiving any guidelines, Henlein pursued the old pan-German policy and became gradually more and more open about it.[85] Otherwise the party platform was cryptic. Henlein was careful not to push the Czechs too far and also to avoid specific pronouncements that might offend some Sudetens even in his own party.[86] During the summer of 1935 Henlein met Robert Gilbert Vansittart, British permanent undersecretary of state for foreign affairs, in Switzerland, which later gave him the opportunity to become acquainted with important English political leaders. Under cover of attending the August 1936 Olympic Games in Berlin, Henlein talked secretly with many of the top Reich leaders, perhaps even Hitler himself.[87] The appointment of Milan Hodža on November 6, 1935, gave new hope to the moderates among the Sudeten Germans. But this hope vanished when Beneš became president of the republic on December 18, 1935. The leadership of Czechoslovakia passed to a man who had opposed in 1934 and would continue to oppose, any cooperation of the government or the coalition with Henlein's party because he was "already convinced about the real objective of that party."[88] Beneš misjudged the situation because in 1936 the domestic political problems of Czechoslovakia, including the minority question, were not yet too pressing.

Comparing the alternatives with the courses selected, we can see that both the Reich German government and the Sudeten German party selected a policy that best served their respective interests: the Reich supporting the ethnic group to preserve its Germandom, the party making use of every contact available to reach its goal of autonomy within the Czechoslovak republic. The German Nazi party, on the other hand, had its own aim: the nazification of the ethnic Germans. Blinded by a narrow ideological approach, it did not hesitate to start a power struggle within the Reich as well as within the newly united Sudeten German party, thus hurting the interests of both the Reich and the ethnic Germans. But with Hitler in control, the party could be sure that its policy would prevail. Finally the Czechoslovak government, with its new prime minister, Hodža, selected the alternative that promised to serve the interests of the republic, but Hodža's desire to pursue that policy was blocked by the ideologically motivated President Beneš. His strong, and outdated, Czech nationalism prevented reconciliation between the German (and other) minorities and the government, and by frustrating the minorities, he pushed the entire Sudeten German population toward more radical demands and solutions.

Hitler—Henlein—Hodža

Was the Sudeten German problem an internal Czechoslovak matter or an international question? The Czechoslovak government maintained verbally right up to Munich that it was an internal affair, but from 1934 on it behaved as though it expected international repercussions. It proceeded with rearmament, fortifications, and a two-year military service requirement.[89] Still, the government expected that this strong defense policy, coupled with assistance from France and Britain, would enable it to confine the problem to its own borders. To deny French and British support of the Czech policy Henlein carried on a successful campaign to reassure the British about his peaceful intentions. He visited London repeatedly from December 1935 to May 1938—with impressive results. His speeches were conciliatory, stressing his support of Czechoslovak democracy, asking only for a "just" settlement. By October 1936 he was able to report to the AA that British support had strengthened the SDP vis-à-vis Prague.[90]

In the meantime, the international situation began to change to Hitler's benefit. The German remilitarization of the Rhineland (March 7, 1936) and the weak French reaction to it proved to friends and foes that the French security system had collapsed. Still, Beneš believed unconditionally in the value of French patronage. Nor did he change his domestic political conceptions. He refused to negotiate with the SDP. The activist parties, now representing a minority of Sudeten Germans, sensed the changed mood of the ethnic Germans and submitted the minority group's grievances to the Czechoslovak government on January 27, 1937.[91]

These demands, theoretically accepted by the government on February 18, 1937, fell short of autonomy and asked only for equality with Czech citizens. Now Henlein and the SDP went into action, publishing their own demands, which included national autonomy for the Sudetenland with reparations for past injustices to be paid to the Germans by the Czechs. As spelled out in the April draft laws presented by the SDP, this program would have created strictly separate nationality groups, each under a speaker who would be answerable to no one[92]—an obvious impossibility in a democratic republic. There was no question of such laws being accepted. According to the Austrian ambassador in Prague, the SDP proposal was made purely for propaganda purposes, and it did serve to dampen enthusiasm for the February 18 reform program. If we accept the ambassador's statement at face value, it is still necessary to find out where the propaganda was organized and how it was executed.

This big propaganda campaign had no centralized leadership. As a matter of fact, forces and personalities opposed to one another tried to exploit the autonomy issue to gain the upper hand. Inflammatory speeches by SDP right-wing leaders raised Sudeten German expectations, and it was clear that they could not possibly be realized without greater political support from the Reich.[93] But even financial support was in danger, since by the spring of 1937 Germany had begun to suffer the economic effects of the forced rearmament.[94] Furthermore, Hitler, in order to divert attention from the economic crisis, wanted to produce a spectacular but easy foreign political success, and Austria was selected as the target. In order to secure the consent and neutrality of the neighboring states, among them Czechoslovakia, Hitler opposed the radical line followed by the Sudeten German Nazis. This attitude of the Reich favored Henlein's plan, according to which the Sudeten Germans had to reach a *modus vivendi* with the Czech government and remain within the framework of the Czechoslovak republic. Henlein tried to reach this feasible arrangement by exerting foreign pressure on the Czech government, as well as through a meeting with Prime Minister Hodža. For that purpose architect Heinz Rutha, the foreign political expert of the SDP, tried to make contact with Vansittart in London. SDP demands were echoed and supported in the Italian press.[95] Henlein explored the possibility of closer relations with Austria, but Vienna's reaction was cool and unfavorable.[96] After much cautious preparation Henlein met and talked with Prime Minister Milan Hodža for the first time on September 16, 1937.[97] A month later, on October 17, an incident at Teplitz gave their negotiations a setback.[98] In a minor skirmish K. H. Frank, a radical SDP leader and deputy, claimed he was beaten by the police.[99] The German press played up the incident for all it was worth. Henlein wrote Beneš a letter of protest, which was broadcast over the German radio before the president received it,[100] timing that was not designed to allay suspicion. "Czechoslovak attitudes visibly hardened, local elections were postponed, and all political meetings banned."[101] Somewhat taken aback by this strong government response, the SDP reduced its activities momentarily.[102]

Though Henlein didn't know it, the choices were now out of his control. On November 5, 1937, Hitler made clear his plan to "settle the Czech question by force" in a meeting with his military leaders.[103]

The Austrian ambassador to Prague had approached the Czech government about Berlin's request for the right to organize the Reich Germans living in Czechoslovakia into Nazi party formations.[104] The Czechoslovak reply was surprisingly conciliatory and expressed only one fear: since the Reich wanted to make enrollment in the Nazi party obligatory for all Reich Germans, the Czech government feared that party officials would misuse their power against the non-Nazi German citizens.[105]

Although these negotiations were concerned only with German citizens living in Czechoslovakia, the direct interference of the Reich had a tremendous impact on the SDP leadership. The power struggle between the Nazi group within the SDP (under the leadership of Rudolf Kasper) and Henlein's moderate group was renewed with vigor. The result was confusion, and there was not a single person in the SDP "who could negotiate with the Czechoslovak government in the name of the entire membership."[106] Now the race began in earnest on the part of both factions for Hitler's favor. Henlein tried to harmonize his group's demands with Hitler's plans for Czechoslovakia. In his long political report to the Führer on November 19, 1937, he expressed doubt about the party's February demand for autonomy.[107] The implied (and preferred) alternative was outright annexation by Germany, though the SDP "would have settled for less if that had been Hitler's aim."[108]

Henlein admitted that the SDP had known from the start that no agreement was possible between the Czechoslovaks and Germans. The party had decided to put forth the 1937 proposal for racial minority protection because it believed it was the only way to put the Czechs in the wrong before the world and to present the Sudeten German question to the Guarantee Powers of the Minority Protection Treaty of St. Germain and, above all, to the British.[109]

On January 1, 1938, Henlein openly tied the Sudeten German problem to German-Czechoslovak relations by stating that the country would find no agreement possible with Germany until the minority problem was solved to the satisfaction of the Sudetens. He offered no specific plan since he had no orders from Germany. His request for an audience with Hitler included in the report of November 19 would go unmet until Hitler had successfully completed the business of first importance to him—*Anschluss* with Austria.

Hitler served notice to the world of his immediate plans on February 20, 1938, in his Reichstag speech. He spoke of the ten million Germans[110] living in "two of the states adjoining our frontiers" who had been prevented by the peacemakers in 1919 from joining the Reich but whose "rights as members of a national community" Germany recognized.[111] Within three weeks 6.5 million of them would be joined to the Reich, leaving the other 3.75 million with high expectations of a similar outcome in the near future.

Attention in early March focused mainly on Austria; still, everyone realized the position of Czechoslovakia in that connection. President Beneš re-emphasized the internal nature of the minorities problem on March 5. Then, thinking perhaps of the impossibility of maintaining this stance without French and British help, he told the *Sunday Times* reporter who was interviewing him that he did grant the "moral right" of Europe to take an interest in the minorities,[112] for the sake of maintaining peace. This apparent contradiction in his statements would play into Hitler's hands when he was ready to force the issue with Czechoslovakia, for if France and Britain had the "moral right" to intervene, surely Germany had also. Austria seemed enough to handle at one time, however, and immediately after the *Anschluss*, on the night of March 11–12, Hitler hastened to reassure Czechoslovakia that Germany had no designs on her. He even took steps to tighten his control over the SDP[113] to prevent any precipitate incidents. Austria had to be digested before he could begin the next meal.

The SPD was overjoyed that Germany was acting at last, and Henlein sent Ribbentrop a letter of congratulation containing praise for Hitler on the Austrian events. He knew the proper way for Sudeten Germans to show their gratitude: "We shall render our thanks to the Führer by redoubling our efforts in the service of the policy of Greater Germany."[114] The significance of Germany's new active foreign policy and of Germany's exclusive relationship with the SDP was not lost on the leadership of the other German parties. For different reasons (opportunism, fear, misguided German patriotism, desperation), they hastened to join the winner. In March the German Christian Social, Traders, and Agrarian parties all fused with the SDP. The Clericals withdrew their representative from the government, while Dr. Spina of the Agrarian party retired in dismay at the failure of his policy of cooperation.[115]

Now there was talk of bringing the SDP into the Czechoslovak government. Ambassador Eisenlohr discussed the situation with Hodža and reported to Berlin that the main condition was that the SDP agree to settle the Sudeten German question within the present constitution and without demanding territorial autonomy. In return, Hodža was willing to grant concessions. He planned to get rid of the minister of health, Dr. Czech, and replace him with another Social Democrat, Wenzel Jaksch, who he assumed would be more acceptable to both the SDP and the Reich.[116] He also pledged that the most distasteful provisions of the National Defense Law[117] would not be enforced against Germans and that the new law for introducing state police into frontier districts would be repealed. There was also discussion of amnesty for German political prisoners. This last concession was signed by Beneš on April 16, 1938. The amnesty benefited only certain political prisoners, not those being held for trial in treason or espionage cases. Released altogether were approximately 1,235 Germans, 930 Czechs and Slovaks, 485 Hungarians, 187 Ruthenians, and 30 Poles.[118] If we compare the number of released political prisoners to the total population in each ethnic group, the percentages are insignificant: Germans, .038 percent; Czechs and Slovaks, .009 percent; Hungarians, .07 percent; Ruthenians, .034 percent; Poles, .036 percent. None of the ethnic groups could complain about political oppression on the basis of these numbers, even if the prisoners had not been released.

The amnesty should have been the basis of an agreement between Germans and Czechs, and it probably would have been if German leaders had been genuinely interested in peace. But meanwhile, Henlein had visited Hitler on March 28, 1938, and had received the impression that it was not just the Sudeten German area but all of Czechoslovakia that he desired—and soon.[119] Henlein and the SDP could further Hitler's plan by spinning out their negotiations, always demanding so much that they could never be satisfied.[120] This they agreed to do. In a meeting the next day with top foreign ministry personnel and other officials, Henlein, Frank, and other SDP leaders were assured of complete German backing. Naturally this backing was to remain covert while the SDP confronted the Czechoslovak government.[121]

In Czechoslovakia German enthusiasm over the recent events in Austria climaxed with great rallies by the SDP on Sunday, March 27, 1938. Eisenlohr reported to the German foreign ministry that some 500,000 demonstrators had turned out. In Eger 25,000 of the total 34,000 inhabitants demonstrated, and in Saaz 15,000 of 18,000 people marched to cries of "one people, one Reich, one Führer!"[122] The police were restrained in their response, obviously on government orders, but further large demonstrations of this type were banned. The number of demonstrators reported by Eisenlohr may have been exaggerated, or it is possible that some of the demonstrators took part unwillingly under pressure from the militant group leaders. When the Czech government banned the demonstrations, these people would have been relieved and happy. Because of the ban the annual SDP meeting at Karlovy Vary (Karlsbad) in April was technically a private affair. Only Reich German supporters were admitted but Henlein's speech reached the public soon enough.

Karlsbad Program and the May Crisis

Following through on the plan to demand the impossible, Henlein proposed a complete reorientation of Czechoslovak foreign policy. Czechoslovakia was to align itself with Germany, a return to what Henlein regarded as the "historic connection" (although the Historic Provinces had never been part of Germany). He called for an end to the role Czechoslovakia had assumed as a barricade against the *Drang nach Osten*. In addition to these general demands, there were eight specific proposals:

> Complete equality of the German and Czech peoples.
> Legal status for the Sudeten German national group as a whole.
> Recognition of the specific territory inhabited by Germans.
> Autonomous administration in public affairs.
> Legal protection for Germans living outside their national area.
> Reparation for injuries to Germans since 1918.
> All German officials in German areas.
> Full freedom of expression for the German *Weltanschauung*.

Henlein's speech also condemned the recent Nationalities Statute, which was basically a codification of the existing legislation affecting minorities.[123] Thus the lines were drawn between the government's moderate proposals and the SDP's immoderate ones. Everything was working out well according to Hitler's plan.

Within a month the picture appeared to have changed drastically. Communal elections were scheduled for Sunday, May 22, 1938, in the German area, and tension increased as the time approached. There were rumors of German troop movements near the border of Czechoslovakia and "Czech fears . . . seem to have derived from detailed and at least superficially plausible reports . . . received just as the Sudeten German party leaders broke off their negotiations with the Czech government."[124] Considering what had happened in Austria scarcely two months before, it was easy to imagine that the Germans might stage a weekend invasion based on some incident related to the election. The first reports on German troop movements reached Czechoslovakia from the British embassy in Berlin on May 20.[125] This fact invalidates the accusation of the Germans that rumors had been spread by the Czechs to excuse themselves from any responsibility for an incident that happened in Eger on May 21, 1938. One class of reservists was called up to reinforce the army along the frontier early on that day. Two German farmers on a motorcycle failed to respond to an order to stop and were shot dead by a policeman, who said he was trying to puncture their tire. The shooting was probably an accident, but the German press made much of it. The press had "hitherto been obliged to content itself with vague accounts of manhunts of Germans in Prague and Brno and of the general failure of the Czech police to protect Sudeten Germans or to allow the singing of German songs."[126] To finally have an actual incident with real victims was a propaganda break.

More important for the entire situation was the fact that the partial mobilization had been completed smoothly and efficiently, even the Sudeten Germans responding when called. This message was not lost on Hitler and probably had the effect of speeding up his plans. He was eager to make use of the gap in Czech defenses opened by the absorption of Austria before the Czechs had a chance to close it. The Eger incident seemed to fade quickly once the public funeral was over, but the effects on Hitler were profound. The foreign press made much of Germany's "diplomatic defeat" by British and French pressure.[127] It has never been clear whether Germany was actually toying with the idea of invasion at that time, but the "rejoicings of the foreign press exasperated Hitler and made him decide to fix a date for the settlement with Czechoslovakia." Only one week after the Eger incident, Hitler reached his decision, and on May 30, 1938, the revised directive for "Operation Green," a surprise attack on Czechoslovakia, was signed.[128] It was to be carried out by October 1.[129] Hitler's plans were unknown to the Czechoslovak government and to the other interested parties; France, Britain, and Russia. Negotiations continued sporadically between the Czech government and the SDP, but the British eventually assumed the lead in trying to reach some solution that would avoid war. Their efforts involved a sequence of four main moves—the Runciman mission and the meetings with Hitler at Berchtesgaden, Godesberg, and finally Munich. During this process France seemed to be swept along in Britain's wake and Russia to be slighted altogether, while Czech wishes were largely ignored. Hitler had everything his way.

The elections passed without further incident, and by the time the last of them had been held on June 12, 1938, the number of soldiers in evidence had been greatly reduced.[130] Contacts between the government and the SDP continued, although the text of the Nationalities Statute still had not been presented by the government. On June 8 the SDP responded to a request from Beneš for a complete statement of its demands with a fourteen-point program based essentially on the Karlsbad plan. When some information about the Nationalities Statute leaked, the Sudeten and Reich German press unanimously rejected it. At the same time, the Czech press as adamantly rejected the SDP proposal.[131]

When parts of the Czech statute were finally published unofficially on July

27, 1938, it seemed to moderates and to foreigners a very generous settlement for the minorities, going far beyond the requirements of the minority treaties or the treatment dealt to minorities by any of Czechoslovakia's neighbors. But the very concept of a dominant majority granting rights to a minority was unacceptable to the SDP. It demanded complete equality of nationalities.[132]

By this time the British had taken upon themselves the mission of sending a special "independent advisor" to Czechoslovakia to deal with the problem between Czechs and Germans.[133] Lord Runciman agreed to accept the task and arrived in Prague on August 3, 1938. He was immediately "inundated with memoranda and appeals" from all sides.[134] The SDP intended to convince Runciman that the problem had no solution within the present confines of Czechoslovakia, and that this was all the fault of the Czechs, who alone were the "disturbers of peace in Europe."[135] The Runciman Mission was made to believe that the Karlsbad program was fair and would provide a genuine solution.[136]

Runciman was apparently also impressed by the moderate and sensible suggestions of the German Social Democrats headed by Wenzel Jaksch. Their memorandum warned that the leadership of the SDP resided in Germany. It concluded that a peaceful and lasting solution would come only from economic improvements in the German area and "conversion of the Sudeten Germans to democratic government by permitting them to see what advantages and what toleration it could bring." The observation of the Social Democratic leadership is frequently disregarded by modern scholars. The Sudeten Germans' turn to extreme nationalism was not instigated only by National Socialist successes in Germany or by the propaganda of the VDA and other German organizations. The Sudeten Germans looked at the actions of Nazi Germany as well as of the successive Czech governments from their own selfish point of view. They had hoped for an improvement in their economic condition through support of the Social Democrats, and only after those hopes had been frustrated did they look elsewhere for help. They turned to Nazism in the depth of the Depression, as the 1935 election results show. Unfortunately by 1938 the Social Democrats represented only a small number of the Germans (eleven of the seventy deputies) and spoke more to future generations who would study the problems in retrospect than to the British mission.

Runciman, who "had not the slightest qualification for a task which would have been beyond a far abler man," viewed the SDP as the equal of the Czechoslovak government.[137] Pressed by London to reach some quick settlement, he urged more and more concessions on the Czechs. In mid-August Beneš decided to intervene personally in the negotiations by presenting his Third Plan. It went far toward meeting the Karlsbad program—so far, in fact, that several SDP leaders admitted that it could not be rejected outright. They promised a reply by September 2, 1938.[138]

Within the government there was conflict between Prime Minister Hodža and President Beneš over Beneš's negotiations with the SDP. SDP Deputy Ernst Kundt speculated that Hodža might reverse his pro-German stance just to undercut Beneš. He feared that the prime minister would reveal to Runciman incriminating evidence against the SDP, which he surely possessed.[139] Such a revelation apparently did not occur.

During August German military exercises were held in order that they might lead naturally into the real thing should an invasion of Czechoslovakia be necessary. Also, agitators and secret commandos were slipped across the border from Germany, and a number of incidents led to the arrest of Germans.[140]

On September 2, 1938, the SDP made a formal reply to the Third Plan—it was a rejection, but with counterproposals. Beneš requested that they continue discussions the next day, but the SDP negotiators insisted on waiting until September 5. Henlein was in Germany consulting with Hitler, and it was obvious that they had to hear the results before they could proceed.[141] Henlein returned in a happy mood, saying that the Führer agreed with him in not wanting war, although he was skeptical about the possibility of a suitable settlement in Czechoslovakia. This was slight encouragement, but with it "the British mediators took up their task once more, with only eight days in which to produce a miracle of agreement before Hitler, having descended from the mountain top, should let fly amid the passionate nationalism of the Nazi Party Congress at Nuremberg and should declare that 'his patience was exhausted.'"[142]

Working under the threat of the approaching Nuremberg Party Congress, the British minister in Prague added his pressure to that of Runciman. Between them they convinced Beneš that he must make the Germans an irresistible offer or else stand alone against the Reich. The result was the Fourth Plan, which essentially conformed to the Karlsbad program—even including autonomy. It was presented to the SDP on September 7, 1938. The SDP leaders agreed among themselves that it was acceptable, but they then "decided to inform the Government that negotiations could not be resumed until an incident which had occurred at Moravska Ostrava (Mährisch Ostrau) during the day had been cleared up."[143] Thus, they got around the embarrassment of suddenly being granted all they had requested when their real desire was to spin out the negotiations to suit Hitler's timetable. Although the incident itself was trivial and strikingly similar to the Teplitz affair of October 1937, it served as an excuse to break off negotiations. It also provided fuel for almost hysterical speeches from Goebbels and Göring at Nuremberg.[144]

By a fateful coincidence, the *Times* of London published a lead article on September 7, 1938, which had buried in it a suggestion that not even Hitler and Henlein had yet dared to offer. The suggestion was to make Czechoslovakia more "homogeneous" by ceding the "fringe of alien population who are contiguous to the nation with which they are united by race." By using the plural, it even opened the door to Hungarian and Polish, as well as German, claims. Although the article was evidently not inspired by the government, it can only have comforted Hitler.

After Hitler's long-anticipated speech at Nuremberg on September 12, which was an invitation to revolt, a number of incidents occurred in the border area of Czechoslovakia. In some places martial law was necessary, but by the fifteenth order was restored. "The whole uprising had been the work of a few desperadoes who could have been rendered harmless very much sooner had not the authorities kept the use of force to the absolute minimum."[145] This judgment of the English experts is not justified in light of new evidence. The uprising and related sabotage and terrorist actions were the work of the *Sudetendeutsche Freikorps*, organized in Germany and deployed in Czechoslovakia in September 1938.[146] On September 13 the SDP had issued an ultimatum that it would not resume negotiations unless martial law ended and the state police were withdrawn from German areas. When the six-hour time limit was up, the party announced to the frantic British negotiators that the old rules were out of date; now negotiations were feasible only on the basis of self-determination and a plebiscite.[147] While the British rushed about Prague trying to force a Czech concession, Henlein, Frank, and other SDP executives slipped across the border into Germany.

Their desertion was a gift that the Czech press and radio quickly grasped. As the news spread, it caused a crisis of confidence in Sudeten German circles. Certain mayors who were SDP members defied Henlein by calling for order and an end to subversion. The rector and deans of the German university and technical high schools signed statements condemning Henlein's "treasonable activities" (possibly under pressure from the Czech minister of education). The news had a "crushing effect in the German area," and the Czechoslovak government was confident and in control.[148] This would have been the opportunity for Beneš to regain the initiative if the true issue had been the treatment of Sudeten Germans. But of course, it was not. The true issue was Hitler's desire to crush Czechoslovakia.

After the sudden failure of the Runciman Mission just as it had seemed to be on the verge of success, the French were left with the responsibility of deciding what to do next. They had treaty obligations to Czechoslovakia, as did Russia. But the Russians would help only if the French did, and their lack of a common border with Czechoslovakia would render any help difficult. France preferred to have British backing before getting involved, although Britain had no treaty obligations to Czechoslovakia. In all the talk between French and British officials about bringing more pressure to bear on Beneš, there was never any mention of pressuring Hitler.

On September 15, 1938, Prime Minister Chamberlain made his first personal visit to Hitler. The Munich crisis had begun.[149]

CHAPTER III

The Swabians of Hungary

Conditions to 1935

Hungary's situation following World War I may be described as complete isolation. She was surrounded on three sides by allies of the victorious powers, and only on the West did she have a neighbor, Austria, which was not a member of the Little Entente. Even with Austria relations were strained because of Burgenland.[1] The Treaty of Trianon sanctioned the separation of large territories from the main body of Hungary in the name of national self-determination. The peacemakers' aim to create homogeneous nation-states was almost fully realized in the case of Hungary. The minorities there were quite small, representing less than 10 percent of the population.[2] The Germans made up the largest group.

Fortunately for the Hungarian authorities the country had no common frontier with Germany. Besides this physical separation, there was also a political one: Germany's democratic form of government was too far to the left for the taste of Hungarians, with their traditional parliamentary system.[3] Although both Hungary and Germany were revisionist states, Germany was too weak to be a useful ally and therefore Hungary preferred Italian patronage in the 1920s. All these factors provided Hungary with a better opportunity than any of the other Successor States to solve her minority problem as she pleased, within the framework of the minority treaties.

The Swabians (ethnic Germans) were faithful and loyal citizens of Hungary and their national consciousness was quiescent as far as political activities were concerned. They used their mother tongue, kept their old customs, and lived in the same little villages that their ancestors had built when they migrated to Hungary under the settlement programs of the Habsburgs in the eighteenth and nineteenth centuries. Although the majority were so-called smallholder peasants, they had a good living standard and had a "proportionally smaller share among the woefully neglected millions than the Magyars who were, ironically, nationals of what is called the dominating ethnic group."[4]

Their chances to make a career for themselves or move upward on the social ladder were as good as those of the Magyars, if they gave up their old customs, learned the Magyar language, and assimilated to the social and cultural customs of the Hungarian state. Even this assimilation did not create a conflict with their German national consciousness.

During the short period of the Hungarian republic (November 1918–March 1919) and during the dictatorship of the proletariat (March 31–August 6, 1919), the Germans of Hungary won considerable cultural concessions. The leader of the moderate Swabian ethnic group, Professor Jacob Bleyer, was the minister of nationality affairs in the provisional governments (August 15, 1919–December 16, 1920) that prepared the way for the regency.[5] The Nationalities Act and Education Act, passed during Bleyer's ministry, promised further improvements for the different minority groups.[6] The Trianon Treaty, which in its articles 54–60 contained regulations for the protection of minorities, secured the rights to use minority languages and to maintain minority schools, and protected the civil rights of minorities. These treaty regulations were incorporated into two Orders in Council[7] of the Hungarian government issued in 1923. These Orders gave specific instructions for the organization of three different types of minority schools, thus securing opportunity and a choice for the German minorities to study in their mother tongue or in Hungarian. Although Hungary, as a result of the territorial reassignments of the Trianon Treaty, was one of the purest nation-states created by the peacemakers,[8] Hungarians looked upon the minority groups with suspicion. This suspicion was created by the different interpretations of the minority policy of preceding years and centuries. While some ethnic German leaders complained bitterly against the forceful magyarization program of the pre-World War I years,[9] the Hungarians argued that the different national minority groups, who—thanks to the traditional liberal minority policy in Hungary—had been able to preserve their ethnicity throughout the centuries, had repaid this toleration with the dismemberment of Hungary in 1919. Thus a forceful assimilation was justified in the interests of national security.[10]

Bound by the minority treaties, the postwar Hungarian government was careful not to violate the words of the international laws. But in practice it used every loophole to magyarize the remaining ethnic groups. Since the authors of the minority treaties themselves saw the solution of ethnic problems in unavoidable assimilation, the government argued that it was only trying to speed up the process.

The organization of an ethnic political party was not permitted for the ethnic Germans since the treaties did not require it. Other organizations that existed before and during World War I in Hungary had their centers in the most numerous ethnic German territories (Bácska, Bánát, Transylvania), which were taken away from Hungary by the peace treaties. Thus the *Volksdeutsche* of Trianon Hungary were left without any organization.

Only in 1924 did the Hungarian government grant the ethnic Germans the right to revive the old *Ungarländisch-Deutscher Volksbindungsverein* (UDV) as a cultural society. Dr. Gustav Gratz, former foreign minister of

Hungary, was elected as chairman of the association. Professor Jacob Bleyer, former minister of cultural affairs, became his assistant. Honorary presidents were Professor Kúnó Klebelsberg, one Evangelical, and three Catholic bishops. Within a year the organizational work produced some 8,000 members in 200 local branches.[11] It also published a weekly *Sontagsblatt.*

Since the UDV was allowed to function only in the field of cultural education, its aim was the preservation of the German language and customs among the ethnic Germans. The main difficulty for the realization of this goal was the magyarization policy of the Hungarian government, which successfully used the schools to assimilate those members of the German Magyars who had reached higher educational levels.[12] If a member of a minority group did "not put his special national feeling above all considerations, Hungary [was] the best country to live in of all the Successor States."[13] Ironically, this school policy worked most successfully during the cultural ministry of Kúnó Klebelsberg and Bálint Hóman, both of whom were assimilated Magyars of German origin.

Thus the struggle for the preservation of Germandom was fought out in Hungary in the cultural field and became a political question only when the German leaders (first Bleyer, then Gratz) sought support for their goals in Germany among the associations that displayed interest in the *Auslandsdeutsche.*

The majority of ethnic Germans in Hungary (55.4 percent) were engaged in agriculture. Traditionally conservative, they accepted the leadership of the Magyars and sought better conditions according to their traditions and experience, i.e., by working hard, buying more land, and keeping away from politics, which was "the villainy of the lords" in their eyes (and in the eyes of the Hungarian peasants). They succeeded fairly well in their attempt to improve their conditions. While the German landowners represented only 2.25 percent of the total population, they owned 8.3 percent of the country's arable land.[14] In industry, commerce, and transportation, they were employed disproportionately to their total numbers, providing 28.8 percent of the personnel in these fields. Only in the civil service were they a small 3.1 percent; and the number of German intellectuals was ridiculously low, 1,761 persons. On the other hand, the number of magyarized ethnic Germans among the Hungarian intellectuals was about 15 to 20 percent.[15]

In the absence of economic stress and hardship the Swabians were disinterested in ideologies and politics and succeeded very well if they played according to the unwritten rules of the official Hungarian magyarization policy.

Magyarization through Education

Hungary's population numbered 7,999,202 in 1920.[16] The Germans, with 551,624, were 6.9 percent of the population. By 1930 the total population of Hungary had grown to 8,688,319, but the number of Germans had declined to

478,630, that is to 5.5 percent of the total population. This represents a net loss of 72,944 persons.[17] This loss triggered a protest on the part of some Swabian leaders, but the majority of them did not display any particular concern. The number of ethnic Germans who died between 1926 and 1930 was 8,102, and the number of emigrant Germans in the same period was about 3,500. The total loss of Germans was 11,602. The number of births represented a yearly growth of 11,000, a total of 44,656,[18] while the number of immigrant Germans was close to 8,000. The final numbers indicate a gain of 52,656 Germans.[19] Unquestionably, the Hungarian statistics indicate that too many Germans had "disappeared."

In principle, the Hungarian government strictly observed the regulations of the peace treaty[20] that protected minority rights, secured the right to use minority languages, ordered the maintenance of minority schools, and protected the minorities' freedom and equality. However, local government officials very frequently watered down these laws, sometimes consciously, sometimes simply through ignorance. If any minority member changed his name to a Hungarian name, professed to be a Hungarian in lifestyle or politics, and did not hesitate to accept the philosophy of the Hungarian middle and upper classes, no barrier would prevent him from reaching the highest rank he could in any field. The basic requirement was good knowledge of the Magyar language. Since minority families used their mother tongue, the only way to learn the Magyar language well was in the schools. Those members of the German communities who wanted to make a career for themselves in Hungary or wanted to see their children do so therefore became allies of the Hungarian government in their desire to learn the Magyar language well.[21] The government skillfully exploited this desire, making the type of school dependent on the decision of the parents. Naturally the school question became the focal point of magyarization policy as well as of the anti-magyarization struggle of the German minority.

According to the 1923 Order in Council,[22] there were three different types of minority schools in Hungary. In Type A the language of instruction was the minority language. The Magyar language was only a required subject for the German minority. In 1930 this meant 47 schools with 5,870 students and 113 teachers. In the Type B schools the language of instruction was the mother tongue, but certain subjects, such as geography, history, civic duties, writing, reading, mathematics, singing, and physical education, had to be offered in Hungarian *also*. Finally, in the Type C school the language of instruction was Magyar, the mother tongue a required subject. There were 387 such schools for the German minority. The number of enrolled students in 1930 was 56,308 with 1,129 teachers. The teacher-student ratio was slightly better in the Type C than in the Type A or B schools.[23]

The Hungarian government and the parent associations naturally favored Type C schools, while the German minority group leaders demanded the establishment of more Type A and B schools. Their main argument was based on statistics: In 1930 there were 67,761 elementary school pupils of ethnic

German origin; only 62,178 of them were enrolled in minority schools, while 5,583 were "forced" according to minority interpretation, to attend pure Magyar schools. The government, on the other hand, argued that this latest figure included students of German ethnic origins living outside the ethnic areas, and their small number within a school did not justify the hiring of German-speaking teachers or the creation of special classes.

Both these arguments had a certain validity. While the percentage of students of German ethnic origin in the elementary schools generally corresponded to the percentage of population of the whole ethnic group,[24] in the bourgeois schools[25] they represented only 2.2 percent. Their percentage gradually declined as they reached the higher educational levels. In the gymnasiums they totaled 1.4 percent; in the academy of commerce, 1 percent; and at the university level only 0.8 percent. The majority of Swabians who reached the university level were magyarized, and "the flow of Magyarized Swabians into Army and Civil Service went on unabated."[26]

The idealistic ethnic German intellectuals, who watched with horror the declining numbers of their nationality group, wanted a program to secure the survival of ethnicity in perpetuity. Confronted with open hostility by the Hungarian government and unable to enlist the support of their own ethnic members, they looked for help outside of Hungary and found it in those official and unofficial organizations in Germany that had been created to help the *Auslandsdeutsche* survive as Germans.

In contrast to the other Successor States, Hungary did not permit the ethnic Germans to organize their own political parties. For a few years after World War I they were not even allowed to organize new cultural associations or continue to work in the old ones.

Only in 1924 did the Hungarian government grant the Swabians the right to revive the *Ungarländisch-Deutscher Volksbindungsverein* (UDV). This was the only ethnic German society permitted by the government. Its leader, Professor Jacob Bleyer, cooperated well with the Hungarian government and there seemed to be no reason for the Germans in Hungary to complain. But Dr. Franz Kussbach, who became the new leader of UDV in 1933, was unable to cope with the rapidly growing dissatisfaction of the more impatient, younger members of his organization who were either pan-Germanists or Nazis. The youths organized a new, more militant, less cooperative society named *Volksdeutsche Kameradschaft* under the leadership of Franz Anton Basch. This organization changed its name to *Volksbund der Deutschen in Ungarn* (VDU) in 1938 and gained a commanding role among the Germans in Hungary.

Thus a split occurred in 1933 among the ethnic Germans in Hungary. The split was precipitated not only by the power struggle of the upcoming young generation for leadership positions in the VDU, but also by the struggle of militant German nationalists against the policy of the Hungarian government, as well as by the series of attempts on the part of Reich German associations and government to help the ethnic Germans in Hungary. The Hungarian government implemented countermeasures to prevent outside interference in what it considered a strictly internal affair.

Swabian Demands

On May 9, 1933, Professor Jacob Bleyer, the leader of the UDV, read a declaration[27] in the Hungarian parliament in the name of the German minority. In strong words he attacked the minority school system, especially the gradual elimination of German as a language of instruction.[28] He objected to the limitations on the autonomy of the UDV and threatened the government that its policy of forced assimilation would trigger resistance by the UDV, including the possibility of a strong desire *to secede from Hungary.*[29]

The declaration created an uproar. There were demonstrations against it in the universities at Budapest and demonstrations for it in Germany.[30] The only positive result of this speech was an invitation from Prime Minister Julius Gömbös to Bleyer to talk over the problems. The meeting took place on August 10, 1933.

Before the meeting, Bleyer made a trip to Munich,[31] where he held negotiations with academic instructors and also talked to Rudolf Hess, deputy leader of the National Socialist German Workers Party (NSDAP). The subject of his negotiations can be reconstructed from the instructions sent to the German embassy in Budapest on August 11, 1933. Bleyer wanted to know "how the leadership of the Reich wishes to treat the question of the German element in Hungary with respect to the Hungarian Government at the present time . . . " He apparently would have welcomed a Reich pressure on the Gömbös government, but the reply was disappointing since it stated that "it is not possible at the present time for the Reich government to exert pressure on the Hungarian government." Conrad Roediger of the Foreign Ministry stressed that it would not be desirable "if the German community in Hungary should get into a hostile position in relation to the Hungarian Government and public."[32]

Bleyer, not knowing about this German reply, took a very firm position at his August 10 meeting with Gömbös, warning the prime minister that unless he solved the problems of the Germans in Hungary, he would not be able to create a rapprochement with the German Reich.[33] Bleyer pointed out that the more he was attacked in Hungary, the more popular he would become in Germany.

But Gömbös insisted that the ethnic German problem was a domestic political question in no way connected with German-Hungarian relations. At the end of the conversation the prime minister declared that he would not tolerate any foreign interference and therefore was demanding respect for the following conditions: Germany should not agitate among the ethnic Germans or financially support the German minority in Hungary, and the Germans in the Successor States should not initiate or support any anti-Hungarian actions.[34]

Although Bleyer described his meeting with Gömbös as friendly, he must have understood that Gömbös judged his relationship with the Hungarian state as bordering on disloyalty, especially since the prime minister demanded that he inform the government *in advance* of any future negotiations with the Reich. Bleyer also mentioned that during this negotiation he had demanded the firing of the *Völkischer Beobachter's*[35] Hungarian correspondent since he was a Jew and tried to discredit the leaders of the ethnic German movement, but Gömbös had remarked that the correspondent represented Hungarian interests.

We may conclude from these two documents that neither the German Reich nor its organizations sought contact with the ethnic German groups in Hungary; Bleyer, as president of the UDV, initiated the contact. Although there is no indication that he offered any services to the Reich for official German support of his organization's policy, it is clear that he tried to exert pressure on the Hungarian government through the German government. He even tried to connect the problems of German-Hungarian relations with the problems of the ethnic Germans (UDV) and the Hungarian government, consciously jeopardizing or making more difficult the realization of Hungary's foreign political aims. This action was a clear violation of the minority laws. In light of this fact, the repeated assurances of loyalty he gave to Gömbös appear to be empty phrases.

Finally, his objection to the reports of the *Völkischer Beobachter's* correspondent and his emphasis on the correspondent's Jewish origin could be interpreted as an attempt to win Gömbös's sympathy and find at least one common conviction with him, for Gömbös was well known for his anti-Semitism. But upon assuming the responsibilities of prime minister, he publicly revised his anti-Semitic views. Judging from Gömbös's reply to Bleyer, he kept his promise and even in a private conversation took the side of a Jew who defended Hungarian interests. The result of the meeting was that instead of becoming friendlier toward Bleyer's demands, Gömbös became more assertive and uncompromising.

The next day, August 12, 1933, Bleyer received information from the German embassy that the German government politely but flatly refused to support the UDV.[36] This disappointment must have made him realize that the discrepancy between Nazi ideology and propaganda and the Reich's official foreign policy was tremendous. He also must have recognized the bitter fact that the Reich was ready to sacrifice the interests of ethnic Germans living in Hungary if support of their interests contradicted Germany's foreign policy.

Reich German Policy

Although by "the summer of 1933 Hitler was complete master of a Government . . . which was independent alike of Reichstag, President, and political allies," his domestic problems were not yet over. On July 6, 1933, Hitler announced that "the revolution is not a permanent state of affairs, and it must not be allowed to develop into such a state."[31] But the SA and its chief of staff, Ernst Röhm, did not agree. Thus from the summer of 1933 to the summer of 1934 their quarrel over the continuation or termination of the revolution became the dominant issue in German politics. Hitler needed time to consolidate his personal dictatorship, win the support of the army, and eliminate the competition of the SA. Under the circumstances he did not want to create foreign political problems for himself because of the fate of ethnic Germans in Hungary.

Hungary played an important role in Hitler's foreign political designs, which were openly revealed in 1931.[38] These plans demanded, at least for the time being, friendly cooperation with Hungary. This cooperation seemed all the more important since Gömbös shared Hitler's views and initiated a rapprochement (June 17–19, 1933) with his personal visit to Germany at a time when Germany was isolated in international politics.[39] Furthermore, Hungary was a client of Mussolini, and since Hitler looked upon Italy as a prospective ally,[40] the mediation of Hungary promised more and faster success in that direction. The cooperation of Hungary was more valuable than the possible usefulness of half a million or fewer ethnic Germans in Hungary. This situation fully explains the negative reply sent to Bleyer concerning his demand to exert pressure on the Hungarian government in order to gain concessions for the German minority in Hungary.

Gömbös felt it necessary after his conversation with Bleyer to notify the German government about his views concerning the minority question. The new Hungarian ambassador to Berlin, Szilárd Masirevich, on his first visit to Hitler, raised the minority question—no doubt at the instructions of Gömbös—on September 20, 1933.[41]

Jacob Bleyer died on December 15, 1933, without having gained any concessions from Gömbös for the UDV. Two weeks later Gömbös received the newly appointed German ambassador to Hungary, Hans von Mackensen, and reaffirmed his convictions. The German minority question was for him, "and he wanted to stress this very clearly to me," reported Mackensen, "a purely Hungarian question and never a German-Hungarian one."[42] Then Gömbös discussed point by point the grievances of the German minority and arrived at the conclusion that "the whole minorities question had been artificially inflated and was the creation of just a few persons who wanted to achieve political importance being active in this field." Gömbös quoted "German press speeches" in Hungary and Germany that, with their "pan-German spirit," provoked considerable unrest among the population. Mackensen tried to convince Gömbös that official German circles were not involved in any way in the pan-German activities.

The next month, on January 14, 1934, Ambassador Masirevich raised the question of German minorities with the new German foreign minister, Constantin von Neurath. The Hungarian complaint was again answered in general phrases and Neurath expressed his regret that "the Hungarian government had not yet found ways and means to satisfy the German minorities in Hungary by appropriate decrees."[43]

Were the Reich's spokesmen telling the truth when they said that German official circles were not involved in the activities of the UDV? Not at all! Upon the death of Bleyer the first general meeting of the UDV asked Gustav Gratz to become the "spokesman for the Germans in Hungary." In this capacity Gratz met with the representatives of the Hungarian government on February 5, 1934, to learn of their reply to the memorandum of Bleyer, submitted to Gömbös after Bleyer's memorable speech in May 1933. The day after this meeting Mackensen sent the detailed text of Gratz's conversation with Hungarian officials to Berlin, on the basis of Gratz's personal report to him.[44] He warned the German foreign office that Gratz had left for Berlin to "take care of his private affairs,"[45] and called their attention to the fact that Gratz did not know anything about *financial aid provided by certain organizations of the Reich to the UDV*. He recommended not informing him about it since this knowledge of financial support would conflict with Gratz's frequently emphasized loyalty to Hungary. Mackensen felt that it was in Germany's interest to preserve Gratz's reputation for loyalty.

Mackensen's report leaves no doubt about German involvement in UDV affairs and influence on UDV-Hungarian relations. It also clarifies the role of Gratz, who came very close to disloyalty, but more through naiveté than conscious decision.

As far as the Hungarian reply to Bleyer's memorandum was concerned, we may say that it was absolutely negative.[46] Gömbös, in his letter to Hitler,[47] repeated the reply given to Gratz, and in his final paragraph straightforwardly demanded that Hitler instruct the German organizations in the Successor States to support Hungarian revisionist aims and cooperate with the Hungarian minority. He demanded that Hitler order the VDA and similar organizations to end their propagandizing and material support of the ethnic Germans of Hungary, and insisted that in the future all German minority questions should be dealt with through the accredited minister or Gömbös himself.

Unwilling either to jeopardize Hungary's goodwill or to stop using the UDV for his own benefit, Hitler left this letter unanswered. He avoided a showdown with Hungary.

At this same time a severe crisis developed within the UDV. The younger ethnic Germans were more responsive to pan-German propaganda than the older ones. This new generation came from peasant stock. Now they were doctors, lawyers, teachers, but they did not want to lose their kinship with the German people. They saw the old, moderate leaders of the UDV as people who were willing to give up their loyalty to the "folk" for the benefit of some authority (secured by the state) or for improvement of their social position. They were torn between Hungarian patriotism and German nationalist feelings.[48] These young ethnic German intellectuals[49] reacted to the magyarization program with hostility, and during the time of Bleyer's leadership they had formed a committee to discuss political questions. Their leader was Franz Basch, doctor of political science and personal secretary to Bleyer. After Bleyer's death this group, now called *Volksdeutsche Kameradschaft*, gained importance within the UDV because of the financial and material support it received from the *Deutsche Auslandinstitut*. Though accepting foreign money was illegal for a cultural organization, certain circumstances made it possible for this group to receive large amounts.

Bleyer was succeeded in the leadership of the UDV by Franz Kussbach, a lawyer and formerly the co-worker and son-in-law of Bleyer, who followed the moderate political line of Gustav Gratz, while Basch was appointed secretary of the UDV. Thus on paper the UDV remained a united organization, while in reality it was composed of two groups: the moderate majority and the radical minority.[50] Tibor Pataky, undersecretary of state for minority affairs, supervised the activities of the UDV for the government.

Basch did not hesitate to continue the fight for "Germandom" and against magyarization. His remark, "Whoever gives up his name does not deserve [to be held] in esteem anymore,"[51] got him a three-month jail sentence for "bringing the Hungarian nation into contempt."[52] This sentence made him a hero among the radical ethnic Germans who were attracted by the "ethical forces of National Socialism in the Reich."[53] The UDV was heading toward an open split, and neither the Hungarian nor the German government's activities helped to prevent it. But for the time being the radicalization of the whole UDV was apparently stopped.

Hitler-Gömbös Confrontation

Gömbös's letter[54] to Hitler of February 1934 had gone unanswered despite the suggestions of Mackensen and Friedrich Stieve, leader of the cultural department in the foreign ministry.[55] In the meantime, the signing of the Rome protocols (March 17), the Nazi *putsch* in Austria, the murder of Dollfuss (July 25), and the German press's hostile attitude toward Hungary after the assassination of King Alexander and Barthou (October 13) cooled Hungarian-German relations. As a result, the Hungarian government did not hurry to fulfill the promises of accommodation of the German minority that Gömbös had given to Gratz. The harsh sentence Basch received indicated that the Hungarians were prepared to use the ethnic German question as a weapon to force Hitler to change his attitude toward Hungary.[56] Ambassador Mackensen understood this change in Hungarian policy and in his letter to the foreign ministry urged officials there to send a friendly reply to Gömbös as soon as possible, if only for reasons of international courtesy.[57] But the reply was not sent.

The spring of 1935 saw ever sharper conflicts between the German and Hungarian governments—not direct but hidden conflicts in which the UDV was the target. The Hungarian government used more and more oppressive methods, while the Reich used more and more conspiratorial ones. Dr. Kussbach was unable to unite the moderate and radical factions of the UDV. Dr. Basch, Dr. Faulstich, and many other members and local leaders of the UDV (the majority of whom were intellectuals with university diplomas) succeeded in curtailing the authority of Kussbach, whose policy was too moderate for their taste. In this intraorganizational power struggle both Kussbach and Basch sought the support of Reich German organizations and the German embassy in Budapest. At the same time each group tried, using demagoguery, to convince the ethnic Germans throughout Hungary that it was the real protector of German interests and that the other group was a puppet of powers acting behind the scenes.

The Hungarian authorities reacted to these developments with anger and warned the UDV leaders to moderate their antigovernment speeches, "or else." When this warning was not heeded, the authorities first withdrew the permit for the traditional Swabian Ball,[58] and then started a criminal investigation of Kussbach.[59] Despite the government's increasing hostility, there were still political leaders in Hungary who advocated a conciliatory tone and the remedying of ethnic German grievances as the best solution of the crisis.[60]

The German embassy in Budapest watched with frustration the struggle of the UDV against the Hungarian authorities. Since Gömbös's letter of the previous February remained unanswered, the embassy had no legal basis for getting involved in the argument. Its situation became even more sensitive with the investigation of Kussbach, since Mackensen was afraid that this would uncover Kussbach's "numerous contacts with organizations of the Reich."[61] No wonder the ambassador again urged that a reply be sent to Gömbös's letter. But still this was not done.

In April 1935 the national elections were the focus of official as well as popular interest. The UDV wanted to sponsor candidates and Kussbach asked the German embassy for additional funds to finance their campaigns. The request was denied, but the Germans allowed him to use the "cultural" funds for this purpose.[62] An agreement with the Smallholder party made it possible for Kussbach and Basch to run.[63] The Reich German organizations and the German press sent observers and reporters in unusually great numbers to monitor the elections. Ethnic German university students volunteered their services to the Reich reporters. Their reports gave a detailed account of the election methods of Gömbös's party and expressed indignation over the terrorism and unscrupulous voting procedures. However, many of these reports proved to be sheer inventions, and Mackensen bitterly complained to the German foreign ministry that the overzealous reporters actually gave ammunition to those Hungarians who accused candidates Basch and Kussbach of being influenced by a foreign power. Mackensen pointed out that Gömbös had used equally unscrupulous methods against opposition candidates, and that since he had won a landslide victory (both Basch and Kussbach lost against the government candidates), it was in the interest of the Reich to congratulate him and stop experimenting with the creation of an opposition minority group.[64] Again he urged a reply to Gömbös's letter.

The Hitler-Gömbös confrontation seemingly ended with Gömbös's victory. But Gömbös was realistic enough to know that he needed the help and cooperation of Hitler to pursue Hungary's revisionist policy. New movements were observable on the scene of European international politics. The Stresa Conference (April 11–14, 1935) disappointed Mussolini, and this and other developments signaled the possibility of a rapprochement between Italy and Germany. Gömbös himself had long dreamed of an international agreement that would provide Hungary with two great revisionist patrons: Italy and Germany. He planned to realize Hungary's revisionist aims north of the Danube with the help of Germany, and south of the Danube with the help of Italy.[65] Gömbös did not want problems with the ethnic Germans to stand in the way of this grand design and he was ready for a compromise.

Ungarländisch-Deutscher Volksbindungverein

Gömbös's landslide victory confronted the UDV leadership with some hard facts: the prime minister was not a man who could be intimidated, the Reich coud not be counted on for vigorous support against Hungarian measures, and divisiveness in the UDV was endangering the organization's effectiveness. The precarious situation required the UDV to review its aims, strategy, and tactics, and if necessary to select new ones in order to serve Swabian intersts better. There were several alternatives from which to choose.

The UDV's policy up to 1935 was based on a certain degree of cooperation with the Hungarian government while relying heavily on the open moral (propaganda) support of Reich German organizations and the secret financial support of the same organizations, as well as of the Reich German government. It seemed a realistic policy in the early 1930s. Leaders of the UDV were awarded honorary membership in the VDA in Germany.[66] The council members as well as Steinacher himself condemned the Hungarian government, "a friend of Germany," for its "cunning methods and administrative treachery."[67] German papers inside and outside the Reich described Hungary as the "gravedigger of Germandom" because the Swabians of Hungary were the most loyal to their government among the ethnic German groups of "all Europe."[68] Editorials warned Hungary that unless the government improved the conditions of the German minorities, the whole revisionist propaganda of Hungary would remain ineffective among other national minorities.[69] But what good did this advice do the ethnic Germans in Hungary? None at all. The doubtful title Our People's Chancellor (*Unser Volkskanzler*), bestowed on Hitler by Bleyer, had brought only hardship to the Swabians and Bleyer himself.[70] In addition, the UDV had to consider the default of open German government help, which left it at the mercy of the Hungarian government.[71] Finally, but most importantly, the UDV's policy had led to the alienation of the younger, more nationalistic Swabians and divided the entire membership.

Conciliation of the Basch-led faction was a precondition to greater political effectiveness for the UDV. It seemed impossible to achieve such conciliation with a continuation of the present policy.

Changing to a more radical policy would certainly have pleased the radical members of the UDV but it would have gained the disapproval of the overwhelming majority of the ethnic German group, who remained loyal to the Hungarian state even after the spectacular rise of Nazism in Germany. Radicalization would lose the UDV members and effectiveness, since it would no longer be able to claim it spoke for the majority of Swabians. The implementation of a radical policy would not be feasible anyway without much stronger support from the Reich government, and stronger support was obviously not forthcoming. It even seemed that Reich support might be discontinued altogether because Germany's interest would be better served by a good relationship with the Hungarian government than by backing the antigovernment activities of a radical German minority. Since Hungary had no common frontier with Germany, communications of the UDV with the Reich German organizations depended on the goodwill of the Hungarian government in granting passports, and on the cooperation of the German embassy in Budapest in forwarding UDV correspondence to Germany. Since neither the government nor the embassy sympathized with the radical Swabians, radicalization of the UDV would probably cut it off from these vital contacts.

To cooperate with the Hungarian government, serving ethnic German interests whenever possible under the given conditions seemed to be the only policy left for the UDV to pursue. But while this policy might guarantee the UDV's survival, it certainly would not satisfy the radical intellectuals. They would do their best to sabotage every attempt to cooperate with the Hungarian government, to prevent reconciliation within the UDV, and thus to paralyze the entire organization. There was only one solution to this problem: the conservative UDV leadership would have to perform a painful operation on their own organization. They would have to remove and isolate the radicals from the leadership of the UDV in order to keep the loyalty of the majority of the members and demonstrate to the Hungarian government their willingness to cooperate.

The basic principle of Hungarian minority policy was this: German minority problems are the internal affair of Hungary; thus they are not subject to negotiations between the Hungarian and German governments. The Hungarians knew very well that the Reich government and Reich organizations were secretly supporting the UDV.[72] The publication of this involvement would have solved once and for all the ethnic German problem in Hungary. But such a radical solution would have embarrassed the German government and strained German-Hungarian relations, which were very important to Hungary for economic reasons.[73] A further political reason for seeking German friendship was Hungary's revisionist aims, which were to be realized against Czechoslovakia with the Reich's help. Radical policy directed against the entire German group in Hungary was out of the question. A complete surrender to the Swabian demands was not feasible: no Hungarian government could have survived such a policy at a time when Hungarian nationalism, under the premiership of Gömbös, was on the rise again. Thus, keeping a close watch on the UDV-Reich relationship and cracking down on the radical faction of the UDV seemed to be the best policy. It enjoyed the support not only of the Hungarians, but also of the conservative, cooperative majority of UDV members.[74] However, the timing of this crackdown was crucial. Germany had no common frontier with Hungary, but the events in Austria in 1934 brought this possibility very near. Any crackdown on radical ethnic Germans once there was a common frontier with Germany would be a risky business. Hungary had to do it now and without any open involvement. The moderate leadership of the UDV seemed to be a good instrument to implement this Hungarian plan.

The Saar plebiscite was the first break Germany had after the setbacks she suffered in 1934. The Franco-Italian mutual assistance treaty (January 4, 1935) still represented the greatest obstacle to the realization of German revisionist aims. Then in October the Italian invasion of Ethiopia created a chance for Hitler to offer his help. The sanctions implemented against Italy for this action further paved the way to a German-Italian understanding. But Italy was the patron of Hungary and Austria, and could not tolerate German interference in the internal affairs of these two states. Thus any provable help given to the Austrian Nazis or to the radical Swabians in Hungary would endanger the Italo-German rapprochement. As always, Hitler did not hesitate to desert the German minorities when his interests demanded it. While delaying a reply to Gömbös's aggressively worded letter, he quietly ordered the German embassy in Budapest to recognize Gustav Gratz, the most prominent Swabian in the leadership of the UDV and a hated "Magyarone" in the eyes of the radical ethnic Germans, as the official head of the UDV. Unquestionably, this move was in Germany's best interests at the time. Other alternatives were not even considered.

The VDA, however, felt that it had to throw its support behind the Basch-led radical group of Swabians. During Basch's trial it flooded Hungary with phony German marks bearing Basch's picture and the words "Hungarian nationality policy: Where his father was not honored and he himself not respected." Dr. Franz Basch was jailed for five months anyway. This and similar activities led to confrontations between the *Auswärtiges Amt* and the VDA, and their disputes were not resolved until 1938.[75] But with a little maneuvering, Steinacher succeeded in securing official German support for the radical Basch group.

The Growth of Reich Influence

Split and Nazification of UDV

The defeat of Basch and Kussbach at the polls did not end their fight within the UDV. On the contrary, it sharpened it. On June 15, 1935, the UDV

Executive Committee, over which Gustav Gratz presided, passed two decisions almost unanimously. The first condemned, without mentioning names, those persons who tried "to drive a spike" into the Hungarian–ethnic German friendship, since the ethnic Germans "consider themselves to be faithful members of the Hungarian nation." The second decision forbade the participation of officials and employees of the UDV in any political action without the knowledge of the presidium. Then, to the surprise of Basch and his supporters, Gratz recommended granting a "vacation" to Dr. Basch until his appeal was decided by the appellate court.[76] Faulstich and Huss[77] rejected the recommendation and claimed it was a political maneuver directed against them as well as Basch. Basch himself refused to accept the proffered vacation. Gratz suspended Basch from his duties and entrusted them to parliamentary deputy (and Canon) László Pintér temporarily. Pintér, naturally, belonged to Gratz's moderate group. The split within the UDV became an open secret. Now a race began for the commanding role.

Gratz wanted to secure that role for the old leadership following his philosophy by cooperating with great meticulousness with the Gömbös government. Kussbach tried to do the same by securing the support of the German government. Thus the German government was courted by both the moderate Kussbach and the radical Basch. Since the affairs of the ethnic Germans were managed by the VDA, which had confidants in every German embassy, the outcome of this race was *ab ovo* decided in favor of Basch.[78]

After the split of June 15, 1935, Kussbach lost the confidence of the Reich. To restore it he planned to visit Berlin and negotiate with the officials of the German foreign ministry in the first days of July. What Kussbach did not know was that Mackensen had sent Dr. Heinrich Kohler, the confidential agent of the VDA, to Berlin two days before he arrived.[79] There Kohler informed the VDA not only of Kussbach's antiradical attitude but also of his "mishandling" of funds and disobedience of embassy instructions.[80] But Mackensen's preemptive strike and VDA intervention both foundered on the stubborness of Kussbach. Since he was popular among the members and enjoyed the support of Gratz (and, through him, of the Hungarian government), Basch's group was unable to remove him from the presidency of the UDV; and the German embassy could only take from him the money, but not the *Deutsch-Ungarische Heimatblätter*.[81] Basch and his group, now enjoying the support of the Reich organizations, turned even more radical and whirled faster and faster in the direction of outlawry in Hungary. It was up to the German government to break the deadlock by seriously considering a compromise.

On September 26, 1935, Gömbös arrived in East Prussia to take part in a hunt to which Göring had invited him. The hunt was only a pretext for Gömbös and Hitler to meet and try to "normalize" their relationship again. On September 29 Gömbös met with Foreign Minister Constantin von Neurath, with Deputy of the Führer Rudolf Hess, with Minister of Propaganda Joseph Goebbels, and with Hjalmar Schacht, minister of economy. Negotiations and letter exchanges during the previous summer had prepared the way for an agreement on the minority question; but since both sides stuck to their own suggestions, success was not on the horizon. The Hungarians' demands, which they were not willing to compromise, were well known: "They wish all direct influence on the German minorities from authorities in the Reich (VDA, party authorities, etc.), to be stopped. Furthermore, they desire close collaboration between German and Hungarian minorities in the Successor States in support of Hungary's revisionist policy."[82]

But German diplomacy considered it to be against the Reich's interest to enter into a general agreement on these questions. Though Gömbös's conversations were fruitless, he was able to get a picture of the Nazi standpoint. Neurath, while denying Reich connections with the ethnic Germans and condemning political agitation, accused chauvinistic elements in Hungary of "constantly trying to force the *German immigrants*... to abandon their mother tongue and their ancient customs."[83] (Italics added.) The most recent German "immigrants" had settled in Hungary in the eighteenth century. Neurath claimed that these chauvinistic attempts had had a "consistently adverse effect upon the goodwill" of Germany toward Hungary.[84] Again they reached a deadlock.

Upon arriving home, Gömbös reported the results to the Hungarian council of ministers. He said that it was his impression "that the German side was beginning to lose interest" in the ethnic German question. At the same time he announced his decision to take sharper measures against German agitators.[85]

It is clear that Gömbös was not telling the truth when he said that the Reich side had begun to lose interest in the ethnic question. He knew very well that the contrary was true: Germany had an increasing interest in the German minority, and the German position was growing less flexible. Gömbös decided to play their tough game and take sharper measures against German interference. Our view is that he lied to his ministers to give them the impression that he had the tacit approval of Germany for this "sharper line." As a result, even those members of his cabinet who were afraid of displeasing Nazi Germany did not oppose his tougher policy. And he certainly took a tougher line. He let loose his agents and they unmasked every detail of the connection between the German embassy in Budapest and the German minority movement. On November 21, 1935, Mackensen desperately reported to Berlin that "there can be no longer the slightest doubt that full information on the system of financial aid from the Reich is now in the possession of the Hungarian government in all its details."[86]

Degree of German Involvement

The German Reich had two channels for pouring money into Hungary for the support of "Germandom" there. The VDA sent RM 86,000, while the foreign ministry sent RM 35,000.[87] Both amounts ended up in the hands of the VDA agent of the German embassy, Dr. Kohler, who decided how the money was to be allocated.[88] He had a huge sum to dispose of after the money was exchanged for Hungarian currency: Some 90,833.1 Pengö.[89] So, the Germans spent in Hungary on the "cultural affairs" of ethnic Germans an amount that equalled 10 percent of the budget of the Hungarian ministry of cultural affairs.[90] Kohler used the money to finance the following:[91]

Deutsch-Ungarische Heimatblätter.
Swabian student associations ("Sjevia").
An economic bureau.
Fostering pro-German propaganda in the Swabian communities by paying expenses and employees, as well as the meeting and travel expenses of the UDV.
People's Education Association of Hungaro-Germans.

And that was not all the money that poured into Hungary. Mackensen wrote: "To these allocations from the Reich must be added the numerous grants for purposes of work and study in the Reich itself, made to Hungaro-German peasants' sons and students; the correspondence regarding those cases is conducted by the various sub-branches of the VDA, partly via Dr. Kohler and partly *direct with other agents in the Swabian communities.*" (Italics added.)

Mackensen was in a panic that the publication of these facts by the Hungarian government would touch off a political scandal. He strongly suggested that his government abandon the present secret system, which was not a secret anymore: "In view of the treachery within our own ranks and the efficient manner in which the Hungarian security service functions, it would be only a very short period during which secrecy might perhaps be maintained." He recommended the continuation of the work to preserve the identity of ethnic Germans in Hungary, "but only in frankness and candor toward the Hungarians."[92] The Germans hoped to clarify the situation during the planned visit of Tibor Pataky (undersecretary of minority affairs) to Berlin in January 1936.

This incident proved that Germany used the UDV for its own purposes against the interests of Hungary. The investigations also revealed that only Basch's small group was involved in activities that were clearly against the interest of the Hungarian state. Why then did Gömbös not utilize this occasion to weed out this group from the UDV? Why was the Hungarian government so anxious to avoid an open political scandal? We do not have documents that would explain this attitude "officially," but the following review of the situation will show sufficient reasons for it.

Gömbös's election victory in April 1935 produced an absolute majority for him in the parliament. Those who lost their mandate were not reconciled. Horthy,[93] Bethlen, and their followers disliked Gömbös's social demagoguery as well as his foreign policy,[94] which seemed to attach Hungary's fate too closely to the German friendship. The legitimists,[95] the liberal intellectuals, and the powerful Jewish press all condemned his totalitarian leanings and pro-German foreign policy. Thus, while Gömbös had a commanding majority in the parliament, he hardly enjoyed unconditional support. Only his chauvinistic revisionism secured his popularity and Gömbös claimed he could pursue his revisionist goals only if Hungary became a close ally of Germany. Revelation of the Kohler affair would have forced him to admit the failure of his foreign policy and caused the immediate fall of his government.

Then, too, Gömbös's open friendship with Germany had already made him hated in the Successor States and in the Western world. A break with Germany now would have left Hungary completely isolated.

Finally, and not least importantly, Hungary's economy was completely dependent on German export and import. German retaliation for the publication of the Kohler affair would have caused a severe economic crisis in Hungary. Thus for domestic, foreign policy, and economic reasons, Gömbös had to handle the affair discreetly. One point in Gömbös's favor is that he did not act as he did because of servility and blind faithfulness to Hitler. On the contrary, when the next year Pataky went to Berlin in order to settle the ethnic German crisis, on Gömbös's instructions he was less compromising than ever. As a consequence, the "conversations led to no concrete results nor could they be expected to do so."[96]

As far as the UDV, the year 1936 formalized the split between the moderates and the radicals. In June 1936 the court of appeal reaffirmed Basch's sentence. On August 21 the general assembly of the UDV, after a heated and bitter debate, voted to expel Basch and his followers. Thus Gratz and his moderate co-workers remained (on paper) the only leaders of the UDV. The reality was different. The expelled radical group went underground and "set up in all forms a rival institution."[97] The Hungarian government pretended that it did not exist. The German government, on the other hand, recognized it as the only true representative of the ethnic Germans in Hungary. Therefore the VDA withdrew all financial support from the UDV and gave it instead to the *Kameradschaft*. Lacking finances, the UDV began to wither away.

UDV Becomes VDU

Stieve, the leader of the cultural-political department of the German foreign ministry, ended his report about his conversation with Pataky with the following conclusions: " ... owing to the 'disastrous activities' of the extremist elements of the UDV, the atmosphere had been so thoroughly poisoned that for a very long time to come the Government's goodwill in respect of making further concessions to the German national group ... would meet with the greatest opposition from both officials and the public."[98] He was absolutely right. Then after the death of Gömbös on October 6, 1936,[99] Horthy appointed as the prime minister Kálmán Darányi, who promised a policy more acceptable to the opposition parties and to the opposition outside the parliament.[100]

"Germany ... greeted the news of Darányi's appointment with an outburst of extreme hostility,"[101] especially since Darányi did not consider Gömbös's verbal promises to be valid.[102] The press war that followed did not help relations between the UDV and the government. On the contrary, since "the German government now officially and vigorously took up the cause of the Swabians, sponsoring their demands as formulated by the *Kameradschaft* to the Hungarian government,"[103] not only the traditional anti-German elements but also the great majority of the population began to profess anti-German sentiment. Many ethnic Germans, hypnotized by the Nazi successes, contributed to the spread of this sentiment by becoming Nazis and professing their loyalty to Hitler. The non-Nazi ethnic Germans left the *Kameradschaft* and, not having other Swabian associations to join,[104] withdrew into passivity or joined Hungarian political parties and associations.

On November 29, 1936, Mackensen sent a long report[105] to the Reich authorities, providing data concerning the minority problems for the upcoming negotiations with the new minister of internal affairs, Miklós Kozma. In his report the German ambassador specified seven points[106] that should be demanded by Germany for the ethnic Germans of Hungary.

The first point centered on the schools. The Gömbös government had corrected the most objectionable shortcomings of the minority school system at Christmas 1935,[107] so the German demands centered on timing and on the question of German-speaking teachers. The Order in Council had used the 1938–39 school year as the target date for the implementation of the new school system. The Germans demanded its introduction at once. Germany also demanded that teachers in the minority schools be of German ethnic origin (instead of German-speaking Hungarians or magyarized Swabians). Furthermore, "to make it possible that the new school system produce the pacification of the minority group, the Hungarian government should pressure the churches to introduce the same school system. To provide enough teachers for the school it would be necessary to organize ethnic German teachers' colleges."[108] The optimum demand was five teachers' colleges at once; the minimum demand was one. Mackensen recommended as a supporting argument the fact that the German minorities living in the other Successor States had teachers' colleges. To prevent the magyarization of children of preschool age, Germany demanded the establishment of German-language nursery schools in every Swabian village.

Germany also demanded complete autonomy for the UDV and the discontinuation of government supervision of its activities. The Hungarian government was also to stop prosecuting leaders of the *Kameradschaft* and promoting the group's dissolution by transferring members to pure Hungarian-populated regions.[109] Germany demanded an end to anti-German propaganda in Hungary. This propaganda had received impetus from the so-called Pan-German Map, which drew the borders of Germany on the northern shores of Lake Balaton (Plattensee). Germany denied this map existed and argued that the Hungarian authorities were never able to produce such a map. However, the map certainly did exist,[110] and a speech by Benno Grat at the VDA meeting in Munich on May 2, 1935, echoed its idea: "The German frontier stands on the Plattensee... We cannot be satisfied only with the Burgenland... German *Kulturboden* must also be German *Volksboden*."[111] Why the Hungarian authorities refused to show the map to Mackensen is a puzzle.

Naturally the Hungarians had replies to all these demands, and their own grievances besides, which Kozma did not fail to present. The main points were the Reich-supported agitation among the ethnic Germans, the hostile articles in the German press, the lack of cooperation between the German and Hungarian minorities in the Successor States, and the excessive demands of both the *Kameradschaft* and the German authorities. During the Kozma negotiations neither party seemed to listen to the other, and neither was ready for inflexibility or action. The negotiations produced only one result from the German point of view: "The Hungarians understand that it is unavoidable to change their attitude toward the German minority... and slowly they will get used to the fact that Germany consistently calls attention to the existing absurdities. Proof for that changing attitude is the open discussions in the recent past concerning these arguments."[112]

In effect, the negotiations produced a deadlock. Each government continued its own policy. The Darányi government paid more attention to the strengthening of connections with Italy, and the Hungarian press and public opinion turned more hostile toward both Germany and the German minority. Some ethnic Germans, under the influence of propaganda spread by German university students on their "study trips,"[113] began to relinquish their loyalty to the Hungarian state and turn instead to the Reich.

Crossing the Rubicon

German policy concerning the *Auslandsdeutsche* went through a dramatic change during the years 1933–37. In 1933 Hitler instructed Mackensen "to handle the German minority question in Hungary in such a way that it would not trouble the general German-Hungarian relationship since the latter was more important from the Reich's point of view."[114] One year later Hitler refused to send a reply to Gömbös's letter written in February 1934 concerning the ethnic German question. By 1936 the minority question had become more important to the Reich than official German-Hungarian relations, and even during the tension of the Kohler affair and its aftermath, the German government avoided granting concessions and remained inflexible. Step by step the Reich maneuvered the Darányi government into abandoning the principle that the minority question was a Hungarian domestic problem, and by 1938 had coerced the Hungarian government into accepting the Reich as the official patron and representative of the ethnic Germans in Hungary.[115]

This *volte-face* by the German government was caused by the successes of German foreign policy between 1933 and 1938. It is enough here to mention the most important events: the Saar plebiscite, Yugoslavia's benevolent attitude toward the Austrian Nazis who murdered Dollfuss; the Marseilles regicide, which furthered the German-Yugoslavian rapprochement; the failure of Mussolini's Danubian Pact; the alienation of Mussolini from a France led by the Popular Front; and the creation of the Axis. All these events worked to make Hungary less important in Hitler's designs, especially in his plan to annex Austria. Italy and Yugoslavia were now much more important. Furthermore, Hitler knew that Hungary's attitude toward Germany had cooled since the rise of Nazism and the totalitarian system. He despised equally Gömbös's chauvinistic Hungarian "anti-swastika" attitude and the anti-Nazi liberals of the Darányi government. And since in the new international grouping Germany did not need Hungary, German policy was revised to push Hungary into the position of obedient vassal. Two factors made this political aim realizable: Hungary's eagerness to secure Germany's support for her revisionist policy toward Czechoslovakia, and the willingness of some Swabians in Hungary to cooperate with the Nazis against their own government.

Thus we may logically draw the conclusion that Hitler and his institutions (the DAI and the VDA) embraced the cause of ethnic Germans in Hungary because they saw in them an instrument to further the good of the Reich. German brotherhood, nationalism, and racism were the slogans they used to lure the ethnic Germans into assuming the role Hitler had designed for them.

For Hungary, unless she was willing to give up her revisionist aims and risk economic reprisals from Germany, only one course remained open: to try to restore Hitler's goodwill through concessions to the radical ethnic Germans, while preserving as much national independence as possible.

For the ethnic Germans, the question of loyalty became the most important problem, although many of them did not realize it at the time. Those who did had to choose between two alternatives: remaining loyal to the state that had secured a good life for their ancestors, or joining those who foresaw great opportunities for the ethnic Germans only within the Reich. The second alternative meant working more or less openly against the Hungarian *patria*. A few took this course because they were true believers, more merely for the promised personal opportunities. But the great majority of ethnic Germans still remained apolitical or neutral, waiting for further developments. One thing is certain: Hungary's vacillating policy toward Nazi Germany, coupled with its hardened line toward the ethnic Germans, did not make it easier for them to reach a decision.

After the creation of the Axis Mussolini, Hungary's long-time patron, recommended that the Hungarian government cooperate with Germany. But Germany was no longer the weak and isolated nation of the early thirties. It had the international authority to force the Hungarians to comply with the wishes of Hitler, one of which was to handle Dr. Basch's group with less open hostility.[116] The German government warned the Hungarians that the German minority groups in Romania, Czechoslovakia, and Yugoslavia would cooperate with the Hungarian minorities of these countries only if the demand of Basch's group were fulfilled in Hungary.[117] International events, such as the annexation of Austria in March 1938, speeded up events in Hungary. Rumors circulated among the ethnic Germans that Hitler would soon annex parts of western Hungary.[118] Hungarian resentment toward the ethnic Germans was nourished by "unfeigned rejoicing among the Swabians of whom many now dropped all pretense of loyalty to Hungary at the prospect."[119] The Swabians expected—and not without justification—that the Nazi German Reich would help them to realize all their dreams. The Hungarians, frightened by the prospect of a hostile German Reich as a neighbor, gave concession after concession.

The first significant concession was granted right after the First Vienna Decision. Dr. Basch received permission to organize the *Volksbund der Deutschen in Ungarn* (the VDU or Bund) in November 1938; and the Bund openly flaunted the fact that it enjoyed the unconditional support of the German government.

Beginning in 1938, international developments (the First and Second Vienna Decisions and the consequences of Yugoslavia's occupation by Germany) played an important role in the history of the VDU. Its ranks were swollen by ethnic Germans who had formerly lived in Romania and Yugoslavia. Their different experiences created new problems. To understand these problems we first must survey the history of ethnic Germans in Romania and Yugoslavia (Chapters V and VI).

CHAPTER IV

Ethnic Germans of Poland

Conditions to 1934

After much discussion, political and diplomatic wheeling and dealing, and power play, the peacemaker at Versailles restored the independent Polish state.[1] Although Polish patriots had hoped for a restoration of the old Polish kingdom's frontiers as they had been before the partitions of 1772, Poland received considerably less territory. The territory of the restored Poland was formerly controlled by three empires: Austria-Hungary, Germany, and Russia. The Germans living in the German and Austrian territories had enjoyed special rights and privileges and dominated the social, economic, and political life of the provinces. In re-created Poland they could not hope for the continuation of these conditions. Although locally they were in the majority in West Prussia, Posen, Danzig, and Upper Silesia, the German ethnic group represented only 3.9 percent of Poland's population.[2]

The rights of ethnic Germans were to be guarded by the minority treaty. The Polish parliament went even further by granting autonomy on July 15, 1920, to parts of Silesia that "might be assigned to the new republic."[3] No such declaration was issued for the territory of West Prussia and Posen, where the Germans made up 42 percent of the population.[4] West Prussia and Posen provided the corridor through which Poland could reach the sea. For this strategic reason, as well as for commercial and business considerations, the people's right to self-determination was disregarded by the peacemakers and no plebiscites were held. At the same time the 96.5 percent German-inhabited city of Danzig (Gdansk) was declared a free city and placed under League of Nations supervision. These arrangements were naturally opposed by the Germans. By the end of 1923 over 800,000 Germans had left Poland and migrated to Germany proper, some voluntarily, some compelled by prevailing conditions.[5] The German government selected "as its first political goal the revision of Germany's eastern frontiers."[6]

The question of Danzig and the corridor dominated German-Polish relations during the interwar years. Since both governments were out to exploit the situation, exaggeration for propaganda purposes distorted the real condition of the ethnic Germans. According to the Versailles Treaty (Articles 100–108), Danzig was under the protection of the League of Nations.[7] The constitution of the free city was also based on the supplementary Polish-Danzig Agreement of November 9, 1920. The constitution was written by the representatives of the free city in agreement with the high commissioner of the League, and then approved and guaranteed by the League Council, which implied that the constitution could be changed only with permission of the League.

Poland had special duties and privileges in Danzig. The Polish government was responsible for its foreign relations, in consultation with the city. But the high commissioner of the League had the right to veto any international agreement that violated the constitution. Danzig and its territory of 1,900 square kilometers was included within the Polish custom frontiers, and Poland supervised the custom service, owned and operated the main railway lines, and had the right to maintain in the port postal, telegraph, and telephone services. The League Council prohibited the city from setting up fortifications or authorizing the manufacture of war matériel. Transit and temporary storage of war matériel was also prohibited with the exception of those items intended for Poland.

Danzig enjoyed autonomy in domestic affairs, had a popular assembly with 120 members and a senate with 22 members. The eight so-called principal senators served also as heads of the city's administrative departments. The city council always had a German majority, which, representing the convictions of the population, regarded the "free city" status as temporary. The judicial system and laws were the same as before the war, that is, Reich German. Danzig was supposed to prevent discrimination against its Polish minority.

Neither Polish nationalists nor German nationalists in Danzig and in the Reich regarded these arrangements as final. The Germans had the more advantageous position. Since Danzig had autonomy and its population was overwhelmingly German, the German institutions dealing with the *Auslandsdeutsche* were able to influence developments in the city. Some open, and even more secret, strong financial ties existed between Germany and Danzig.[8]

Culturally and politically Danzig mirrored developments in the Reich. Among the twelve eminent political parties in 1920, the Nationalist (Pan-German) was the strongest, closely followed by the Social Democrats. By 1930 the Nationalists as well as the Social Democrats had begun to lose power and the young NSDAP was close in strength to the Social Democrats, pushing the Nationalists into third place. Then in 1933 the NSDAP won the election with thirty-eight mandates, gaining the majority of votes against the rest of the parties led by the Social Democrats.[9] After the 1934 elections the NSDAP controlled 50 percent of both the senate and the popular assembly.[10] With this change in political leadership the *Gleichschaltung* of the city was a relatively easy task for Hitler. The prominent conservative Dr. Hermann Rauschning could not withstand the attacks of the extremist Arthur Greiser and his group.[11]

In November 1934 the Nazis forced Rauschning to retire, and with the election of Greiser, Danzig's coordination was theoretically completed.

With Greiser as president of the senate and Albert Forster *Gauleiter* (district leader) of the NSDAP in Danzig, the German leadership was ready to establish a Hitlerian one-party dictatorship in the city. But Hitler was not yet ready to challenge the conditions laid down by the peace treaties, mostly because of his great sensitivity to Poland's concern for every matter connected with Danzig. "Hitler demanded from the National Socialists of Danzig that they conduct their policy in a restrained and cautious way in order not to create difficulties for the Reich."[12] Hitler's caution was justified in light of the aggressive attitude taken by Josef Pilsudski, marshall of Poland, toward Germany.[13]

The situation of ethnic Germans living outside of Danzig in Poland was entirely different. First of all, they lived under Polish authority, which was strongly nationalistic and carefully observant of the behavior of ethnic Germans. At the first sign of disloyalty to the Polish state the Germans would be investigated, and if found guilty, punished. The second difference was a complex one created partly by the prewar conditions and partly by the war itself, the peace treaties, and the economic crises of the 1920s and early 1930s.

Socially the Germans provided the ruling classes in Prussia and Silesia. The big landowners[14] were and remained Germans even in the new Poland, since the peace treaty had forbidden confiscation of their property by the Polish state. The land reforms enacted by the Polish governments could distribute to landless peasants only those lands that had formerly belonged to the Prussian state or been deserted by Germans who opted for Germany and emigrated from Poland. Thus German landowners kept their economic power and, following their pan-Germanic sentiments, were openly or secretly for the revision of the Versailles Treaty.

The big industrialists, who like the landowners became "double proprietors," actually profited from their inclusion in Poland.[15] The great markets of unindustrialized Poland were opened to them, while the tariff war between Germany and Poland freed them from Reich German competition. So although they shared the pan-German sentiments of the estate owners, their business interests prepared them to cooperate loyally with the new Poland.[16]

The middle class was hit hardest by the change from German to Polish rule. The Polish state naturally tried to replace the Germans in the state administration, bureaucracy, industry, postal service, and transportation with Polish patriots. It instituted special prerequisites for these positions that had the effect of excluding a great number of Germans.[17] The German middle class, being strongly nationalistic, left Poland voluntarily in great numbers, hoping that the Versailles Treaty would soon be revised in their favor so that they could return to Poland as privileged citizens.[18] Those who remained in Poland felt insecure, and while some of them chose to accept the *fait accompli* or were willing to be "polonized," others looked to the Reich for their liberation.

The workers and peasants were almost exclusively native Poles. If they spoke German, according to the Polish interpretation they were "Prussianized" Poles. Their numbers were relatively large and they always played an important role in the propaganda campaigns of both Germany and Poland. The workers were more concerned with their own economic well-being than with nationality questions. Their often opportunistic attitude further confused the political picture.[19]

The Polish government recognized the existing German political parties. The National party was controlled by the big industrialists and its aim was to preserve Germandom in Poland; the Catholic party was based on church affiliation and Church influence, which was still strongly German; the Socialist party was the remnant of the old Social Democratic party of the German empire.

Besides these political parties the Germans had numerous local clubs, and cultural, recreational, sports, and religious associations as well as unions. These local organizations were united in the *Volksbund* which served the entire German minority. The number of the *Volksbund*'s local member organizations grew to over 300 by 1932.[20] The *Volksbund* had two organizations of its own: the *Kulturbund*, which, as its name suggests, was to serve the cultural needs of ethnic Germans; and the *Schulverein*, which had the special task of funding and maintaining private schools for the ethnic Germans.

The *Volksbund* became influential in 1926 when its complaints against the Polish school policy were heard by the League of Nations. In Poland parents had the right to decide which school they wanted to send their children to, but the State Board of Education had to give final permission for the students to register. This situation practically invited bribery and intimidation of parents. The *Volksbund* tried to enlist Polish children as German students to keep German schools open.[21] They were successful during economic crises because they provided extra financial help for their members out of the financial aid given them by Reich German organizations. Poles were accepted as members of the *Volksbund* if they were willing to register their children for the German schools.[22] Intimidation of parents by their German and Polish employers, as well as by the Polish authorities, was a common practice. Thus the entire educational program became a political football between the Polish state and the *Volksbund*. The *Volksbund* filed 9,942 complaints against the Polish authorities with the League of Nations' Mixed Commission.[23] The gravity of these complaints can be judged by the fact that only forty-three of them required action by the League Council. Many of the complaints lamented the scarcity of German teachers, although the shortage had been partly created by the German teachers themselves. Of 3,300 ethnic German teachers, almost 2,500 had left Poland voluntarily by 1922.[24] The teacher-student ratio was 1:37, which was not bad at all in East Central Europe.[25]

Polish-German Nonaggression Pact

Both Polish and German state actions contributed to the ever-growing hostility between ethnic Germans and Poles. On June 15, 1925, Germany refused to renew the coal convention that secured markets for Polish coal producers. Warsaw retaliated five days later with an embargo on German products, to which Germany replied with a boycott of all Polish goods.[26] The effects were temporarily devastating to the Polish economy: by the end of 1925 unemployment had reached the 80,000 mark.[27] Revisionist propaganda was stepped up and the German press forecast the economic collapse of Poland. Luckily the British coal strike enabled the Polish coal industry to find a substitute for the lost German market. However, relations between the two countries remained tense because of the unsuccessful Pilsudski-Stresemann negotiations in 1927. The German minority papers (supported by Reich German subsidies), the *Gazetta* and *Courier*, openly attacked the Polish government and engaged in a bitter press struggle with the Polish papers, *Polonia* and *Western Poland*. This press war exacerbated the ill feeling between the Polish public and the ethnic Germans. Two of the German-language papers, *The People's Will* (published by the Socialists) and the *Weekly Post* (published by the Catholics), displayed more moderation.

At the beginning of 1930 more and more ethnic Germans were accepting the status quo and their moderate leader, Senator Eduard Pant, in a series of articles published in the Warsaw daily *Polska*, deplored the hostility between Germans and Poles and suggested steps for conciliation.[28] Senator Pant's influence was strong among the Germans because he was a member of the *Volksbund* leadership. His plan was greatly helped by the end of the German-Polish tariff war and the signing of a new trade agreement in March 1930.

The Depression put an end to attempts at conciliation, and with Hitler's coming to power in Germany, a split occurred even within the *Volksbund*. A group of young ethnic Germans, mostly the followers of Otto von Ulitz, executive secretary of the *Volksbund*, began to publish a weekly paper called *Der Aufbruch*. In this paper they attacked and criticized the moderate leadership of the *Volksbund* and "demanded a total change" in the Bund's, as well as Poland's minority policy.[29] The "Young Germans" rejected the idea of complete loyalty to Poland and looked for their ideals to the growing Nazi movement in Germany.

Only two months after his appointment to the chancellorship Hitler learned some lessons from Poland. Though Germany did not guarantee the Polish frontiers, as she did the French and Belgian borders in the Locarno treaties, obviously for revisionist reasons, this "nonguarantee" proved to be a two-edged sword. Pilsudski was not the man to give in to German propaganda demands or to tolerate the slightest violation of the Versailles Treaty. Insured by the Polish-Soviet Nonaggression Pact (July 25, 1932) against a possible attack from the rear, Poland pursued an aggressive foreign policy. In case of war the Polish army could easily overrun the weak German military forces,[30] and Pilsudski, as the Westerplatte incident of March 1933 proved, was prepared to fight against Germany.[31] In order to secure the necessary time for the buildup of her armed forces, it was in Germany's interest to reach some kind of understanding with Poland. The result was the Nonaggression Pact signed by Germany and Poland on January 26, 1934.

The dreams of Reich and ethnic German revisionists and pan-Germanists concerning the early repossession of the Danzig Corridor, Posnan, Pomerelia, and Silesia, lay in ruins, destroyed by the Führer. The Germans living in Poland also suffered practical consequences, for the Polish authorities interpreted the pact as Hitler's consent to deal with their German minorities as they wished.[32] "Repolonization" of the germanized Poles was speeded up and there was a series of official and unofficial harassments of ethnic German organizations and individuals.[33] Naturally, these Polish actions triggered an ethnic German reaction, especially on the part of the younger generation, which began to organize—against the advice and will of their elders—"active defenses."[34] Thus, the Nonaggression Pact indirectly strengthened those forces that threatened the German minority with an internecine struggle and a deepening split.

The Reich German organizations that had been encouraging ethnic German activities to help "preserve their Germandom" were made to look ridiculous in the eyes of many ethnic Germans by the Nonaggression Pact. Their efforts to keep the revisionist spirit alive were in vain. A year earlier, in 1933, this spirit seemed to be catching the imagination of more and more Germans. The "freedom flight" of two sport pilots from Danzig to Germany in February 1933 was skillfully used by the *Verein für das Deutschtum im Ausland* (VDA) and *Deutsche Auslandinstitut* (DAI) in a revisionist propaganda campaign.[35] The pilots were taken on a lecture tour in Germany. Their lectures, as well as the introductory speeches of their hosts and the headlines in local newspapers, served to give a simple message to the Germans, to Poland, and to the entire world: *Danzig bleibt deutsch* (Danzig remains German).[36] VDA pamphlets had called on the Reich Germans to help their brothers in Poland. Now these requests seemed phony. After all, the Führer himself had directed the negotiations for the Nonaggression Pact. The authority of the VDA was on the decline.[37]

As had happened in Czechoslovakia, so also in Poland: the leaders of Reich German organizations and officials of the foreign ministry did not comply faithfully with the guidelines of the government's foreign policy. The VDA and DAI continued to "help" the Germans in Poland. The *Auswärtiges Amt* (AA) poured money into the "Separated Eastern Territories" under the guise of commercial aid, but counseled the recipients in Poland to use the sums for the "deepening of German ideas and community feeling among the [ethnic] German peasants."[38] The *Volksbund* leaders in Poland were scolded because of their ineffectiveness: "Germany had received very little benefit for the

RM 37,000,000 she invested in Upper Silesia. Berlin was growing impatient."[39]

The Poles, in possession of the Nonaggression Pact, continued their drive to solve their minority problem once and for all no matter what the VDA, DAI, or even the AA thought about it. Besides their nationalist convictions, the Poles had very good international reasons for trying to eliminate the threat represented by the German minorities.

On May 5, 1933, Germany and the Soviet Union renewed the 1926 Treaty of Berlin, which was clearly directed against Poland. On October 14, 1933, Germany withdrew from the disarmament conference and left the League of Nations. France, the great friend of Poland, was submerged in her own internal problems and thus both unable and unwilling to pursue an aggressive foreign policy toward Germany.[40] She had already rejected Pilsudski's preventive war plans against Germany and seemed more and more to care only about her own security.[41] Poland had to consider the possibility that France would not honor her promises in case of war. Thus the Nonaggression Pact with Germany served Poland's basic national interest. But the pact had a duration of only ten years[42] and its extension was not at all certain. Undoubtedly within the ten-year period the German army would build up its forces to the point where it represented a serious threat to Poland, especially since the German minority groups in Poland lived near the German frontier, and there were numerous signs[43] that their loyalty and sympathies were with Germany. The Polish government had to find a solution to this problem, if necessary by changing its minority policy.

The signing of the pact was primarily in Germany's interest—Hitler intended to use it to buy time to build up his army. Thus no matter what the Poles did to the ethnic Germans of Poland, Germany could not protect them. After all, the strongest response she could make to the speeded up "repolonization" program would have been the cancellation of the Nonaggression Pact. But it was in Germany's interest not to cancel it.

Therefore the protection of the ethnic Germans was left to the organizations dealing with the *Auslandsdeutsche*. These organizations were at this time involved in internecine battles to gain the leadership position within the Reich. They supported, morally and financially, those ethnic German organizations that seemed to share their philosophy. In other words, the Reich German organizations, instead of promoting unity among ethnic Germans, contributed to the existing conflict, and perhaps even sharpened it. If they really wanted to serve the Reich interests, they would have to revise their policy. So the year 1934 also represented a dilemma for these organizations.

The German-Polish Nonaggression Pact found the German minority in disarray, an almost natural state for them since 1919. The few unification efforts following World War I had not borne fruit because of the special, complex composition of the ethnic group, its geographic dispersion, and its history. The Germans lived in six large, more or less solid blocks in Poland. Those living in central Poland and Wolhynia had been subjects of the Russian tsar from the eighteenth century. Experiencing for generations the disadvantages and sometimes hopelessness of minority life, they were the least self-conscious and the hardest to organize of the ethnic Germans living in post–World War I Poland. The ethnic Germans of Galicia, part of the Habsburg lands from the eighteenth century, were mainly peasants. From this group the Austrian government appointed many Jews as civil servants.[44] These Jews continued to identify with the German minority even after World War I, and until the spread of Nazi anti-Semitism they helped to elect German representatives to the Sjem. On the other hand, the Germans of Posen-Pomerelia, Silesia, and Teschen had belonged to Prussia and later to the German empire, under which they enjoyed benefits of first-class citizenship. They experienced minority conditions only after World War I, and so had very little in common with their brethren farther to the east. The Germans of Teschen, Silesia, Posen, and Pomerelia living near the Reich could expect a better life if the peace treaty of Versailles should be overthrown. It is no wonder then, that the majority of them were revisionist, and that they acted politically, as well as culturally, to preserve their Germandom.

The Germans of Silesia, Teschen, Posen, and Pomerelia had in 1934 four political parties: the *Deutsche Katolische Volkspartei* under the presidency of Senator Eduard Pant; the *Deutsche Socialistische Arbeitspartei*, made up of social democrats; the *Deutsche Partei*, conservative and close to Pant's party; and the *Jungdeutsche Partei*, which before 1931 was called *Deutscher National-Socialistischer Verein für Polen*. The president of this last party was Rudolf Wiesner from Bielitz. In central Poland there were two additional parties: the *Deutsche Volkspartei*, founded in 1918, and a more important party called the *Deutscher Volksverband in Polen*, founded in 1924 and led by August Utta.

After the 1928 elections these parties, with the exception of Wiesner's *Verein*, in alliance with the Jews, Ukranians, and White Russians, were able to send 5 senators to the senate (total membership: 111) and 21 deputies to the Sejm (total membership: 444). So although the representatives of the minority block were negligible in number, they could voice the grievances of their constituency. In the elections of November 23, 1930, however, the bloc elected only three senators and five deputies. This decline is explained by some Germans as the result of election terrorism by the Polish government.[45] However, such a sudden loss cannot be explained altogether by Polish terrorism. Bierschenk[46] points out rightly that other causes, seemingly unimportant at the time, contributed to the defeat. Among these were the struggle among the German parties, the alienation of Jews because of the spread of anti-Semitism among the Germans, and the insensitivity of the formerly elected representatives to the needs of their constituency.

The widespread disillusionment of the younger and idealistic generation, who were influenced by the successes of National Socialism in Germany, led them to join the *Jungdeutsche Partei* (JDP), which in 1933, while following Nazi ideas, still professed loyalty to the Polish state and denied any connection with the Reich.[47] The party's popularity increased and in the December 1934 local elections the JDP became the strongest German party in Silesia. From that time on the JDP tried to organize its own branches everywhere in Poland and attempted to unite all the ethnic Germans in the spirit of National Socialism.

In this unification effort the JDP found itself confronted not only by the political parties, but also by the old leadership of the *Volksbund* (Dr. Hans Heinrich, prince of Pless, president, and Otto Ulitz, secretary). The old leaders condemned the JDP for limiting the party's activity to the "political activization of the masses and the political indoctrination of the membership."[48] The *Deutsche Vereinigung* (DV), under the leadership of the energetic Dr. Hans Kohnert, also opposed the JDP and declared that its members could not be members of the *Deutsche Vereinigung* at the same time ("exclusivity" clause). The JDP accused these old organizations of being "meeting places of reactionaries and of Marxists."[49] The VDA leader Steinacher tried to reconcile the JDP with the old ethnic German parties and organizations during his trip to Poland in 1933, but because of the stubbornness of Wiesner the split was not healed. On the contrary, the JDP found its patrons in the *Auslandabteilung der Reichsleitung der NSDAP* (later the Ausland Organisation der NSDAP, or the AO) and among certain officials of the AA, while the VDA continued to support the traditional organizations.[50] The ethnic Germans were hopelessly divided at the time of the German-Polish Nonaggression Pact. They had to decide what kind of policy would further their interests, and what ideological foundation would best support this new policy—cooperation, pan-Germanism, or Nazism.

Aims and Needs of Polish Policy

The Nonaggression Pact secured Poland against German aggression for ten years. But this decade gave Germany the time to close the existing gap between German and Polish military strength. In an armed conflict a well-prepared German army could do battle against the Poles with a greater than 50 percent chance for victory. To deny that chance was the primary interest of the Polish state.

From the military point of view, Poland needed additional allies. The support of Czechoslovakia would have been beneficial, as would that of the Soviet Union.[51] As far as the deployment of the Polish Army was concerned, the main problem was the German settlements near the German border in Posnan, Pomerelia, and Silesia. If they were to become disloyal to Poland, the communications and supplies of a Polish army on the frontiers woud be endangered. Since a mass resettlement program for the Germans was impossible (it would have alienated even those Germans who were ready to cooperate), the Poles' alternative was to strengthen the loyalty of the ethnic Germans. They chose to use the method of "repolonizing" the "germanized"

Poles, that is, eliminating step by step by the political and economic influence of the pan-German leaders and fighting an open battle against the spread of Nazi ideas. The results were satisfactory. The number of people who professed to be ethnic German declined from 1,059,194 in 1921 to 741,000 in 1931.[52]

Another method of eliminating the danger for the Polish army in the German-inhabited territories was the policy of divide and conquer, which seemed to work well. The Germans had used their freedom of association and assembly to form many political parties and cultural, sport, and other associations. Yet they did not have a summit organization that could harmonize their activities. Divided according to political parties, church affiliations, economic interests, and social positions, the German group was powerless. It was in Poland's interest to encourage this division by supporting those Germans who loyally cooperated with the Polish state and neglecting those who were hostile.

Finally, it was Poland's primary interest to secure the Danzig Corridor and with it the free flow of commerce to and from the outside world, and the free transportation of mostly French-manufactured war supplies to Poland. Since the free city of Danzig seemed to be lost to Poland,[53] Poland built a modern seaport, Gdynia, just north of Danzig on Polish territory. With this new seaport Danzig lost some importance militarily, though not politically.

Ethnic Germans' Policy

Because of the division of the ethnic German population, no unified and generally accepted policy existed. The present haphazard policy seemed to be disastrous for the Germans. Their number decreased day by day, their disunity was exploited by the Poles, and their living standard was declining. The first precondition for a changed policy was the unification of all ethnic Germans in a mass organization, but this looked impossible because of the different experiences, geographical locations, occupations, religious affiliations, and political convictions of the German individuals and groups. There seemed to be only one way to accomplish unification, and that was step by step, starting with the Germans living in the borderlands and then extending the process to the east. But even if this method worked, two questions would have to be answered: Which organization should become dominant? And which ideology or philosophy should be adopted by the whole German minority? The leaders had very little control over these two questions, especially since the Reich German organizations to which they turned for advice and help were also very much divided. Logic dictated following the dominant ideology of Germany, that is, Nazism, but this was repulsive to many Silesian, Galician, and Wolhynian Germans who had lived in peace for centuries with their Jewish neighbors.[54] Furthermore, the JDP, which did profess the Nazi ideology, was led by people who could not gain the confidence of the majority of Germans.[55] It could also be expected that Polish reaction to a nazified German summit organization would be violent. It looked, then, as though the best policy for the entire German group was a "nonpolicy"—that is, toleration of present divisions coupled with the exploitation of every opportunity to more effectively preserve German identity in Poland.

German Reich Policy

The official German political line was decided by the Nonaggression Pact. Of course this did not mean that secretly or under the guise of cultural or charitable activities the German government could not and should not try to help the ethnic Germans of Poland keep their German consciousness, or even to use them for the promotion of German foreign policy. One aim would be to prevent the success of the repolonization program. The economic crisis of 1933 provided an opportunity to pursue this policy without creating suspicion. After all, who could object to the Reich Germans' aiding their less fortunate brethren in Poland? They really were in need of aid. For example, 43 percent of *Volksbund* members in Silesia were unemployed in December 1933.[56]

There were no obstacles to money transactions. The *Deutsche Stiftung* (German Foundation) and OSSA[57] had been organized for this purpose, and the *Oberschlesien Bankverein* (Upper Silesian Bank Association) and the *Kattowitzer Vereinbank*, not to mention the seven German-controlled financial institutions in Danzig, made money distribution easy. The government and the Reich German organizations (AO, DAI, AA) poured millions of marks into Poland with limited results; the number of Germans continued to decline.

In order to spend the money in a more profitable way it would have been advisable to centralize all activities (cultural, political, and financial) in the hands of one organization. But the power struggle for such control was so great among the Reich German organizations that German policy concerning the ethnic Germans in Poland was destined to remain ineffective for a long time to come. In conclusion, the best course for the Polish government seemed to be the continuation of its present policy, for the ethnic Germans a policy that would lead to their unification within Poland, and for the German government a policy that would promote unity among the ethnic Germans.

Course of Events after 1934

The German-Polish Nonaggression Pact was unwelcome news to the anti-Nazi forces in Europe, especially in France. Without taking into consideration the assurances given by Poland to Barthou during his Warsaw visit of April 22–24, 1934, that Poland would honor its mutual assistance treaty in case of German aggression against France, leftist French circles attacked Pilsudski's policy and tried to turn public opinion as well as government policy against Poland. Unfortunately for France, Barthou himself believed that the Poles were no longer trustworthy allies.

The visit of the Nazi propaganda minister, Joseph Goebbels, to Poland

(June 12–15, 1934) fueled French antagonism. Since Goebbels was an unofficial visitor, the Polish government ordered that only the minister of interior, Bronislaw Pieracki, greet him upon his arrival and bid him farewell upon his departure. On June 15 Pieracki was assassinated. The murder was followed by the wildest speculations about the reasons for the assassination and the persons involved. Polish National Socialists were suspected, as well as the German secret service, which had long patronized Ukrainian separatists living in Poland.[58] The murdered Pieracki was a close collaborator of Pilsudski and used "an iron hand" against the Polish National Socialist party, as well as against the Ukrainian separatists.[59]

The investigation discovered that the assassin was a Ukrainian indeed, a certain Mikolaj Lebed, who escaped from Poland to Germany aboard the German ship *Preussen* with a new visa issued by the German consul in Danzig. The extradition proceedings created justifiable doubts in the Polish leaders concerning the goodwill and honesty of Germany,[60] and suggested to them a more radical course. The government began this new course with the establishment of concentration camps for elements hostile to Poland.[61] The next step was even more radical: in September Poland denounced the minority treaties. The timing of this act was interesting— it occurred only a few days before the League of Nations admitted the Soviet Union into its membership.[62]

The year 1935 began badly for Polish foreign policy. The Laval-Mussolini agreement followed by Mussolini's Danubian Pact plan, which foresaw the possibility of revision, was disturbing news, especially because France seemed to favor it.[63] In order to restore France's confidence Poland again reassured Laval in March 1935 that she would honor her treaty obligations. However, relations between the two countries did not improve, and with the signing of the French-Soviet assistance treaty (May 2, 1935), a new cause for friction was created: Poland was asked to permit Soviet troops to march through Poland against Germany in case of war. Poland was not prepared to grant such permission.

In March 1936 Germany reoccupied the Rhineland. The reaction to this flagrant violation of the Versailles Treaty was much stronger in Poland than in France. Beck hurried to reassure France that Poland would observe the French-Polish mutual assistance treaty; however, the French government and public seemed to acquiesce to the *fait accompli*. Not so in Poland. Large anti-German demonstrations were organized by the West Marches Society (a Polish veterans' organization) all over Poland "with the tacit consent of the authorities."[64] The demonstrations and anti-German propaganda continued throughout the summer. Anti-German feelings were fed by the events occurring in Danzig. The newly elected Nazi senate of Danzig, under the presidency of Arthur Greiser, disregarded Hitler's directives for its conduct of policy toward Poland.[65] It ventured to pass and implement measures that violated Poland's rights in Danzig. These measures, which were of a commercial nature, coupled with violent Nazi activities against the Poles in the city, triggered similar violence against the Germans in Poland. This violence was of such dimensions that Neurath thought it necessary to express concern about the safety of the German minorities and the impact of these demonstrations on German-Polish relations. Joseph Lipski, Polish ambassador to Germany, "expressed his profound regret," but his regret did not ameliorate the prevailing conditions of the ethnic Germans.[66]

Conditions in Danzig

Both Greiser and Forster wanted to see Danzig annexed to the Reich and did their best to prevent the League's high commissioner from fulfilling his duty. In 1936 the high commissioner, Sean Lester, recognized that he had been rendered powerless by the lack of cooperation from the senate and the merely lukewarm support of the League of Nations during the 1936 crisis.[67] He resigned in the fall.

The new high commissioner, Carl J. Burckhardt, a Swiss diplomat and historian, accepted the position only after receiving assurances of cooperation from both the Polish and German governments, as well as from the Danzig senate.[68] Burckhardt assumed his position in March 1937.[69] He soon learned that his efforts to preserve Danzig's free city status were opposed by all the parties concerned.

Poland had tried in 1935 to wring from Germany a statement recognizing the need to establish a Polish protectorate over Danzig in case the League of Nations should withdraw its protection. Hitler declined to give such a statement. During the negotiations for the Minority Declaration of 1937, Beck presented a less ambitious demand to Hitler. This was for German guarantees of the inviolability of the status of Danzig and the upholding of Polish rights within the city.[70] Hitler refused even this moderate Polish demand.[71]

In light of these developments, it is interesting that Beck, even though he had lost confidence in the League, wanted it to withdraw its protection from Danzig, still hoping that the negotiations with Germany would produce better protection for the status of Danzig. His visit to Berchtesgaden and Ribbentrop's visit to Warsaw in January 1939 produced no agreement concerning Danzig.[72] But German diplomacy tried to quiet Polish anxiety over Danzig by emphasizing that Germany would not produce a *fait accompli* in the city. Danzig's senate president Greiser also tried to calm the situation by publishing an article in which he warned the Danzig Germans "not to expect immediate political results from the slogan 'Back to the Reich' since the political status of the Free City would remain."[73]

Ethnic German Developments

The struggle for leadership among the various German factions in Poland reached the crisis stage during this period. Everyone agreed that the *Volksgruppe* should be united—but under whose leadership? Richard Wiesner's JDP considered itself the only genuine purveyor of Nazi ideas in

Poland and, as such, the obvious choice to unite all the ethnic Germans. At the beginning of 1935 the JDP included about 100 *Ortsgruppen* (local organizations) with some 13,000–15,000 members.[74] However, the *Deutsche Vereinigung* under Dr. Hans Kohnert had 130 *Ortsgruppen* with 20,000 members. Each side still had its advocates within the Reich: Ernest Wilhelm Bohle and the AO supported the JDP, while Hans Steinacher and the *Volksdeutscher Rat* (VR) sided with Kohnert. The main issue of contention was still the "exclusivity" clause.

The old *Volksbund*, now led by Dr. Otto Ulitz, rallied under the strong attacks of the JDP and broadened its influence during this period. The JDP called Ulitz "the monstrous product of reaction combined with Jewry, the personification of folkish aberration—of liberalism."[75] In central Poland the JDP's principal rival was the *Deutsche Volksverband* (DVV) of August Utta and its youth leader Ludwig Wolf. Wiesner's representative there, Dr. Walter Gunzel, was rejected, especially by the younger people. In the 1936 election in central Poland the DVV received over 13,000 votes to the JDP's 3,000. By 1937 DVV membership totaled 25,450 with some 550 *Ortsgruppen.*[76]

In the assessment of the Austrian ambassador to Poland there was little to distinguish between the rival factions. Both the JDP and the DVV appeared to be Nazi, and he suspected both were financially dependent on the Reich.[77] Their rivalry led the Reich finance ministry to threaten to cut off funds,[78] which supports the ambassador's assumption. That the VDA had been channeling money to its clients is suggested by its statement in mid-1936 that RM300,000 was needed for Poland for the rest of the year.[79]

Bohle's attempts to reconcile the different factions in favor of the JDP alarmed the AA. Neurath feared the Polish government would crack down on the entire ethnic German group if the connection to the Reich was called to its attention. He wrote in April 1935 to remind Hess of his 1933 announcement that the party would not interfere in the affairs of other countries.[80] Göring seemed at pains to reassure Lipski along these lines, saying that although he could issue orders to prevent anti-Polish incidents in Germany, he had no control over German minorities in Poland. He further confided that leading elements among the minorities there opposed Hitler because of the Non-aggression Pact. Lipski, perhaps ironically, surmised that orders from Göring might nevertheless "reflect on the behavior of Germans in Poland."[81]

Various governmental and party departments in Germany reminded one another, as well as the ethnic Germans in Poland, that the *Volksgruppe* itself would have to decide between the rival factions. Still the Kursell Bureau felt it necessary to discuss and influence their decision. Represented at a meeting on June 5, 1936, besides the JDP and DVV from Poland, were several organizations including the *Deutsche Stiftung*, AA, ministries of the interior (RIM) and propaganda (ProMi).[82] One remarkable argument offered here in support of the JDP was that it had always paid its own way and was not subsidized by the Reich. Since the JDP had begun from a base in former

Austrian territory and, furthermore, was fighting the traditional recipients of German funds, it was handicapped in trying to tap these sources for itself.[83] The government ministries supported this party, while Krahmer-Möllenberg of the *Deutsche Stiftung* favored the DVV. The ProMi representative observed that the most important German press was that of the JDP, which was threatened with bankruptcy if not aided. ProMi was considering such help on condition of press neutrality in the power struggle.[84]

After considerable discussion the meeting adopted a program that it hoped would settle the matter: dual membership in the two groups, an end to public accusations, and the presentation of a united front in the Polish parliament. In November 1936 Fritz von Twardowski of the AA suggested dividing responsibilities so that the JDP would handle all political affairs. Twardowski's overview of the German finances provided for ethnic work in Poland (millions of marks annually) pointed up the seriousness of the problem. He suggested that the ethnic Germans should be prepared to rely less heavily on outside help.[85]

Neither the June nor the November suggestion seemed to affect the quarrel in Poland. Those Poles who had hoped that the freedom permitted under the 1934 agreement would weaken the German minority through internal dissension were perhaps disappointed that membership in the German organizations continued to grow despite the rivalry. There was, for example, a great increase in membership in the *Verband Deutscher Genossenschaften in Polen* between 1936 and 1937.[86] On at least one occasion even the JDP urged cooperation among all German groups, for the *Winterhilfsaktion* in 1935, designed to alleviate some of the great hardship in the industrial areas.[87]

On the other hand, those ethnic Germans who had expected more freedom of activity for their organizations in Poland as a result of the Nonaggression Pact were certainly disappointed. Emphasis in the Polish press in late 1935 on what it called the germanization policy of the Reich toward the minority in Poland caused anti-German demonstrations. The government began to place difficulties in the way of minority organizations. Youth groups were especially hard pressed. No distinction was made between political, religious, and athletic groups. Many were dissolved outright, some youth homes were closed, and meetings were dispersed.

As early as April 1935 blows were exchanged in northern Pomerelia when Poles overran a German youth meeting and several people were seriously injured. A similar incident at a JDP meeting in Upper Silesia in May 1936 left seventy persons injured, including women.[88] In July 1936 the police in Katowice dissolved the Upper Silesian *Wanderbund*, which was closely connected to the JDP. In November some of the former members, together with members of the Tarnowitz (Tarnowskie Góry) *Wanderbund* and a youth group of the German Catholic Union—altogether forty-nine youths—were charged with conspiracy. Twenty-seven were sentenced to terms of eight months to two and a half years; fifteen between the ages of fifteen and seventeen were sent to a Polish reformatory. The incident led to the prohibition of youth organizations. A similar trial in Konitz (Chojnice) in July 1937 brought sentences of up to two years for twenty defendants.[89]

Even more influential in their consequences were the repressive measures that the Poles implemented against the German minority churches. The border settlement of 1922 left 522,713 German Protestants in Poland.[90] The number of German Catholics was approximately 134,287. Voluntary migration over the years modified these numbers.

In both the Catholic and Protestant churches the real problems were not so much religious as national. German Catholic complaints centered around the following conditions: In Polish Upper Silesia the German Catholics came under the jurisdiction of the German cardinal in Breslau, since the administrative boundaries of the church did not coincide with the national boundaries. Although the cardinal tried to supply German clergy for the German Catholics and Polish clergy for the Polish Catholics, voluntary migration of the clergy hindered his plan. For example, in 1932 there were only five German priests for the 120,000 German Catholics in Upper Silesia, while on the German side twice as many Polish Catholics had only three Polish priests.[91] Neither the Germans nor the Poles wanted this situation to change because they saw it in a nationalistic rather than a religious light. Thus the religious question was politicized. With the appointment of Bishop Adamski in 1930, and the founding of a new seminary in Cracow, which was farther away from Warsaw, the center of Polish nationalism, the situation changed rapidly. By 1933, in fact, the Poles were complaining that the Silesian Catholic Church was not Polish enough.[92] The end result was that both German and Polish clergy became more nationalistic and politically involved, thus contradicting the international character of the Church and inviting the disapproval of both governments.

The Polish Protestants in the newly attached territories of Silesia were given special status as an autonomous unit with a separate synod. Financially they were quite well off and did not need to use the yearly grant provided by the Polish government. While this financial strength ensured independence and protection, it kept these Polish Protestants from joining with the other Protestant churches in Poland. Although the number of Protestants in Poland was never large, in the borderland areas the number was considerable because of the influx of Protestant Poles from Czechoslovakia after the annexation of Teschen. At first they were accepted for membership in the German Protestant churches, but in 1930, as a result of growing German national consciousness, the synod in Katowice refused to admit any more Poles.[93] This decision split the German and Polish Protestants. Eventually the Polish government became involved in the argument because of the inflexibility of the German and Polish Protestants. In 1937 the government passed a law depriving the German churches of the right to elect their pastors, giving it instead to the *wojewoda* (governor). Thus the government was able to appoint Polish Protestant pastors as leaders of the German Protestant churches. The growing nationalist spirit within the German Protestant churches made it possible for Poland to implement this law by accusing some German pastors of disloyalty to the state. This accusation was justified by the fact that the *Osthilfe* (special fund for preserving Germandom on the eastern frontiers) was managed through the German Protestant churches.[94]

From 1935 to 1937 the German minority was represented in the Polish senate by Erwin Hasbach and Rudolf Wiesner, who were both appointed senators by the Polish government.[95] Their appointment did not meet with the approval of either the VDA or the larger minority organizations in Poland. At that time the war between the DVV and the JDP sharpened. According to Steinacher's interpretation, the intention of the Polish government in appointing Wiesner was to give greater weight and authority to the otherwise small and insignificant JDP in its fight against Ulitz who, as a leader of the *Volksbund*, represented the majority of the Germans. The appointment was also a gesture toward Germany that cost the Polish government nothing.[96] In the 1938 elections Hasbach kept his seat but Wiesner was replaced with Max Warnbeck by the Polish government.[97] The two German senators spent most of their official time protesting the Polish *Verdrängungs und Assimilierungspolitik.*[98]

Polish assimilation policy was apparent in the way land reforms were enforced. There was general agreement on the need for these reforms, which affected Polish as well as German owners, since in 1930 Poland had an estimated "surplus" agricultural population of 51.3 percent, or about ten million people.[99] Besides distributing state-owned lands, the Polish government asked for voluntary offers of land to implement the reform plans. The reaction to this approach was varied: in some districts it ran ahead of expectations, in others it fell far behind. To make the land reform bill a success, it became necessary to resort to forceful expropriation in those districts that lagged in voluntary offers and this method presented an opportunity to discriminate against the German landowners.

In 1936 the reform hit hardest at those areas that needed it least. Almost one-fifth of the annual redistribution occurred in Posen and Pomerelia, where there were neither dwarf holdings nor latifundia; rather there was sound, intensive production on primarily medium-sized farms. Thus the program was political as well as economic.[100] At least half of the forced redistribution in the western provinces annually fell on German estates. The plan for 1937 called for an increase by half in the amount of land to be redistributed (from 100,000 to 150,000 hectares), but the share to come from the western provinces was nearly doubled (from 18,000 to 32,000 hectares).[101]

The Austrian ambassador reported in January 1936 that after two years the Nonaggression Pact had enabled the Germans to halt the polonization of the German-inhabited territories, though not much else.[102] As the figures show, however, land reform speeded up after January 1936—and it would increase even more drastically beginning in 1937. Although the Germans held only 40.9 percent of the total land in Posen and Pomerelia in 1926, they had been forced to contribute 66.5 percent of the total share of land redistributed in the two provinces by 1936. In contrast, the Polish landowners possessed 59 percent of the land, but their share for distribution amounted to only 33.4 percent in that ten-year period.[103]

The situation of the German schools in Poland was complicated by economic conditions. There was a general downward trend in the number of German schools, which continued after the Nonaggression Pact. There had been a striking decline in the number of German state schools between 1929–30 and 1934–35, from 768 to 490, a loss of 278 schools. The number of pupils decreased in the same period by 7,700.[104] By 1937–38 a further 62 schools and 15,500 pupils had been lost because of the orders of Polish authorities.[105]

Such intervention by the Polish authorities may have been justified by *Volksbund* (VB) recruiting methods. Children of VB members were registered for the German schools as a matter of course, and in times of economic hardship and unemployment the extra dole given to VB members attracted Poles as well as Germans. The Polish authorities tested the children on their knowledge of German and rejected many on this basis. In Upper Silesia in 1926–27 there were 8,649 applicants for the German schools (twice as many as in any previous year) and the Board of Education rejected 5,000 of them.[106] The *Volksbund*'s challenge prompted an investigation sponsored by the League Council, which partially confirmed the Polish decision: 811 of the 1,685 children tested knew no German. In 1929–30 sixty German teachers were dismissed from the state schools for accepting monthly subsidies from Germany (which they had collected at the Deutsche Bank in Bytom [Beuthen]). In 1932 a mining community that was 98 percent Polish qualified for a new German school—the effect of unemployment.[107]

There was some dissatisfaction with the state minority schools because of inadequate teaching and mixed languages,[108] as well as because many of the principals and some of the teachers were Polish. In Upper Silesia in 1933 only 11 of the 54 school principals were German, and there were 88 Polish teachers out of a total of 243.[109] Private schools provided an alternative, although they were too expensive for many parents.[110] Some of the private schools were built with the aid of the Reich; the Goethe school in Grudziadz (Graudenz), for example, was the work of the VDA aided by contributions from local Germans. Even private schools with German instruction were decreasing. Those with between twelve and twenty-two hours per week of instruction in German declined by 11 schools and 500 pupils between 1936–37 and 1937–38.[111]

Besides the outright closings, some German schools were changed over to Polish instruction, teachers were dismissed, and parents were prosecuted for failing to send their children to Polish schools.[112] The *Volksbund* feared that the decreasing number of German schools and the continuing attacks on German youth organizations would lead to assimilation in the next generation.

Of more pressing importance to many ethnic Germans were the economic hardships, particularly unemployment, which they faced along with their

Polish neighbors. Economic conditions were the reason for the secret organization whose discovery in Katowice in February 1936 led to a sensational trial in June.[113] The NSDAB (*Bewegung* instead of *Partei*) was organized by one Manjura of Friedenshütte among simple people, long unemployed, who were attracted by the promise of work. Since part of the initiation ceremony was an oath of unconditional loyalty to Adolf Hitler, they could assume that there was some official backing from Germany. Manjura advocated joining eastern Upper Silesia to Germany. The trial failed to show any connection between the NSDAB and the *Volksgruppe* organizations, but there was some evidence of contact with lower-level officials in Germany itself. As the Austrian ambassador pointed out, the support (if any) from Germany must have been very slight, otherwise the movement would certainly have been larger.

Manjura did not appear at the trial and the police announced that he had committed suicide. The process showed that the great majority of the 120 members arrested considered themselves Polish. They had pure Polish names, gave their testimony in that language, and sent their children to Polish schools. Many received severe sentences, from six to ten years, as a warning to others. Ambassador Hoffinger blamed the fiasco on the divisions and rivalries within the *Auslandsdeutsche* leadership in Germany itself, which "had once again brought a number of compatriots into calamity."[114] Because the entire episode demonstrated the severe economic distress of Upper Silesia, Poland could gain little from publicity about the case and the press showed considerable restraint.

The frequent changes of governments in France and the economic crisis in 1936 exacerbated Poland's economic problems, since the Polish zloty was closely tied to the franc. The crisis brought about a moderate change from Pilsudski's deflation policy. However, the change brought only gradual improvement in the unemployment figures. The year 1937 was the worst, with 470,000 registered unemployed.[115] In particular industries, such as mining and iron and steel, where 1933 had been the worst year, there was improvement, but the German minority failed to benefit from it. Senator Wiesner reported that 1,100 jobs had actually been lost by Germans in eastern Upper Silesia in 1937, although employment in mining there had increased during the year by 9,100 jobs and in the iron and steel industry by 3,200. This deterioration in minority economic conditions forced the Reich government to intervene in behalf of the ethnic Germans in Poland.[116]

Economic hardship made the German minority group in Poland care less about ideological and political considerations and more about their daily bread. The simple workers, that is the "polonized" Germans (or "germanized" Poles), changed their national affiliation according to their everyday financial needs. Reich German work aimed at the preservation of German consciousness was often met with apathy. In January 1937 the VDA heard reports from its scientific circle about the disinterest of German minorities in nationality questions.[117] At the same time the circle recommended to the VDA a new tactic: first use the social aspects of German ideology among the Silesian workers, since they were unemployed; and then, after gaining their sympathy, make them aware of the fact that as Germans they, too, belonged to the Third Reich. Once they felt that way they could be used by the Reich (either as voters in a plebiscite or as active supporters of military operations in case of war).

There was another reason for the declining effectiveness of German work among the *Volksdeutsche*: the struggle for predominance among the VDA (Steinacher patronized by Hess), the *Volksdeutsche Mittelstelle* or VoMi (Lorenz patronized by Himmler), and the Kursell Bureau (under the supervision of Ribbentrop) had reached crisis proportions by January 1937. Since the competition of those different Reich German organizations influenced the *Volksdeutsche* organizations they supported, their differences hindered the effectiveness of the ethnic German organizations everywhere in eastern Europe. The result was that the ethnic Germans in Poland lost support exactly at the time when their situation became critical. Hitler needed the goodwill of the Polish government because of his future plans. Nevertheless, seeing that the Reich German organizations were powerless to provide protection for the German minority in Poland, he had to do something to rescue the German cause in Silesia and elsewhere. The only way to do that while preserving Polish goodwill was to begin negotiations for a new minority agreement.

The Minority Declaration

To relax the tension between Germany and Poland caused by Polish actions against the German minorities was in Hitler's interest for various reasons. Hitler had no more revisionist claims against France. Thus German revisionist policy, if it was to be continued, had to be directed eastward. In order to implement any revisionist policy toward the east, it was necessary to remove the "dagger directed at the heart of Germany," that is, Czechoslovakia.[118] Military operations against Czechoslovakia would be feasible only if Germany took control of Austria and secured the neutrality of Poland.

Germany had another reason for trying to ease the tension between Poland and Germany, and that was to better the conditions of the German minority. The Polish-German agreement concerning the rights of Germans in Upper Silesia was due to expire on July 15, 1937. In order not to leave the German minority group without protection, Germany had to open negotiations with Poland. It seemed advantageous to use the new negotiations to protect not just the Silesian Germans but rather the whole minority group in Poland.

The negotiations began with Hitler's proposal, made through his ambassador to Warsaw, Hans Adolf Moltke, on June 19, 1937, to relax the atmosphere surrounding the minority question. Hitler hoped to secure this relaxation by issuing a common German-Polish declaration that "would set an example for the local authorities to follow in selecting a proper line of conduct."[119] Since German law and practice prevented Poland from helping or protecting the Polish minority in Germany (which numbered about 1,300,000

people, most of whom lived in poor economic conditions), the Polish government accepted Hitler's proposition in the hope that the declaration would
better the conditions of these Poles.[120] The negotiations were complicated by
the desire of certain Polish foreign ministry officials to connect this minority
declaration with an agreement that renewed the recognition of Polish rights in
Danzig. The German negotiators did not reject this Polish precondition
outright, but neither did they accept it. Thus the agreement was delayed.

On November 5, 1937, Hitler informed Lipski that he was willing to comply
with the Polish demands, stating that: "(1) in the legal-political situation of
Danzig no changes will occur...; (2) the rights of the Polish population in
Danzig have to be respected; (3) Poland's rights in Danzig will not be
violated."[121] Thus the status of the German minorities in Poland and of the
Polish minorities in Germany was settled, not within the framework of the
minority-treaties, but by agreement between the two governments. The
bilateral agreement acknowledged that the minority question was not just an
internal matter within each country.

The Minority Declaration was signed on November 5, 1937, after summer-
long negotiations. The Polish government correctly concluded that the
agreement was of greater benefit to Germany than to Poland. On the same day,
Hitler outlined to his staff his plans concerning Austria and Czechoslovakia.
He realized that the possibility of war with France presented an added danger:
"Should Germany have any setbacks, then an attack by Poland against East
Prussia, perhaps against Pomerania and Silesia, must be taken into
account."[122] Thus a precondition of his plan was the neutralization of
Poland.[123] Besides concluding the Minority Declaration, Hitler pursued this
policy by assuring Lipski on November 5, 1937, and Beck on January 14,
1938, that he had no intention of altering the statutes of the free city of Danzig,
and took steps to calm the situation there.[124]

Poland wanted to use the thaw created by Hitler's attitude to further her
foreign policy. This policy had been determined by Marshall Pilsudski, and
Beck had not changed it. Briefly we may summarize it by saying that while
Poland was ready to cooperate with France and to honor her treaty obligations
in case of a French-German conflict, she was not ready to compromise her
"third road" policy by opposing Hitler's designs alone in the case of Austria
and Czechoslovakia. Since no firm opposition to Hitler seemed to be emerging
from France and Britain, Beck's foreign policy was to try to obtain from Hitler
the highest possible price for Poland's neutrality. This price included the
security of Danzig, participation in the dissolution of Czechoslovakia,
creation of a common frontier with Hungary, and the right not to participate in
the Anti-Comintern Pact in order not to undermine the cool but correct Polish-
Soviet relations.[125] Noticeably missing from these plans were any concessions
to the German minorities in Poland.

By signing the Minority Declaration Poland had conceded that the minority
question was intergovernmental rather than domestic. From that moment the
Reich became the advocate of the German minority group. But since Germany

was seeking rapprochement with Poland, this concession did not seem too serious. Poland paid only lip service to the declaration. Ardent nationalists among local officials continued their repolonization campaign and the land redistribution program went on at the expense of German landowners. German families were even relocated or expelled from areas considered strategically important. German objections, if they were voiced at all, were mild considering the unchanged Polish attitude toward the German minorities throughout 1938. The deal made in 1937 seemed, in the short run, to serve Poland's interests well.

From Hitler's viewpoint the Minority Declaration was a complete success. In return for quieting down the Nazis of Danzig and promising Poland a small share of Czechoslovakia, Germany had gained the right to champion German minority affairs in Poland and had secured the rear for her upcoming diplomatic and military operations in Austria and later on in Czechoslovakia. At the same time she had avoided taking on any obligations for the future and had left the door open for the continuation of her aggressive foreign policy of obtaining *Lebensraum* in the east at the expense of her neighbors, among them now Poland. If there were losers, even temporary losers, because of the Minority Declaration, they were the ethnic Germans of Poland.

The German-Polish Nonaggression Pact of 1934 had disappointed the ethnic Germans. After experiencing the Polish attempts to assimilate them forcibly and realizing that the minority treaties did not give them the desired protection, they were happy to learn about the minority agreement between the Reich and Poland. They expected that with the signing of this treaty their period of hardship had ended and their complaints would now be remedied.

The complaints may be grouped in the following categories: economic grievances caused by the Polish land reform program and by the acute unemployment problem; curtailment of the right of parents to send their children to German schools and thus preserve their Germandom; limitation of the rights of association, cultural, and even religious work.

The Minority Declaration dealt with several areas in the relationships between minorities and governments. Its articles prohibited forced assimilation, especially of the young, and any hindrance of membership in the minority group. It also guaranteed the right to use the minority language in personal and business matters, press, and assemblies. The third article guaranteed the right of association, including cultural and economic unions. The next article granted the right to establish schools and organize religious groups using the mother tongue, and said that there was to be no interference with beliefs or charitable works. The final article concerned economic matters. It stated the right of minority members to the free choice and exercise of an occupation or business. It also called for equal treatment of the minority with the *Staatsvolk* in the economic area, mentioning specifically the possession or acquisition of land.

Since the agreement touched on all three main categories of complaints— economic, educational, and cultural—the ethnic Germans were understandably hopeful that their situation would improve after November 1937. They expected an end to the Polish pressure for assimilation. This would have meant proportional equity in land reform, job security, and rehirings in industry, free choice of schools by the parents, and unrestricted associations. (Naturally, these improvements were to be within the prescribed bounds of loyalty to Poland.) In fact, none of these expectations was realized. The German minority continued to have complaints in all areas after 1937.

German Complaints after the Declaration

Economic grievances, particularly concerning execution of the land reform, were many and justified. The Polish authorities expropriated land owned by Germans disproportionately and distributed it among landless peasants, favoring the Poles. In west Poland German owners held about 30 percent of the land available for compulsory distribution in 1925 when the program began. During its first ten years they contributed 66 percent of the parceled land.[126] The compulsory distribution lists for west Poland called for 53 percent of the land to come from German owners in 1936, 72 percent in 1937, 61 percent in 1938, and 65 percent in 1939.[127] The volume of German land distributed also greatly increased, from 8,444 hectares in 1936, to 20,325 hectares in 1937, 22,254 hectares in 1938, and 22,732 hectares in 1939. In the western provinces almost as much land was parceled between 1937 and 1939 (99,230 hectares) as in the entire decade from 1926–36 (101,206 hectares).

One other aspect of land reform affected the Germans in particular. For obvious military and national security reasons the Polish government wanted to remove the untrustworthy (at least in their view) German landowners from the vicinity of the border with Germany. The frontier zone decree of January 22, 1937,[128] was the legal basis for such action. It provided that within thirty kilometers of the border *Volksdeutsche* could not make land transactions, and in Posen and Pomerelia could not even inherit land.[129] They would instead be compensated for the land, which would then be awarded to trustworthy Poles.

The land reform had two detrimental effects on the conditions of ethnic Germans: first, by reducing the size of German holdings it weakened the economic and financial position of the entire minority group; second, the reduction in the size of estates limited the capacity of German owners to employ landless peasants as farmhands, thus creating unemployment among the agricultural workers. Since the expropriated land was distributed in small plots, the new owners were also unable to hire farmhands.[130] Lack of skill and job opportunities condemned such workers to live in misery—even to face starvation.

The ethnic Germans fared no better in industry. Here on many occasions the political goal "degermanization" was pursued even more openly than in agriculture. For example, during the period March through October 1938 some ninety-six members of the Trade Union of German Workers in Upper

Silesia were dismissed and replaced with Polish workers. On March 8, 1938, Senator Wiesner had reported a 62 percent unemployment rate among members of the Trade Union of German Workers, and the rate ran to 80 percent in other German organizations. The overall unemployment rate in Upper Silesia at the time was 16 percent.[131]

In the Olsa territory, acquired from Czechoslovakia with German help in October 1938, many German employees were dismissed if they couldn't prove mastery of the Polish language within three months or show identification cards from Polish organizations. Others were simply given notice for December 31, 1938.[132] It seemed that the Minority Declaration of November 5, 1937, had not improved ethnic German economic conditions in the slightest degree.

The school question and the minority's grievances associated with it were quite complex. The number of German schools and pupils continued to decline after 1937. In light of the methods used by the *Volksbund* to recruit pupils, here perhaps the Polish authorities' actions were correct. Germany, however, took up the cause of the minority schools and issued frequent complaints to Poland. Many of them concerned the carrying out of the gentleman's agreement reached by Beck and Moltke during the negotiations for the Minority Declaration. In return for the opening of a secondary school in Marienwerder (Kwidzýn), the Poles were to restore public rank to the secondary schools in Königshütte (Królewska Huta),[133] Graudenz (Grud-ziąz), and Posen (Poznán) and allow construction to continue on a secondary school in Bromberg (Bydgoszcz). The Germans claimed that the Poles had delayed and obstructed the implementation of the agreement; for example, public rank was secured for Graudenz only, and while the building permit for Bromberg was granted, the building inspection department had used technicalities to halt construction once again.[134] The complaint regarding the school in Posen had still not been settled months later. The consul general there said that four of the six German private schools, including the Schiller School, were deprived of the right of public rank "for which they had fought so long."[135]

Other complaints concerned the closing of schools, including some large ones; economic pressure, even punishment of parents for not sending their children to the Polish schools; and the transfer of German teachers to the interior.[136] Minor harassments included prohibition of certain literature for use in the schools—"Goethe's Childhood" from *Dichtung und Wahrheit*, the *Nibelungenlied* and *Edda*—and the sudden cancellation of a Christmas play.[137] More serious was the closing of Hostel Association buildings in Graudenz, including one that had housed eighty needy students at the Goethe School there.[138] At the beginning of November 1938 only about half the German children in west Poland were in German schools; the number had declined to 30 percent in Silesia and about 12 percent in central Poland.[139]

In the Olsa territory there were numerous complaints about the schools.[140] In November 1938 many German schools were still closed, although the Polish schools had opened weeks earlier. Obstacles were placed in the way of their opening: summonses to parents to enroll their children in Polish schools within twenty-four hours or face punishment or expulsion; language examinations; obstructionism by local officials—even violence; higher fees than for the Polish schools. Before the Polish occupation of Teschen there had been one private and four public elementary schools. Now there was only one elementary school. Enrollment was down in the secondary school of Neu-Oderberg from about 680 to 150, and the intermediate school was still closed. Only about one-tenth of the German children had reentered German schools. The Poles replied in December that more than 1,000 German children in the Olsa district were enrolled for German schools, that six schools would be opened in Oderberg and Teschen, and German classes would be established in the Polish school in Pudlow. They said there were too few German students in Karwin and Freistadt to qualify those districts for German schools. The German response seized on these figures to compare the 1,000 students in six schools with the earlier 3,000 students in thirteen schools. There were reports that qualified children in Karwin and Freistadt had been refused admission and that meetings of the *Schulvereine* for the purpose of founding new schools had been prohibited at the last minute.

German churches and other organizations felt the same pressures as the schools. In December 1937 Ambassador Moltke reported that clergy of ethnic German origin in Upper Silesia were being dismissed and even expelled. Beck responded to his protests by saying that he "saw no possibility of a satisfactory solution" at that time and that the problem was being intensified by the "intransigent attitude of the Protestant clergy."[141] The Protestant clergy openly rejected a new church law that withdrew the right of the parishes to elect their own clergymen and placed it in the hands of a provisional church council controlled by the *wojewoda* of east Upper Silesia, who was a Catholic. A year later this problem was still unresolved.[142] In March 1939 Germany once again requested an end to the "political proceeding" against Evangelical pastors, and again Poland replied that such influence on the church authorities "was not within the power of the administration."[143] In June the German Order of St. John was dissolved and its two hospitals taken over by the Polish Sisters of St. Vincent.[144] In July Moltke furnished the foreign ministry with a list of seventeen incidents against German Protestants, some of them involving violence.[145] Finally in August it was announced that the Protestant Theological College in Posen would close on January 1, 1940.[146]

During the same period other German societies were being dissolved and their assets confiscated. In December 1938 the Graudenz Hostels Association was ended and its property, valued at 250,000 zloty, attached.[147] In January 1939 the head office and local organizations of the German Union (*Deutsche Vereinigung*) were searched,[148] apparently without further consequences. During the summer, as tension increased, so did the pressure on the ethnic Germans. More and more of their organizations were either dissolved or left without meeting places: the German Home at Karwin (valued at 160,000 zloty),[149] the Evangelical Hostel in Posen (worth several hundred thousand zloty), the Casino House in Bromberg, the Men's Choral Society House in Lodz, and the German House in Tarnowitz.[150] The German Dramatic Society in Teschen was prohibited and its property, valued at 500,000 zloty, taken.[151] Like the hostel in Posen, the theater in Teschen was the center of German culture in its district. In August the remaining German organizations were dissolved: the Library Association in Posen and all of its locals in west Poland;[152] in Bielitz the Gymnastic Club, Choral Society, Hiking Club, and Apprentices Association.[153]

The Minority Question in 1939

In the year 1938 the map of Europe was redrawn according to the will of Hitler: Austria was annexed by Germany, Czechoslovakia was reduced in size to the territory inhabited by Czechs, Slovaks, and Ruthens, Teschen was ceded to Poland, and the southern parts of Slovakia and Ruthenia went to Hungary.[154] The Western powers looked upon these events passively, and even assisted Hitler unintentionally. After Munich France hurriedly signed a Franco-German agreement in December 1938 in which Germany announced that she had no more territorial demands against France, recognized the Franco-German frontier as final, and agreed to consult the French government from time to time on political matters.[155] Halifax, Britain's foreign secretary, believed that the right policy was "to let Hitler go ahead and do what he likes in Central Europe" as long as he did not interfere with the British Dominions.[156] In other words, the democracies deserted their East Central European allies.

The most sensitive situation was that of Poland. Because of Polish participation in the dissolution of Czechoslovakia, France considered Poland an untrustworthy ally. French irritation grew even stronger because of Poland's renewed refusal to grant passage rights to Soviet troops in case of war.[157] Britain displayed almost complete indifference toward Poland. Germany seemed friendly for the time being, and though there were disagreements over the interpretations of the Minority Declaration and the status of Danzig, the preservation of friendly relations seemed to be a feasible goal.

In October 1938 Polish relations with Germany took a sharp turn for the worse. Ribbentrop made a surprising proposal for the "normalization of German-Polish relations."[158] According to this proposal, the free city of Danzig would revert to the German Reich. To secure transportation and communication with Danzig and East Prussia through the Danzig Corridor, the Germans wanted to build an extraterritorial superhighway and a multiple-track railroad, offering similar privileges to Poland through the Danzig territory leading to a free port. The proposal also suggested a new consultation clause for the Minority Agreement to regulate Polish-German relations on a continuous basis; expected Poland to join the Anti-Comintern Pact;[159] and offered, after the recognition of the new Polish-German frontiers, an extension of the 1934 Polish-German Nonaggression Pact from ten to twenty-five years.

Ribbentrop's proposal was very liberal and reasonable from the German point of view. The principle of self-determination had been accepted as the guiding spirit of the Munich agreement by the Western powers. Since Danzig had a majority German population,[160] would not the city's annexation by the Reich eliminate an injustice of the Versailles Treaty and remove a dangerous point of friction in Polish-German relations? The proposal solved the transportation problem on the basis of fair reciprocity. The consultation clause would serve as a safety valve to prevent the development of crises, and membership in the Anti-Comintern Pact would provide additional security for Poland against a revisionist Soviet Union, which had a greedy eye on the Ukraine. Finally, the recognition of new boundaries in the extended Non-aggression Pact was more satisfactory than the Locarno Treaty's provisions, and the pact would assure security and peace for both countries for a quarter of a century.

Poland, of course, interpreted the proposal very differently. Though Beck personally regarded Danzig as a "lost post" since early 1938, vital Polish interests demanded that he hang on to it.[161] The corridor and Danzig were Poland's lifeline to the sea; 60.5 percent of her imports and 55.1 percent of her exports passed through it.[162] The territorial routes and the waterway (Vistula River) both crossed Danzig, and these were essential not only for trade but also for the transport of French arms that were needed to modernize the Polish army.[163] The annexation of Danzig by the Reich would have put Poland's defense and economic well-being into the hands of Germany. To Polish eyes Ribbentrop's proposal looked like a Trojan horse hiding a *Drang nach Osten* policy. Neither the Polish government nor people had forgotten the lessons of history, and the German proposal was regarded as a covert attack on national security.

The Anti-Comintern Pact directed against the Soviet Union, contradicted the basic principle of Polish foreign policy, which was to keep Poland neutral between her two great neighbors. That is why Poland had declined the original German invitation in November 1937.[164] During the Munich crisis Polish-Soviet relations deteriorated to such a degree that armed clashes occurred on the frontiers.[165] Thus, joining the Anti-Comintern Pact would most likely have produced a complete break in Polish-Soviet relations, leaving Poland with only one course to follow: complete reliance on Germany for protection against the Soviet Union. Signing the pact was clearly against Poland's interest. No wonder Beck rejected the German proposal. Unfortunately, his counterproposal suggesting the "replacement of the League of Nations guarantee and its prerogatives by a bilateral Polish-German Agreement" unintentionally played into Hitler's hands.[166] It was precisely Hitler's aim to discontinue the League's guarantees of Danzig.

Upon receiving Poland's refusal of the proposal, Hitlerian diplomacy turned to a combination of promises and indirect threats. While giving concessions to Poland by stopping the German-supported Ukrainian anti-Polish propaganda,[167] it unleashed the German press, which began to attack the Polish minority policy.[168] At the same time it heated up the crisis atmosphere in Danzig.

On March 15, 1939, in a surprise move, Hitler occupied the Czech lands, Slovakia declared its independence, and Hungarian troops, against German objections, occupied Ruthenia, thereby restoring the traditional Polish-Hungarian frontier. These events created an entirely new situation in East Central Europe. With the sharpening disagreement between the Reich and Poland, the ethnic Germans of Danzig and of Poland were nearing the time when they would have to make a clear choice between the Reich and Poland.

In the eyes of almost 50 percent of Danzig's population the threatened annexation of the city by the Reich was unwelcome. The Danzig Nazis were afraid it might result in a Polish takeover of the city, while the non-Nazi Germans feared it altogether. Thus if the city leaders really wanted to represent the interest of their constituency, they had to work for the preservation of the status quo, that is, a continuation of the League of Nations' guarantees. However, neither the population nor the senate, nor even the League, was in the position to decide the future of Danzig. It was in the hands of Hitler, who declared his plans to Greiser in these words: "If the Poles will behave, we shall wait for a while with an action in Danzig and Memel. But if they don't then they will find out who is the boss."[169]

In Poland proper events in the spring of 1939 alienated some of the German minority group members from their Polish neighbors who, under the influence of Polish nationalistic propaganda, looked upon them as enemies.[170] At the same time, international events proved to the ethnic Germans that the Reich stood up in their defense only when its own interests were not prejudiced.[171] Thus, while domestic events suggested to the ethnic Germans that they could not hope for the betterment of their situation through the goodwill of the Polish government, international events indicated that they could not expect deliverance from the German Reich for their own sake. The dissolution of Czechoslovakia, the creation of the Slovakian protectorate, the occupation of the Memel territory, and the weak Western reaction to all these moves seemed to indicate that Hitler could have his way with Poland if he so decided. The German group did not have a united organization, so the separate organizations, as well as every individual member, had to choose whichever side— Poland or Germany—seemed more beneficial.

The great majority of ethnic Germans were disinterested in nationality questions. They changed their national affiliation according to their narrow personal interest. Therefore both the repolonization efforts of the Polish nationalists and the nazification efforts of the few self-conscious ethnic Germans supported by the Reich organizations seemed to gain wide support depending on the circumstances. Very few of the leaders realized that their "mass support" was only temporary, since the majority of people have only one thought in mind—survival under the best possible conditions. This desire was typified in the statement one peasant made to Bülow[172] after the occupation of Poland: "Your lordship! We were Germans before and that passed away. Then we were Poles and that passed away, too. Now we are Germans again, and that, too, will pass." This conviction prevented people from participating in activities directed against Poland, and also from challenging the Polish authorities. When the time came, they even obeyed the mobilization orders.[173]

Those *Volksdeutsche* such as Dr. Pant who sided with the Polish government did so because they were anti-Nazi. They were the tragic figures of the German minority group. Their pan-German convictions were the original motivation making them work for the revision of the peace treaty and for the preservation of Germandom, but their humanistic views and democratic political convictions separated them from the aims of the Reich as soon as the Nazis gained control.[174] Unfortunately, the Polish government did not realize that their loyalty was based on firm anti-Nazi convictions, and beginning in 1935 it appointed senators from the *Jungdeutsche Partei*. The small loyalist group lost influence with both the other *Volksdeutsche* and the Polish government; thus its work was in vain.

International events up to March 15, 1939, as well as Hitler's statement to Greiser that he would "show who is boss,"[175] indicated to the Nazi elements in the German minority that the future was theirs. Through diplomatic negotiations or war, sooner or later, Hitler would liberate them from Polish rule. It was in their interest to organize the *Volksgruppe* for a Nazi takeover and thus promote the diplomatic aims of the Reich. In light of the strong Polish reaction to Nazi activity, they had to decide whether it was worth the risk to act openly or whether it was better to work as a fifth column. Furthermore, they had to know how the Reich wanted to realize the annexation—by peaceful means or by force.

The continuation of overt opposition and pro-Nazi activities would have given the Polish state police the opportunity to arrest and eliminate the entire pro-Nazi leadership, so this was not a practical alternative. Therefore, underground activities seemed the best way to help in their own liberation. Their underground work was halfhearted and not too successful, however, because of the different attitudes of the German AA and the Nazi party concerning the use of minority group members.[176]

Unquestionably, it was in the interest of the whole German minority group to see that annexation, if it occurred, was by peaceful means. This would preserve their occupations, property, and lives. However, the stiffening Polish attitude toward German demands made the possibility of war very real. To survive the war with the smallest losses it was advisable for the minority to organize itself for defense against the arbitrary actions of the local Polish authorities. For this purpose it needed arms, which meant Reich support.

After the signing of the Anglo-Polish alliance and the renunciation of the German-Polish Nonaggression and Anglo-German Naval pacts (April 28, 1939), there was not too much hope the German-Polish differences could be solved by peaceful means. But Hitler's speech in the Reichstag on April 28, 1939, was surprisingly conciliatory, even in the interpretation of Lipski. It held out some hope for a peaceful settlement. Beck, however, in his address to the Diet on May 5, displayed a certain inflexibility by stating that "I have already made clear our attitude."[177] The German government interpreted this speech as a closing of the door by Beck "and, until he himself reopened it, there was nothing to be done."[178]

Diplomatic activities continued in other fields, none of them contributing to the relaxation of tension. Britain, after signing mutual assistance treaties with Poland, Greece, and Romania (April 6 and 13), extended her guarantees to Turkey (May 12, 1939) and conducted negotiations with the Soviet Union. Germany signed a military agreement with Italy (May 22, 1939) and mutual assistance treaties with Estonia and Latvia, thus gaining a dominant position in the Baltic region. The Germans also carefully watched the Anglo-Soviet negotiations, ready to jump in if the parties could not agree.[179]

German-Polish relations reached a deadlock. As proved by developments between May and August, 1939, each side tried to break this deadlock by using public opinion against the other. The means to mobilize public opinion were found in incidents, staged or accidental, true or untrue, that occurred in Danzig and in the German-inhabited border area of Poland.

Poland was in the more advantageous position: Polish hostility to Germany prevailed in all circles[180] and the hardship caused by the partial mobilization was blamed on Germany. Thus Polish local officials and nationalist groups often found the police sympathetic when they broke the law involving German minorities.

Germany was in a less advantageous situation. Since ethnic German economic power and educational institutions in Poland were much greater than those of the Poles in Germany, a systematic policy of reprisals for Polish actions would have ended up hurting the ethnic Germans much more than the ethnic Poles.[181] Fear for the well-being of the *Volksdeutsche* was especially noticeable in the AA, DAI, and VDA, which had in 1938 objected to the use of ethnic Germans by the Army Intelligence Service because they feared this woud bring on massive resettlement of ethnic Germans by Polish authorities in case of war.[182] The army did not stop the practice, however. Besides building up a network of confidential agents, the majority of them volunteers, it established a few wireless stations to help the invading German army.[183] But these agents played no role during the early summer months of 1939.

The German minority group in Poland, outside of Danzig, could not hope to receive any effective protection from Hitler's Germany. The traditional minority complaints of unjust treatment over land, schools, and unemployment gave way to much greater complaints. Beginning in 1939 the relationship between ethnic Germans and Poles on the local level worsened, under the influence of war psychosis, so much so that the Germans were afraid to speak their mother tongue in public. German minority papers were censored, then confiscated, and finally closed down.[184] Polish authorities, as well as the common people, boycotted German businesses.[185] As a result bank accounts of individual businessmen declined rapidly by 90 percent. Professionals, industrialists, and small manufacturers lost almost all their Polish customers. The AA feared that for lack of financial reserves the ethnic German business communities would not be able to survive without help. Help came only in meager amounts from the *Deutsche Stiftung*, which distributed through the German consulates in Poland the RM300,000 donated by VoMi and the Reich finance ministry.[186] Because of heavy Polish pressure, the Germans who only two years before had displayed disinterest in nationalism and Nazi ideology, began to accept more directions from the *Volksbund*, which was designed to become the chief organization of the German minority group.[187] It did not help. As international events moved closer to the great crisis of August 1939, attacks against the Germans increased. At first the Polish authorities used discrimination and took into custody only those Germans whose names appeared on the list of suspects already drawn up by the state in April and May 1939.[188] They were marched under guard to the eastern parts of Poland. Their total number estimated by unofficial German sources varies between 50,000 and 58,000.[189] Many died during the march or were murdered by hysterical mobs along the roads, despite the best efforts of the guards. The German minority lived in fear and those who could joined the *Reichdeutsche* families on their route to Germany.[190] But the great majority remained and secretly prayed for the appearance of the liberating German armies.

As international events and the Danzig crisis came to a climax at the end of August 1939, impatient young *Volksdeutsche* (their average age was well below twenty-two), who were organized by *Abwehr* agents, equipped, and armed for action at the rear of the Polish army, fell victim to their own carelessness and thus to the Polish authorities. On the night of August 25–26, several groups of *Reichdeutsche* saboteurs guided by *Volksdeutsche* were arrested along the Polish frontier. In Łódź a saboteur group of *Volksdeutsche* was arrested, and the dynamite, weapons, and a wireless they carried were confiscated.[191] The very same night a German commando group crossed over from Slovakia to Poland to occupy in a surprise attack the strategically important Jablunka Pass. They were to hold the pass until the arrival of the German troops the next day, but since Hitler postponed the attack of his army until September 1 (which these commandos did not know), they were soon overpowered and forced to retreat.[192] All acts of sabotage on the eve of the war were carried out by specially trained troops of the German army,[193] but incorrect reporting by the Polish press and radio ascribed these acts to the ethnic Germans. This news, coupled with a secret document[194] found in a downed airplane on September 3, triggered panic in Poland. Suddenly, every German became a "fifth columnist" who should be dealt with as such and executed without trial. This new wave of violent attacks on the ethnic Germans made even those who had once loyally cooperated with the Polish state welcome with flowers the invading German armies and help their advance, sometimes actively participating in the military operations.[195] The atrocities and hysterical mob actions disappointed even many Polish patriots, who risked their lives to offer asylum to the hunted *Volksdeutsche*.[196]

German governmental circles opposed from the beginning the involvement of *Volksdeutsche* in the actual operations and kept up their opposition until the outbreak of the war. As late as August 22, 1939, the foreign ministry disapproved the plan of Rudolf Wiesner (leader of the *Jungdeutsche Partei*) to broadcast a violent anti-Polish speech on the Danzig radio station.[197] The next day *Gauleiter* Forster asked the AA if the *Volksdeutsche* in Posnan-Pomerelia "should be called upon to resist" or should be advised to go into hiding during the critical days. The AA, after consulting the High Command of the Armed Forces, replied the next day that they did "not consider the arming of the *Volksdeutsche* advisable."[198] Because of the moderating influence of the AA and other Reich authorities, the ethnic Germans (with a few exceptions when they acted on their own initiative) were not actively involved in sabotage activities, the surprise occupation of towns, the destruction of railroad lines, or the creation of confusion in the rear of the Polish army. The Reich German authorities and the army successfully executed these kinds of partisan activities with well-trained commandos of the special forces.[199]

On September 1 the Germany army invaded Poland, and contrary to unfounded optimism of the Polish political and military leadership, the Polish army not only failed to march on Berlin,[200] but was unable even to withstand the attack of the Germans. Nor did the German people revolt against Hitler, as Lipski had expected.[201]

The ethnic Germans, after the unbelievable happiness of the first few days, went through a bitter period of awakening. Their "liberating" Reich German brethren behaved no better than the demoralized retreating enemy troops. Many ethnic Germans were arrested and promptly executed without trial for their cooperation with the Poles, or simply on the basis of reports submitted by their personal enemies.[202] Houses were plundered, property was confiscated. The Reich Germans displayed great arrogance toward the ethnic Germans, who called them with malicious irony "the Right Germans." The destruction of Catholic religious monuments, usually done at night, not only provided good propaganda material for the Poles but also alienated the *Volksdeutsche*. The oversimplification of the religious issue and the ignorance of some commanders in the lower ranks of the German army heightened the antagonism; Germans who followed the Evangelical faith were considered Germans; German Catholics were regarded as Poles, that is, enemies. The handling of the Jewish population also created animosity. Suspicion and distrust grew to such a degree that, in contrast to the Sudeten, in the occupied territories of Poland not a single *Volksdeutsche* was considered trustworthy enough to be appointed to a higher position by the Reich authorities.[203]

Role of the Ethnic Germans in the Prewar Crises

It is almost impossible to reconstruct the prewar crisis in Poland objectively. The available sources, such as the *German White Book*, the *French Yellow Book*, the *English Blue Book*, the *Polish White Book*, and the *Lipski Papers*, contain only diplomatic documents. Some of these documents reflect the domestic conditions of Poland and describe certain actions of both the Polish authorities and German minority, but always they mirror the convictions and sympathies of the reporting diplomats. Thus there are few facts; instead, there are reports based on hearsay. Of equally doubtful value are the memoirs and reminiscences of the Polish and ethnic German "common people" who wrote about their personal experiences long after World War II, at the request of West German researchers. (Their reports are deposited in the *Ost Dok. 2* files of the Bundesarchiv in Koblenz.) The following description, based on these available sources, is therefore more an illustration of the overheated crisis atmosphere than an unchallengeable historical survey.

Until the time of the Czechoslovak crisis the "German minority proved its loyalty in the most exemplary way. One would have said that the minority question no longer existed." These were the words in which Leon Noël characterized German minority behavior in Poland.[204] The occupation of Bohemia, the establishment of the German protectorate over Slovakia (March 15, 1939), and the occupation of the Memel territory (March 22) did not bring any change in their atttitude. But these events greatly changed the attitude of the Polish population, which "suddenly recognized" the German threat. Under the influence of the press, as well as "of patriotic women [!] the patriotic sentiments of the Poles... were exalted."[205]

Although these sentiments were first directed only against the Reich, soon all the Germans became the object of suspicion and dislike.[206] Fanatical Polish patriots expressed their general anti-German feelings in violent actions against the local ethnic Germans. Anti-German demonstrations were reported from Thorn (March 25) and Bromberg (March 26). Ethnic Germans registered complaints about the economic boycott against them in Bromberg (March 27 and 30) and in Graudenz (March 30 and April 4). Property was destroyed in Pomerelia (March 30), and there were reports of physical injuries from Thorn the same day. Between March 30 and April 4 the ethnic Germans complained that Polish police and other officials failed to halt or actually participated in these actions, and that the Polish press aggravated the situation (Posen, March 31).[207]

Ironically, the ethnic Germans were suffering not for their own behavior but for what was happening in Danzig. From the end of February arms were openly transported almost daily to the barracks of the Nazi-controlled Danzig police.[208] On March 13 and 14, 500 officers and sergeants from East Prussia made a reconnaissance trip on a road leading from East Prussia to Danzig. Local SA troops marched around the city in uniform and with weapons in hand. The Polish authorities implemented countermeasures and, beginning March 17, the French consul in Danzig reported a "great influx of Polish troops to the frontiers of the territory." Around March 25 Polish artillery batteries were positioned around Danzig because of widespread rumors concerning a possible Nazi coup there.[209] Poland mobilized two army corps and tried to justify this action by pointing to the German troop movements in

Slovakia and the occupation of Memel. However, there were no German troop concentrations on the frontier with Silesia, Posen, or Pomerelia. Thus Poland's military measures could be interpreted more as a threat than self-defense.[210]

The Polish authorities also used economic measures to intimidate the Germans of Danzig[211] and stopped restricting the arbitrary actions of some local Polish authorities against the German minorities outside of Danzig. In fact, some local officials, confronted with ethnic German grievances, defended their actions by saying that their orders came from higher up.[212]

Hitler's denunciation on April 28, 1939, of the German-Polish Non-aggression Pact gave Poland the excuse to denounce on May 2 the Minority Declaration (of November 5, 1937).[213] In effect, Poland now had a free hand in dealing with the German minorities. The cancellation of the Minority Declaration meant that henceforth complaints had to be based on the Polish constitution—which nevertheless should have give the minority adequate protection.[214] No serious incidents involving physical injury to ethnic Germans occurred before the Polish denunciation of the Minority Declaration. On May 3, according to the French ambassador, the German minority press still summarized German grievances in these three points: dismissal of German workers in Upper Silesia, land reform directed against German landlords, and the closing of certain German schools.[215] The Polish press objected only to the desire of the German minority to create a unified minority organization at the instigation of Berlin. Only the head of the JDP radicalized his party's program by demanding *Volksgruppenrecht* for the entire German minority group.[216] Even this was not a new demand on his part.

Suddenly the tension created by international events produced an eruption of violence on May 13–14, 1939, in Lódź. At an organized anti-German demonstration aggressive, emotional speeches created an uncontrollable anti-German atmosphere leading to mob actions against the local German population. The result was not only property damage but also bodily injuries and even death. The event frightened members of the German minority to such a degree that the German consulate received numerous requests for immigrant visas.[217]

Just before the outbreak of violence, Senator Erwin Hasbach and the head of the JDP, Rudolf Wiesner, appealed directly to the president of Poland, asking him to instruct the Polish authorities to obey the laws and "secure for the German minority the rights to which they are entitled under the constitution."[218] But Polish authorities continued to implement measures against the German minority throughout June and July. These unprovoked meaures caused the ethnic Germans to lose faith in the Polish government and, instead of eliminating the minority problem, actually escalated it. The German minority became more and more united and aggressive, even as the Poles determined to show them that they were the masters. This confrontation ended only when a new crisis in Danzig turned attention to the international competition between Germany and Poland.

Results of the Forced Assimilation Policy

Reviewing the history of the ethnic Germans of Poland, we may now draw conclusions concerning our vital questions.

The German government's policy (and here we may include the policy of Reich German organizations dealing with the *Auslandsdeutsche*), paid greater attention to the needs and interests of the ethnic Germans in Poland than it did to those of the Germans in Czechoslovakia and Hungary. Though Hitler unquestionably sought a rapprochement with Poland and therefore did not use any kind of diplomatic or economic pressure to better the conditions of the ethnic Germans during the 1930s, the Minority Declaration of 1937 was intended to improve their situation.

The Reich German organizations did a better job, thanks to their cooperation with the AA and Reich finance ministry. Their financial aid, sent through the *Deutsche Stiftung* and diplomatic channels, lightened the burden of many unemployed and bankrupt *Volksdeutsche*. In the crisis year of 1939 the Reich German authorities, with the exception of the Army Intelligence Service, continued their policy of not using ethnic Germans for assignments that could endanger their lives or property.

The question, however, turns not on the method of the Reich, but on its goal, and its goal was the revision of the Versailles Treaty and the annexation of the lost German-populated territories. This was also the goal of the *Volksdeutsche* associations and, without doubt, of many self-conscious ethnic Germans. But as our investigation has shown, the great majority of the *Volksdeutsche* displayed a remarkable disinterest in the nationality question and were ready to accept Polish rule, even at the price of assimilation, until economic hardship and unemployment made them more susceptible to nationalistic ideas. Thus, if the Reich government had wanted to help the ethnic Germans as they themselves would have liked to be helped, it would have stopped seeking revision, given up its annexation plans, and reached a permanent agreement with Poland that would secure a better life for the ethnic Germans. As we saw, the Reich hesitantly pursued this line until Hitler decided to occupy Poland. And even after reaching this decision, Hitler took every precaution not to make the life of the German minority harder than it already was.

This caution of the Reich was unique in East Central Europe and can be attributed partly to the ethnic Germans themselves: By refusing the ideas of Nazism and rejecting the encouragement of the Reich to unite in one huge (Nazi-controlled) mass organization, they were able to secure for themselves a greater degree of freedom than any other German minority group in East Central Europe. It is ironic that the Polish government did not appreciate the loyalty of the majority of ethnic Germans and, beginning in 1935, always appointed one Polish senator from among the members of the *Jungdeutsche Partei*, which represented only a negligible number of the *Volksdeutsche* in Poland.

The problem of Danzig was almost independent of the general ethnic

German problem. The majority of the city's population was German and Nazi ideas were accepted by a great number of its inhabitants *before* Hitler came to power in the Reich. Because of the free city status, they enjoyed the protection of the League of Nations, which prevented the Polish authorities from interfering with the domestic policy of the city. Thus *Gleichschaltung* was realized in Danzig without great difficulty.

The location of Danzig, too, made it a desirable target of German revisionism. Besides the German character of the city, which made the self-determination argument plausible, the German government, even before Hitler, appreciated its economic and strategic importance. Economic control of Danzig would have meant the control of traffic and transportation between Poland and the world, providing additional income and riches not only for the city, but also for the Reich. Thus the interest of Danzig coincided with that of Germany, and the pro-Nazi sentiment of the city's population made it a most convenient tool of German revisionist policy.

The Polish government's policy regarding the German minorities supposedly served Poland's interest. Its beginning in the 1920s was not a fortunate one. Local Polish authorities, strongly influenced by their nationalism, very often implemented Polish minority laws in a distorted way. Many ethnic Germans interpreted this type of action as an ultimatum: Either assimilate or accept an inferior position for the rest of your life—economically, politically, and socially. Thousands of Germans chose a third course by emigrating to the Reich. There they provided strong support for a harder revisionist line, and on occasion even influenced the German government in that direction.

By renouncing the minority treaty, the Polish government freed itself from the restrictions of the League of Nations, but at the same time closed off the only safety valve the German minority had for their grievances. Thus Polish policy contributed to the radicalization of the minority group. Worsening economic conditions speeded up this radicalization process.

After the successes of Polish diplomacy with the Soviet and German Nonaggression Pacts, Poland maneuvered herself into a neutral position that already in 1934 projected the possibility of isolation. As time passed, France had less and less confidence in Poland, and there was no other acceptable great power in sight that could provide security for her against Germany. Polish policy firmly held that her participation in the destruction of Czechoslovakia would secure not only economic and strategic benefits but also the goodwill and friendship of Hitler. In possession of the Minority Declaration, she continued the strong polonization policy that was designed to eliminate unfriendly minority groups near the frontiers. It was an unrealistic plan, for stronger Polish actions always triggered stronger *Volksdeutsche* resistance. A deadlock developed and the Reich began to display more and more interest in the conditions of the ethnic Germans. With Beck's proposal, Poland voluntarily recognized the minority question as an intergovernmental problem instead of a domestic affair. By that recognition, she opened the door to stronger Reich influence on the *Volksdeutsche.*

During the crisis of August Polish diplomacy seems to have lost sight of reality and actually to have played into the hands of Hitler, making it easier for him to realize his imperialistic aims. The early partial mobilization, the drawing up of the lists of German ethnic suspects, the signing of the Anglo-Polish Mutual Assistance Treaty and counting on its value (though Britain had only two combat-ready divisions and Chamberlain proposed compulsory military service only on April 26), the tragic overestimation of the strength of the Polish army, and the refusal of the Soviet offer of military help, left Poland isolated between enemies on the west and on the east. Government propaganda to raise Polish morale went to such anti-German extremes that it created hysterical fear among the ethnic Germans. The unexpected collapse of the Polish army, the successful raids of the German army special forces, and the capture of the famous Lahousen document made the existence of a German minority fifth column an accepted if not well-proven fact.[219] The gap between Poles and ethnic Germans became irreconcilable. This policy did not save Poland from defeat. It heightened emotions so much that the vengeful behavior of the victorious Germans in 1939 and the similar behavior of Poles close to the end of World War II were predictable.

CHAPTER V

Saxons and Swabians of Romania

Conditions to 1935

Romania was in a different situation concerning her German minorities than the other East Central European countries: she did not have common frontiers with Germany. Thus Romania did not have to fear a German invasion and could select a minority policy that would best serve her own interests. On the other hand, Romania had enemies on her frontiers that demanded the revision of the peace treaties (Trianon and Neuilly), and as a consequence the mutilation of the newly created Greater Romania. Bulgaria, Hungary, and the Soviet Union demanded the return of their territories (Dobrudja, Transylvania, Bánát, Bessarabia) and their revisionist demands marked the course for Romanian foreign policy, which was to enter alliances against these revisionist powers in order to maintain the status quo. The Little Entente treaties concluded in 1921–22, plus French patronage (from February 10, 1926), secured Romania against Hungary as well as Bulgaria. Against the Soviet Union, Romania found relative security in the Polish-Romanian mutual assistance treaty (March 3, 1921).

German-Romanian relations had been correct but cool since World War I, even though the Romanian king, Carol II, was from the Hohenzollern family.[1] However, German-Romanian trade relations grew, and by 1934 Germany ranked as Romania's first trading partner.[2] This development made it natural for the consecutive Romanian governments to favor the German minority, which in the 1918 Karlsburg Declaration[3] voluntarily joined the new Greater Romania. Ethnic German-Romanian understanding was also promoted by common experiences in the past: numerous groups of both nationalities had lived in Transylvania and the Bánát before 1919 and been exposed to the strong magyarization policy of the Hungarian state. Both nationalities, or at least their most idealistic leaders, wanted to secure a successful and fruitful cooperation between the two groups in the new Greater Romania. It was also in Romania's interest to prevent by favoritism toward the German minority any possible agreement between the Germans and the other minority groups

(Hungarians, Russians, Bulgarians) in order to weaken the impact of revisionist demands. On the other hand, the desire on the part of the Romanian patriots to eliminate the minority problem once and for all by, if necessary, forcible assimilation of all minorities contradicted the preferred policy.[4] Thus there were great contradictions between the text of the laws and governmental orders and their practical execution.

Minority Policy

The Karlsburg Declaration, created and accepted by the ethnic German representatives and association leaders on December 1, 1918, foresaw "complete national freedom for all the people" of Romania, securing for them the right to study in their mother tongue and to "have their own representatives in the legislative bodies."[5] It also anticipated religious freedom, freedom of the press, association, assembly, and of thought, including in the latter the right to make propaganda for all human ideas.[6] However, the Romanian parliament in Bucharest, contradicting the desire of the Romanians living in Transylvania, never ratified the Karlsburg decisions. Thus the ethnic Germans had only one protection against forced assimilation and that was the minority treaty that had been incorporated into the Versailles Treaty (December 9, 1919). The treaty obliged Romania as one of the signatories to grant certain rights to all minority groups. While Romania signed the treaty, it was never ratified by the government. Thus a legal gap was created, opening up the possibility of practical discrimination against all minority groups.[7]

The Romanian government was not exempt from the strong nationalist spirit that generally dominated East Central Europe, and naturally used every available means to secure a privileged status for Romanians in every field of life and in the newly acquired territories.[8] But instead of practicing open discrimination and using forced assimilation measures against the minorities, the government employed more refined methods. In some fields it granted more privileges for the minorities than the minority treaty required; in other fields it sought the destruction of the ethnic groups. Especially hard hit were the Jews. Those living in the newly acquired territories of Transylvania, Bánát, and Máramaros—which formerly belonged to Hungary—had enjoyed full economic, cultural, and political freedom since 1867. This freedom "led to the rise of strong assimilationist tendencies."[9] The overwhelming majority of Jews professed to be Hungarians, a smaller number of them Germans. The Romanian government, as a matter of routine procedure, granted citizenship to the populations of the annexed territories, except for the Jews. They had to go through a long naturalization process and as a result thousands of them became legally stateless in Greater Romania. Naturally these Jews felt at home among the ethnic Hungarians and Germans, played an active role in minority life, and supported the minority organizations financially. Only a negligible number, 2.9 percent, professed to have Yiddish as their mother tongue in the 1930 census.[10]

Belonging to a religious minority group did not mean that the Jews escaped the disadvantages of not being Romanians. Those Jews who belonged to the German minority suffered from the measures that the Romanian government implemented against the entire German minority group. The Germans were allowed to organize their own political parties but at the same time they were exposed to heavy attacks directed against the financial and material foundation of ethnic German life.

From First Settlement to Greater Romania

The population of Romania numbered 17,819,500 according to the December 29, 1930, census.[11] The majority of ethnic Germans lived in territories formerly belonging to the Austro-Hungarian and Russian empires, which had been awarded to Romania by the peace treaties following World War I. While in 1912 the old Romanian kingdom (including Dobrudja) had only 29,400 Germans, by 1920 the number of Germans was 715,900, representing 4.5 percent of the population.[12]

The official Romanian statistics referring to *all* German-speaking groups living in Romania as "Germans" creates the impression that Germans were a united, homogeneous ethnic group. In reality the "Germans" were made up of easily distinguishable groups whose land of origin, history, tradition, and geographic location created differences in lifestyle, occupation, religious affiliation, political views, culture, and sometimes even in language since different groups spoke different dialects.

The Saxons settled in the southern part of Transylvania at the invitation of the Hungarian king Géza II (1141–62).[13] In 1224 the Saxons received a "Gold Freedom Charter," which placed them under the direct command of the Hungarian king and secured for them extensive rights of self-government.[14] Thanks to these rights, the Saxons were able to preserve their language, culture, and firm control over their territories by denying the rights of immigration and citizenship in their cities to other ethnic groups, even to Hungarians.[15] In the sixteenth century the majority of Saxons accepted Lutheranism[16] and enjoyed religious freedom under the rule of the Transylvanian princes.[17]

Although a certain amount of jealousy and competition existed between the Saxons and Hungarians throughout the long period of their common history, the first serious (and almost irreparable) split occurred in 1848. The Saxons took the side of the Habsburg dynasty, hoping that for their loyalty they would receive further privileges and even autonomy. But the Habsburgs were never to fulfill these dreams; and the Hungarians never forgot the Saxon "treachery."

After the 1867 compromise the Hungarian government tried to assimilate all the different national minority groups with an official magyarization program, but had only limited success.[18] The economic and cultural significance of the Saxons of Transylvania surpassed "not only the Romanian average, but in some respects also that of the Magyars."[19] This fact forced the

Hungarians to treat the Saxons more leniently. However, this lenient policy did not pay off either. On December 1, 1918, the Saxons of Transylvania joined the Romanians and signed the Karlsburg Declaration, which announced the separation of Transylvania and the Bánát from Hungary and their annexation to the Romanian kingdom.

The Swabians of the Bánát and Bácska came to Hungary after the peace treaty of Passarovitz (1718). They left their homes in Trier, Cologne, Mainz, Hessen, Alsace, the Black Forest, Styria, and Tyrol with imperial help.[20] In 1848 the Swabians, politically divided, fought on the side of the Habsburgs as well as of the Magyars. Upon the defeat of the revolution, the Swabian leaders rushed to restore the goodwill of the emperor and asked him to separate their lands from Hungary by attaching them directly to the crown lands as an autonomous province.[21] Their petition, like that of the Saxons, was refused, exposing them to the magyarization policy of Hungary after 1867.

In 1918 the Swabian leaders also signed the Karlsburg Declaration and wanted to join the Romanian kingdom. Serbian troops, occupying the Bácska and the western parts of the Bánát, forestalled them and gained recognition from the peacemakers who divided the Swabians, attaching some to the Serbian and others to the Romanian kingdom.

The Germans settled in smaller numbers in Bukovina and Moldavia during the thirteenth century. Although there was continuous immigration during the following centuries, their number grew considerably only after the consecutive partitions of Poland awarded this territory to the Habsburg empire.[22] The German settlers can be divided according to their place of origin into four groups: the Swabians, the Zipsers, the Bohemian Germans, and a mixed German group coming from the different provinces of the Habsburg empire.[23] The political awakening of the Bukovinian Germans began in 1848 when they started their long struggle against Habsburg absolutism and for autonomy. However, their number (68,100 out of a total population of 811,700) was too small (8.4 percent) to carry significant weight.[24] Realizing that fact, the Bukovinian *Volksrat* (German Folk Council), acting as a national asembly in Czernowitz, decided at a meeting on October 27, 1918, not to object to the annexation of their land by Romania. Instead they only demanded minority rights in accordance with the principle of self-determination.[25]

In Bessarabia the German settlers appeared only in the nineteenth century at the invitation of the imperial Russian government after the territory was annexed by Russia in the Bucharest Treaty of 1812. Their number reached 79,000 in 1920, representing 3 percent of the population of the province. Under tsarist absolutism these Germans had no opportunity to gain significant political or even economic experience.[26] Thus the annexation of Bessarabia by Romania after World War I did not create too great a shock since they had already experienced minority life.[27]

The Germans in Szatmár and Máramaros counties, located within the former Hungarian kingdom, shared the experience of the German minorities of Hungary up to 1918. Their number in 1920 was close to 48,000.[28] Because of the location of their territories and their relatively unorganized institutional life, they were the forgotten Germans, even for the Reich German organizations. Very strong, almost stubborn German national consciousness developed only among the Transylvanian Saxons, the Bácska and Bánát Swabians, and the German minority in Bessarabia.[29]

The different ethnic German groups (or, more accurately, their pan-German leadership) decided in favor of the Romanian kingdom instead of Hungary because they wanted to end magyarization and to secure far-reaching privileges for themselves. The Romanian authorities, afraid of Hungarian revisionism,[30] "favored the German minorities at the expense of the Hungarians."[31] They granted them almost unlimited freedom of assembly and organization. In the 1920s hundreds of local independent clubs, associations, orchestras, choirs, and amateur theater companies were organized.[32] The aim of these groups was mainly entertainment without politics or history lectures. Up until 1933 many performances were organized in cooperation with the Hungarian minority organizations. The leadership in these activities belonged to the different church groups.[33]

Ethnic German Politics

With the exception of the Transylvanian Saxons, none of the ethnic German groups within Greater Romania had political experience. Thus the Saxons were the first to organize an association that had more than cultural purposes. The *Verband der Deutschen in Grossrumänien* (Association of Germans in Greater Romania) grew out of the desire to implement the Karlsburg resolutions. It was intended to coordinate the activities of all German groups in Romania. These groups were: the *Volksgemeinschaft der Deutschen in Bessarabien* (German People's Community) and the *Volksrat of Bukovina* (People's Council), both representing the local communities: the more ambitious *Deutsch-Schwäbische Volksgemeinschaft* (German-Swabian People's Community) was organized in the Bánát to protect the rights and interests of all Germans of Romania without regard to their religious or party affiliations.

In reality the organization that represented all the ethnic Germans politically in the Romanian parliament was the *Deutsche Partei in Grossrumänien* (German party in Greater Romania), which in the 1928 elections won twelve seats in the parliament and four in the senate. The most prominent of these German political representatives were Senator Hans Otto Roth from Transylvania and Senator Kaspar Muth from the Bánát. The political representatives evaluated the situation of the ethnic Germans realistically, and knowing the Romanians' point-blank refusal of the Karlsburg Declaration, they were willing to compromise to find a *modus vivendi* for the ethnic Germans within Romania.

These old leaders of the German party were opposed by the radical nationalist and idealist dreamers of the younger generation, who wanted to see the Bánát and Transylvania autonomous ethnic German territory. Having no hope of legally taking over the party since they were in a minority, they began to organize their own associations. In Transylvania the *Selbsthilfe Wirtschaftorganisation* (Self-Help Economic Organization) was founded and led by Friedrich Fabritius, who took the idea of self-help—politically and economically—from a pan-German Transylvanian Jewish banker, Dr. Karl Wolff. Fabritius had become acquainted with Hitler in 1922–23 and by 1927 he was an "idealistic, platonic" admirer of the National Socialist Party (NSDAP).[34] In the Bánát Hans Beller and Professors Hans Eck and Anton Valentin organized the *Jungschwäbische Bewegung* (Young Swabian Movement) in 1926. They also claimed to stand above parties and the goal of the new organization was to fill the already existing organizations with "a new and healthier spirit."[35] Both new organizations competed for young membership with the Bund[36] and with the churches which generally controlled the youth through associations such as the *Katolische Jugendbund* and *Katolische Mädchenkränze.*[37]

These movements were especially successful at recruiting new members from among the Bund membership. Thus a power struggle started within the Bund, as well as between the Bund and the two new organizations. The struggle became sharper and sharper under the influence of events in Germany,[38] which became known in the ethnic German communities through the activities of ethnic German students who pursued their studies in Germany and then returned home as admirers of Nazism.[39]

With the help of these students the *Selbsthilfe* and the *Jungschwäbische* movements merged into one organization called *Nazionalsocialistische Selbsthilfebewegung der Deutschen in Rumänien* (NSDR). Its leader was Fabritius, who wanted to use the organization to "revitalize the national self-consciousness of Germans."[40] Though this revitalization (*Erneuerung*) movement was supposed to be founded on the principle of self-help, its name clearly indicated that it accepted Nazism as its ideal, and thus it became more and more a political organization.

Economy, Churches, Schools

The German minority group in Greater Romania had a total of 1,300 consumer companies, 4,696 credit and financial institutions, and 550 different art, timber, real estate, and other companies.[41] The number of German farmers was over 80,000,[42] and they were overwhelmingly smallholders. The ethnic German peasants lived considerably better than their fellow peasants of Romanian or other nationality. The German peasant clung "stubbornly to his language and customs... resisting any attempts made to denationalize him."[43]

The natural leaders of the ethnic German peasants were the village priests; parish and other religious institutions were important. The majority followed the Catholic faith (412,600), especially the Swabians; the Saxons were members of the Evangelical Church (340,082).[44] The majority of Romanians, on the other hand, belonged to the Greek Orthodox or Greek Catholic Church. State-church relations were regulated by three legal documents: the Constitution of March 28, 1923, the General Cult Act of April 5–6, 1928, and the Concordat ratified by the senate on May 25, 1929. These laws, by declaring the Greek Orthodox and Greek Catholic churches the "ruling Romanian churches," practically divided the population into two groups, granting extra privileges to the Romanian churches, while curtailing the equality of others.[45] The government used the law skillfully to attack the other churches, which were the citadels of Germandom. For example, each orthodox bishop was made an ex officio member of the Romanian senate, which favored the more hierarchical Romanian churches (the Evangelical Church had only one bishop in Romania).[46]

The curtailment of rights of the "nonruling" churches was also implemented through financial and economic measures. The law permitted all churches to tax their followers, but reserved the right to fix the amount of the church tax. Since the collection of this tax by the churches themselves was prohibited, the government collected it for them. This gave the state authorities a chance to practice double discrimination against the nonruling churches, first by fixing the amount of the tax and then by collecting the tax in an inefficient way.

Under the rule of Austria-Hungary financial support of the churches had been the duty of the magnates, who enjoyed patronage rights.[47] The Romanian land reform of 1918 divided the large estates in territories formerly belonging to Hungary. "Over 4,000,000 hectares of arable land had been distributed to smallholders of landless peasant laborers,"[48] who were exempt from the obligations of patronage rights. Thus the churches, besides losing their estates, were also deprived of the donations of rich patrons, which was up to that time their most important source of income.[49]

The state gave subsidies to the churches to compensate them for their loss of property and income. The largest subsidies[50] went to the Unitarian Church (28.41 Lei per person) followed closely by the Presbyterian Church (26.68 Lei per person). But these two churches represented only a small minority of the population. Among the churches representing the majority, the Greek Orthodox Church received 21.87 Lei per person, the Evangelical Church 17.56 Lei per person, and the Catholic Church only 12.68 Lei per person. These numbers suggest strong discrimination against Catholics, that is, Swabians and Hungarians, and more moderate discrimination against Protestants, that is, Saxons. Thus most of the ethnic Germans lived in a double minority status through nationality and religion.

The limitation of the churches' economic and financial capacities influenced first of all education and teaching. At first glance the Romanian government's school policy seems to have been much more liberal than, for example, that of the Hungarian government. But on closer examination this liberal impression dissolves. For example, schools belonging to the different Catholic orders were not recognized as minority schools and Julius Maniu's government made an attempt to force them to use Romanian as the only language of instruction.[51]

By refusing to comply with this government plan, the schools exposed themselves to loss of accreditation. Other religious schools, not belonging to a religious order, had the right to use their minority language for instruction, but the students had to take a final high school examination (*Bakkalaureat*) in front of a state-appointed committee, usually in the Romanian language. The results were tragic from the minorities' point of view. An average of only 40 percent of the candidates successfully passed the exam.[52]

Some minority schools were maintained by the Romanian state. In these schools the languages of instruction were Romanian and the minority language in a one-to-one proportion. The problems here were caused by the shortage of licensed German-speaking teachers. Both the Romanian government and the German minority group leaders recognized the importance of secondary schools. In the 1930s in East Central Europe the requirement for a better position in the professions, as well as in the state and local administrations and bureaucracy, was a high school diploma. By usually insisting that the high school final examination be conducted in Romanian, the government created a problem for the minority group. The government claimed that knowledge of Romanian was necessary for minority intellectuals to find positions anywhere in the state administration, that ignorance of the language would restrict them to positions within the German-language territories. The German minority schools produced more high school graduates than the administrations and professions of these territories needed. So—the Romanian argument continued—knowledge of Romanian served the self-interest of the German minority intellectuals.

The minority group's interpretation, naturally, was different. Seeing the effects of similar national minority policy in Hungary (where it had been used since 1867), they wanted to prevent the unavoidable results of such language requirements. Those Germans who spoke Romanian and found jobs in Romanian society were more apt to assimilate than those who remained within the German communities. Furthermore, the loss of intellectuals through assimilation deprived the minority group of young leaders, thus making them less prepared to resist assimilation.

Parents were theoretically free to select a school for their children (as in Poland), but the local authorities always tried to "convince" them not to send their children to German schools.[53] The teacher-student ratio was 1:18 in the high schools and 1:44 in the elementary schools.[54] This proportion in the high schools was better, in the elementary schools the same, as the general East Central European average. Since the German minority enjoyed the special privilege of having its own political party, the leaders never created a real crisis out of the education question. It is also true that while it was hard for a Saxon or Swabian peasant's or worker's son to enter the middle class, he enjoyed more freedom within his own community than was possible in any of the other Successor States. A great majority of the ethnic Germans reciprocated the relative toleration of their ethnic freedom with loyalty to Romania, while retaining strong connections to their country of origin. "Lecturers, scholars and politicians came in great numbers from the Reich to contact the *Volksdeutsche* in Romania; and hundreds of German students, teachers, and others were invited from that country to visit Germany or to study there."[55] The financing of these activities came from the *Volksbund für das Deutschtum im Ausland* (VDA) and the *Deutsche Auslandinstitut* (DAI), and the money was distributed with the help of different Reich German commercial and financial enterprises established in Romania.

Besides the political and cultural associations described, the ethnic Germans had five additional cultural and four social associations, five commercial organizations, and many church-organized culture groups, choirs, and amateur theater groups. Equally if not more important for the preservation of Germandom were the ethnic German press and publications. With two daily newspapers and twenty-two weekly, monthly, or annually published magazines and journals, the ethnic German group of Romania was the best-organized minority.

In the early 1930s, as in the other East Central European countries, the ethnic Germans of Romania fought a bitter struggle for control of the nationwide minority organizations and for predominance among these organizations. It started out as a power struggle between the old leadership and the matured young generation. As time passed, this generational fight became more and more a war of ideologies. The outcome of the struggle was strongly influenced by Romanian domestic political developments, as well as by the reorientation of Romania's traditional foreign policy.

Changing of the Guard

Senator Hans Otto Roth, the leader of the German party, had reservations concerning cooperation with Nazi Germany and the NSDAP. Roth, who was at the same time the president of the Association of German Folk Groups in Europe, visited Hitler with Hans Steinacher on June 15, 1933.[56] Both men came away much impressed with Hitler's personality. But to promote Nazi ideas among the *Volksdeutsche* in Romania, where even Romanian extreme nationalist groups such as the Iron Guard were disliked by the king, would have been unwise on the part of Roth.[57] However, his cautious policy was viewed with disapproval by the younger ethnic Germans. They wanted to see the direction of the Bund, of which Roth was also a leader, in younger, more militant and nationalistic hands.[58] The leader of these impatient nationalists was Friedrich Fabritius. Since his *Erneuerungsbewegung* (revitalization movement) was "burdened by many unqualified elements," even the VDA was hesitant about giving it unconditional support.[59]

In December 1933, during the parliamentary elections, the old conservative political leaders of the *Volksgruppe* had made a pact with the Romanian Liberal party led by Nicolae Titulescu. After the election victory the new government ordered the dissolution on July 11, 1934, of the *Erneuerungsbewegung*, which was already under heavy attack by the "Jewish Press, written in Bucharest."[60] By 1935 Fabritius had enough followers among the younger members of the Bund to take over the presidency of that "old umbrella organization" (*Verband der Deutschen in Rumänien*).[61] Thus Fabritius, although his *Erneuerung* movement was dissolved, gained control of the largest nationwide ethnic German organization. Within it was created the National Socialist Labor Front. It was a "tightly organized party group which played the role of the real 'Movement.'" Fabritius completely reorganized the Bund on the basis of the "leadership principle." The previously loose federation of different ethnic German associations was reorganized as a *Volksgemeinschaft* (people's community) led by a *Volksrat* (people's council) to which the chairman of all associations were subordinated. The *Volksrat* "demanded that the National Socialist ideology should permeate all spheres of life of the ethnic groups."[62]

Within the *Volksgruppe* some of the old conservative leaders such as Kaspar Muth from the Bánát showed some understanding toward the new Bund (*Volksrat*), but the majority were generally cautious, while the leaders of the different church organizations openly condemned the movement for its socialistic ideas, which created the impression that they were against the rich in general.[63] On the other hand, the more radical Germans, who were formerly members of the *Erneuerung* movement, judged Fabritius to be too moderate, and after the voluntary dissolution of the extreme rightist *Jungschwäbische Volkspartei* in the Bánát, they founded on February 10, 1935, the *Deutsche Volkspartei Rumäniens*. With this the split within the old, the middle-aged, and the young leadership of the ethnic Germans became a fact of life. The leader of the conservatives remained Kaspar Muth, who was head of the traditional German party. The "moderate rightists" in the Bund were led by Fritz Fabritius, while the Nazi-oriented members of the *Volkspartei* followed Dr. Alfred Bonfert.

Among the Reich organizations only the VDA tried to prevent this alienation of different groups of ethnic Germans and invited the quarreling leaders to the VDA rally in Königsberg for Whitsun 1935. But by that time the VDA was struggling against the pressures of the Nazi party and the *Hitlerjugend* and therefore could not influence the leaders very much. They did agree to recognize Fabritius as their leader, but a few months later the radicals broke away and under the leadership of Bonfert joined the *Deutsche Volkspartei*.[64] The VDA continued to support the Bund and Fabritius; the *Auswärtiges Amt* (AA) provided him with funds. The SS, the DAI, VoMi (*Volksdeutsche Mittelstelle*), and the AO (*Ausland Organisation der NSDAP*), on the other hand, supported the Bonfert group.[65] This division of Reich German patron organizations seemed to make the division of ethnic Germans in Romania permanent, or at least to ensure it would last as long as Germany did not adopt a uniform policy toward both Romania and the ethnic Germans of Romania.

Conditions after 1935

Fabritius's Principles and Actions

After the "palace revolt" of June 1935, staged by Dr. Alfred Bonfert and Waldemar Gust, Fabritius found his support greatly weakened and still diminishing. The reasons for the revolt and declining support can be found first of all in the changes that occurred in Fabritius's principles. In 1923 he was one of the few ethnic Germans who had become personally acquainted with Hitler and with Nazi theories when Dr. Wolff, a Saxon Jew, who was the director of a Transylvanian bank, sent him to Germany to "look for new ideas, which may save the Saxons from losing their German identity."[66] Fabritius's sponsor and his purpose in this trip suggest that he started out from the old pan-German spiritual cradle. He found Nazi ideology easily acceptable because many of its ideas were similar to or the same as the ideas of pan-Germanism. When he arrived back in Transylvania he wanted to implement some of the ideas he thought would serve his aim: "the revitalization of national self-consciousness and making the Germans aware of the fact that they belong to each other, must help and stand up for each other."[67] This was the old goal of pan-Germanism. What was new in Fabritius's program was the socialistic and anti-Semitic doctrines of Nazism.

The Saxons of Transylvania were rich compared to the Romanians and Hungarians living among them. Even the Swabians of the Bánát were mostly well-to-do farmers. Thus socialist ideas alienated them. In Transylvania many German Jews were respected members of the Saxon business world who carried a great share of the financial burden of keeping the different ethnic German associations and clubs functioning. These Jews regarded themselves as Germans, and what was even more important, the Christian Saxons and Swabians also regarded them as Germans. Therefore the anti-Semitism of the *Erneuerungsbewegung* alienated not only the Jews but also many of the Germans. Finally, the churches without exception condemned the antichurch principles and attitudes of Nazism. Since the ethnic Germans grew up accustomed to regarding their priests as their natural leaders in the diaspora, the Nazi ideology deprived the movement of the very important moral support of the churches.

Fabritius realized the effects of his Nazi ideas and in order to save his movement from complete deterioration he was ready to compromise. He only preached Nazi doctrines. In practice he remained a "platonic admirer" of Nazi ideas and of the party partly for realistic considerations and partly because of the international situation in the mid-1930s.[68] At that time Germany seemed to be isolated internationally, and even within Germany the power struggle did not seem to have been finally decided. At least this was the impression Fabritius probably received when he saw Steinacher successfully defend him in 1935 from the attacks of the SS-supported faction of Bonfert. Furthermore, the Reich seemed to be disinterested in or unable to protect the Germans of Romania. Thus the way of the old conservative leadership promised more success, since the Romanian government was less ready than ever to recognize the old Karlsburg Declaration.[69] Fabritius began a rapprochement with the conservatives by toning down his statements directed against the rich and the churches. This concession secured some conservative support but alienated the young generation in his own *Erneuerung* movement. The palace revolt was the work of devoted Nazis, supported by the SS of Germany. They wanted the *Erneuerung* movement to follow a more radical and nationalistic policy. These people were strongly influenced by the domestic and economic successes of the Hitlerian regime in the mid-1930s. The Berlin Olympic games of 1936 were used by the Reich German Nazis to further impress their ideas on the receptive young ethnic Germans. Thus they returned to Romania as well-educated agitators for Nazism.

The Reich institutions were not satisfied with this first step. They followed it with financial support, which was temporarily cut off in 1934 when the Reich finance ministry suspected mishandling of funds sent to the *Erneuerung* movement through German-controlled banks in Romania.[70] Two years later financial aid was restored to the by that time nazified Bund, and participating in it now were not only the AA and the finance ministry but also the NSDAP. Thanks to this help the former *Erneuerung* movement was transformed into a mass movement as part of the Bund by 1936.[71] However, the split between the Bund and the radicals, who had left the movement on February 10, 1935, and organized themselves into the *Deutsche Volkspartei*, remained.

Now even the Reich German institutions, the VoMi, SS, NSDAP, as well as the VDA, urged the unification of the folk Germans of Romania in a great mass organization, preferably in the German *Volkspartei*. Since all the Reich German organizations dealing with the *Volksdeutsche* were *gleichgeschaltet* by 1937, Fabritius no longer had real support in Germany. Himmler himself lectured him about the duties of folk Germans, saying that all Germans would be incorporated into the future "Great German Reich," while the non-German population would have to "disappear or be subjugated." Fabritius believed that this plan could only be realized by war, which was certainly not in the interest of the German *Volksgruppe* of Romania. Thus he refused to allow the Bund to join the German *Volkspartei* and continued to lead the Bund until 1939 when he was released from his duties and ordered to Berlin.[72]

It was not only Fabritius's movement and the conservatives that stood in the way of the unification of all folk Germans of Romania. The effects of different traditions, experiences, lifestyles, and so forth, continued to separate the Swabians of the Bánát, the Germans of Bukovina, and the Swabians of Szatmár and Máramaros from the politically active Transylvanian Saxons. It was no wonder that the *Deutsche Volkspartei*—that is, the ethnic Nazi organization—looked for help outside the German minority group and in 1936 got in touch with the Iron Guard.[73] These contacts, however, failed to produce any positive results.

The Rightists of Romania and Carol's Policy

After the remilitarization of the Rhineland on March 7, 1936, Romania noted the lukewarm reaction of her allies and the passivity of the League of Nations and decided that it was advisable to reconsider her foreign policy. Because of the economic ties that made her dependent on a friendly Germany, she decided to withdraw her unconditional support from French foreign policy and maneuver herself into a neutral position between Germany and the Western powers. With Nicolae Titulescu's forced resignation (August 29, 1936) and the appointment of Victor Antonescu as foreign minister, Romania took the first steps along this new path.

King Carol was careful to separate this new Romanian foreign policy from his domestic policy. Because of the growing unemployment, young intellectuals swarmed into government offices, where there were not enough positions for all of them. Those who sought professional employment found many of the professions occupied by Jews. The establishment of a quota system at the universities in 1935 was to change this situation, but for the present this situation and the observation of Hitler's political and economic successes in Germany made the Romanian nationalist and fascist movements advocating Nazism very attractive to young intellectuals. Great numbers joined the National Christian party as well as the Iron Guard, thus increasing the political significance of these parties.

King Carol had no intention of allowing the establishment of an extreme rightist dictatorship.[74] Therefore, while seeking German friendship, he was careful to see to it that German influence would not grow strong within these rightist movements. Another way for Germany to influence Romanian domestic policy lay in the use of the *Volksdeutsche* in Romania. To check this influence was a more delicate matter for the king because the activities of the Reich German organizations dealing with the *Auslandsdeutsche* had long been tolerated. Transylvanian Saxons and Bánát Swabians visited and studied in Germany with the knowledge and permission of the Romanian authorities. Furthermore, the German minority was favored over other minorities in Romania because "the relationship of the German *Volksgruppe* to the Romanian state and people was always loyal and correct."[75] Carol had to find a solution for this problem without forcing an open confrontation with Germany.

In July 1936 he asked the German ambassador to see him and told him "most gravely that he would in no circumstances tolerate" German interference in Romanian domestic policy. The interference Carol referred to was German propaganda promoting Nazism in Romania. He retaliated against the propaganda by expelling the representative of the *Völkischer Beobachter*. He

further demanded the discontinuation of German subsidies for the modernization of the right-wing press and the bribery of leaders of the different rightist
parties as an incentive for the unification of all the rightist parties of Romania.
The funds were sent to Romania not by the foreign ministry but by the Nazi
party. The German ambassador denied the charges but in his report to the
foreign ministry he warned the German authorities that the Romanian secret
police had knowledge of the whole operation and the continuation of financial
support would be "an intolerable burden on our relations with this country and
might in particular do us grievous harm with the King. It might also render the
position of the German minorities in Rumania particularly difficult."[76]
Judging from this German reaction, King Carol had successfully stated his
objections without risking Romania's good relationship with Germany.

  The Iron Guard[77] was by no means the only rightist organization in
Romania, but by 1937 it had become perhaps the most powerful. The growth
of its power was promoted by the dissatisfaction of Romanian peasants with
the existing economic conditions, by the great number of unemployed
intellectuals, and by Romanian nationalists' fear of their great communist and
revisionist neighbor, the Soviet Union. An equally important factor in the
growth of the Iron Guard's influence was King Carol's ambition to secure a
free hand in Romanian politics. His first targets were the traditionally strong
and powerful Liberal and National Peasant parties. To curtail them, Carol
tolerated the Iron Guard as a temporary ally.

  Since the Iron Guard stood firmly on a Romanian nationalist base, its
foreign political principles excluded *ab ovo* a rapprochement with the Soviet
Union, with revisionist Hungary, and with Hungary's patron, fascist Italy.
Because of its strong social reform program, anticommunism, and anti-
Semitism, the Iron Guard was much closer in ideology to German Nazism
than to any other rightist movement in Europe. Still the guard did not enjoy
German support. The most plausible explanations for that lack of communication between the Nazi party and the Iron Guard can be found in the
personality of Corneliu Codreanu, the founder and leader of the Iron Guard,
and in the conduct of German foreign policy in the 1930s.

  Codreanu was an idealist whose nationalist and anti-Semitic ideas, fused
with religious beliefs, attracted many students, intellectuals and even lower
clergymen in the 1920s. This group was transformed into a mass movement in
the early 1930s and the participation of Iron Guard members in the Spanish
Civil War provided the organization with "the political-military experience
and exposure to militant fascism that was to place the Legionaries in direct and
mortal combat"[78] with the forces (Communists and Jews) that it believed
endangered the "spiritual and historic values which formed the texture of
Rumania's national existence."[79] Codreanu and his successor Horia Sima did
their best to preserve the independence of the movement from every foreign
influence. Therefore "the Guardists were shunned by Berlin."[80]

  The German foreign ministry preferred to cooperate with King Carol, while
the foreign office of the Nazi party (under Alfred Rosenberg) spent its time,

money, and energy on the project of uniting Octavian Goga's National Christian party with I. C. Cuza's movement. They were successful indeed. The next project, the uniting of the National Christian party (Goga president and Cuza honorary president) with the Iron Guard, failed because of the "insurmountable personal incompatibility of Cuza and Codreanu."[81]

However, the "Nationalists' foreign policy, secretly projected by Germany," did not fit into King Carol's plans. After the 1937 elections, in which the Iron Guard received 16 percent of the votes, Rosenberg made a new attempt to gain the Guard's cooperation. Carol's prosecution of the Guard was fast proceeding, however, and the foreign office was unsuccessful in its attempts to convince the AA to intervene in behalf of Codreanu, so all it could do was to offer political asylum to the most exposed and militant members of the Iron Guard. The AA and even the party leadership "condemned the entire project of the Bureau in Rumania."[82]

After the execution of Codreanu extremist elements transformed the Guard into a terrorist organization, and it kept this character even after Carol's abdication, when General Antonescu formed a coalition government with the remnants of the Legionary movement in 1940. The power struggle between the general (supported by the army) and the extreme Legionaries under the leadership of Horia Sima, who demanded from Antonescu "total power for the Legionnaire movement,"[83] involved the Germans again. The SS, SD, AO, certain members of the German legation close to the SD, and a number of German journalists encouraged the Iron Guard to overthrow Antonescu.[84] The putsch of the Iron Guard of January 21, 1941, was spoiled, however, and the German foreign ministry, alarmed by the possibility of losing Antonescu's goodwill, complied with his demands: Those who had been involved with the Legionary movement were recalled to Germany,[85] and about 400 Legionaries who fled to Germany were interned in the camps at Dachau and Buchenwald. [86] Antonescu remained the unchallenged "Führer of the State."

German Interests in Romania

Since the German army was largely mechanized, fuel was the key to the success of Hitler's plan to invade and occupy Poland. Germany might have tried to secure petroleum supplies from Hungary, the Soviet Union, or Romania. However, development of the Hungarian oil fields was only in the initial stage, Hungary could not yet provide enough oil even for home consumption, and acquisition of oil supplies from the Soviet Union seemed an unrealistic goal because of the antagonism between the two countries. For Germany this left only one choice: to secure Romanian oil deliveries. Hitler could not accomplish this so long as Romania was not entirely in the German camp. Therefore it was in Germany's interest to interfere more and more in Romanian domestic affairs to bring about a pro-German government. Traditionally, German opinions were divided over the best candidate. In order to promote a better understanding with Romania, and understanding that could open the road to even closer trade relations, the AA considered it best not to interfere with Romanian domestic politics.[87] The foreign ministry hoped to reach an understanding with King Carol, but the SS increasingly placed its confidence in the Iron Guard and the National Christian party.

The election results in 1937 seemed to indicate that SS support of the Iron Guard would bring returns; however, King Carol "cleverly finessed the results,"[88] and Germany was forced to pursue its political goals through direct negotiations with Carol. The best the Rosenberg bureau (foreign office of the Nazi party) could do was to offer refuge to Iron Guard members who had fled to Germany.

Even this was not the end of German political setbacks in Romania. The Romanian police discovered documents linking the Iron Guard to the Nazi party, and King Carol "regarded any such contacts with the Iron Guard as directed against himself."[89] To preserve the king's goodwill the German foreign ministry stated not only to the foreign office of the party but also to the AO, VoMi, *Hitlerjugend*, and the propaganda ministry that it was "absolutely necessary that these relations [with the Iron Guard] be broken off at once."[90]

There were two factors working in Germany's favor in gaining King Carol's support. One was the growing feeling of insecurity in Romania concerning Soviet plans. The other was the failure of Romanian-English economic negotiations, which left Romania with a wheat surplus of 400,000–500,000 tons. Germany now had an opportunity to offer Romania a "friendly service" by buying wheat, and in return to secure the quantity of petroleum she needed.[91] By November 1938 Carol was so eager to improve relations with Germany that he visited Hitler in Berchtesgaden. During his conversation with the Führer Carol complained about the activities of certain Germans in Romania and Hitler promised to correct the situation.

Two days later Carol met with Göring. During their conversation Göring warned him that good relations between the two countries depended upon the king's treatment of the German minorities. Carol promised a reexamination of the Romanian minority policy and said that he intended "to give the German minority groups who were good Rumanian citizens the same rights and living opportunities as the Rumanians." Discussing the role of the Iron Guard and possible German support of it, Göring "asked the King to bring any complaints directly to him."[92] At the same time Carol appointed a Romanian committee to conduct economic negotiations.

Ethnic Germans at the Crossroads

Strangely enough, during all this foreign and domestic political maneuvering very few words were said concerning the ethnic Germans in Romania. The Goga government as well as King Carol tried to improve the conditions of the ethnic Germans, hoping thus to secure the Reich's support. Even though the old democratic parties looked upon the Fabritius-led Bund with suspicion, on February 6, 1938, the Goga government recognized the *Volksgemeinschaft der Deutschen in Rumänien* (the nazified Bund under Fabritius) as sole spokesman for the ethnic Germans.[93]

The unification of the ethnic German group on October 27, 1938, was not achieved through a reconciliation between Fabritius and Bonfert. Rather it was achieved through the actions of the Reich organizations, which at that time were all *gleichgeschaltet* (coordinated). Fabritius remained the leader of the Bund and Dr. W. Brückner became his deputy. Bonfert dissolved the *Volks* party and rejoined Fabritius. But since the VDA and Steinacher lost control over *Volksdeutsche* affairs, Fabritius was left without official patronage in the Reich.

Brückner regarded the ethnic Germans as "an outpost of the Reich and therefore always looked for the approval of Berlin."[94] "Berlin" meant VoMi, and VoMi meant SS *Oberführer* Hermann Behrends. The unification of the *Volksgruppe* was hardly completed when Behrends began to use the ethnic group as an instrument to further the foreign political aims of the Reich. On November 23, 1938, he held a meeting in Berlin at which it was decided to instruct the *Volksdeutsche* in Transylvania "to maintain their previous loyal attitude toward Rumania and... not enter into any electoral alliance with the Hungarian minority."[95] While the Reich was pleased by the unification of the ethnic German group, Romania regarded it as an added danger. Ardent nationalist government officials, trying to limit German infiltration into responsible positions, considered instituting anti-German employment acts,[96] but the acts were never passed. King Carol, upon his assumption of dictatorial power, dissolved all political parties and organized a single party of National Rebirth. This meant the dissolution of the German party led by Kaspar Muth, so now even the conservatives joined Fabritius. Carol accepted the representatives of the united ethnic German group into the party and the ethnic Germans were able to send twelve deputies to the Romanian parliament in June 1939.[97]

The maintenance of the unity of the *Volksgruppe* and their complete subordination were the primary goals of the Reich. To prevent a split, at the demand of Himmler, chief of the SS and of the German police, Fabritius was not allowed to return to Romania after his visit to Berlin in early 1939.[98] His successor, Brückner, continued to lead the *Volksgemeinschaft* to the satisfaction of VoMi.

King Carol, after accepting the British-French offer of guarantees, was eager to prove his trustworthiness and loyalty to Germany. Therefore the Romanian authorities, "in particular the military authorities, were leaving the Germans complete freedom." The unification of the *Volksgruppe* was completed when Hans Otto Roth, with the conservatives, joined the new National Socialist Labor Front (NAF), making it the only ethnic German organization in Romania. Brückner was so eager to please VoMi (and through it the SS) that he began to organize the *Volksdeutsche* into "active squads," which were "a sort of defense organization" and "also a sort of SS." He also set up an intelligence network "through the agency of the national group organizations."[99] Such eagerness alarmed even Twardowski, the deputy leader of the cultural department of the AA, who warned Brückner "sharply and severely" that the organization of such militant groups might endanger the whole *Volkstumorganisation.*[100]

As far as the members of the *Volksgruppe* were concerned, the time between 1937 and 1940, that is, from Carol's appointment of Goga as prime minister to his abdication from the throne, was not an easy period. Not only because of the power struggle within their own ranks, but also because of the interference of the Reich, particularly by the Nazi party's foreign political office (*Aussenpolitisches Amt der* NSDAP) led by Rosenberg. Their unsuccessfully disguised support of the Iron Guard not only triggered diplomatic protests, but created economic difficulties for the Reich and retaliation against the *Volksgruppe* as well. Beginning in December 1937, and continuing through the next year, the Romanian government constantly considered introducing anti-German employment measures, which greatly alarmed Ambassador Fabricius.[101]

In 1939 the ethnic Germans were shocked to learn that the Führer planned to resettle the Germans living outside of Germany, instead of protecting them by occupying the German-inhabited territories.[102] In 1940 they learned of the experience of the Germans in Bessarabia and Bukovina. The leaders had been warned in advance and evacuated to Transylvania, but the ethnic group was left to the mercy of the occupying Soviet troops.[103] Negotiations for the resettlement of the entire *Volksgruppe* of Bessarabia and Bukovina resulted in the emigration of some 9,000 ethnic Germans. The new immigrants were looked upon with suspicion by the Reich German authorities and their refugee camps looked like concentration camps. Their bitterness was expressed in the following reproach: "You should have left us at home, here we are treated like slaves."[104]

So as the crisis developed between Hungary and Romania in 1939, the Saxons and Swabians feared that the Reich would abandon them also and, neglecting their wishes, award their territory to Hungary. The Transylvanian Saxons as well as the Swabians of the Bánát petitioned Hitler and the German minister in Romania "to do everything to prevent their reincorporation in Hungary."[105] They awaited the Second Vienna Decision with bated breath. The Decision seemed to be in their favor. Only a small group of them (46,000 according to the Romanian census of 1927), the ethnic Germans of Szatmár, were subjected to Hungarian rule. Those who remained within Romania saw the realization of their dream—the recognition of the Karlsburg Declaration. The government of Antonescu went even further to please the German minority (and through it Hitler) by issuing a decree on November 21, 1940, that recognized the German folk group as a legal entity with public rights. The Nazi party became the guardian of their will, and the ethnic Germans were allowed to display swastika banners beside the Romanian national flag.[106] The whole folk group was reorganized along Nazi lines and Andreas Schmidt, an SS officer and the son-in-law of SS General Berger, was appointed the new

Volksgruppenführer of the ethnic Germans in Romania. With his appointment the independence of the German folk group in Romania ended.

The German-Romanian protocol attached to the Second Vienna Decision
of August 30, 1940, contained a provision for the improvement of the
conditions of the ethnic German group.[107] The protocol accepted the
Karlsburg resolutions as a basis for this improvement. Consequently, on
November 20, 1940, General Antonescu issued an ethnic group law to
implement the protocol.[108] The German ethnic group in Romania was
recognized as a corporate body officially entitled "German Ethnic Group in
Rumania." Articles 2 and 3 of the law exempted the German ethnic group
from the earlier ethnic laws and made it almost a state within a state. The
leadership of the ethnic group was given the right to decide who was a member
of the group by including or excluding names from the national register it would
draw up. Exclusion meant denial of the new privileged status. The previous
construction of democratic institutions among the ethnic Germans was wiped
out and a quasi-military hierarchy was established.

The only spokesman for the ethnic group was to be the NSDAP of the
German Ethnic Group in Romania. With this rule, and with the appointment
by VoMi of Andreas Schmidt to the position of *Volksgruppenführer*, the
nazification of the ethnic Germans was completed and their obedience secured
for Berlin. The arrangement confused the simple ethnic German about where
his loyalty should be directed: toward Romania or, through the ethnic leaders,
toward Germany. Although the Reich and Antonescu had wanted to improve
the conditions of the minority group, the law had an adverse effect among the
Romanians. Recognition of the NSDAP as the only German party
representing the ethnic minority, plus permission to use the swastika flag as its
official emblem, alienated both Romanian nationalists and the Romanian
government, which began to use its arianization policy against the Germans.[109]

The personality of the new *Volksgruppenführer*, Andreas Schmidt, caused
further friction between Romanians and ethnic Germans and also between
VoMi and the German foreign ministry. Schmidt came from a Transylvanian
Saxon peasant family. He had received his education in Klausenburg,[110] and
continued it in Berlin.[111] There he became a fanatical National Socialist
through his contact with the SS. He gained the attention of the SS higher
leadership by marrying the daughter of SS General Berger. He rose rapidly not
because of creativity and ability but because of his blind obedience and
unquestioned loyalty to the SS.[112]

Upon his appointment as *Volksgruppenführer* in Romania Schmidt
reorganized the entire folk group on the basis of SS principles and on the Reich
German model. He even began to organize the folk group into an "SS type"
special unit.[113] This idea had alarmed the German ministry a year earlier, since
it considered it a threat to good Reich-Romanian relations. Schmidt was
attempting to make the isolated *Volksgruppe* in Romania into an experimental
field for a possible future SS state.[114] Schmidt's contacts with Horia Sima,
Codreanu's successor as leader of the Iron Guard, pleased the AO and

Gauleiter Bohle, who visited Bucharest on December 3, 1940.[115] But they embarrassed the German foreign ministry because Antonescu discovered the Iron Guard conspiracy and dismissed the Legion from the government. Beginning in the spring of 1940 Schmidt also secretly promoted SS recruitment among *Volksdeutsche* youngsters who "were smuggled out to the Reich under the guise of participating in sport and physical fitness programs."[116] The foreign ministry learned about these activities of the SS from desperate parents who requested the return of their sons in letters addressed directly to the Führer. The ministry recommended that this practice be discontinued.[117]

In spite of Schmidt's more than doubtful activities the Romanian government fulfilled the obligations it had accepted in the Vienna Decision. With its Decree Law No. 977–1941,[118] which regulated the German ethnic schools, it granted cultural and educational autonomy to the Germans. The law widened the gap between the Romanians and the *Volksgruppe*. The minority organized a "School Office of the German Ethnic Group," which had the duty of informing the Romanian ministry about the opening of schools, but approval of these schools rested with the ministry. The School Office took over the professional training of teachers and became responsible for the primary and secondary schools as well as the teachers' colleges. Article II of the school law stated that "The purpose of education and teaching in the German schools is to train and educate the members of the German Ethnic Group in Rumania *to be good and loyal citizens of the Rumanian state*" (italics added). It did not explain how the German schools could educate good and loyal citizens when, according to the Karlsburg Declaration, these citizens were free "to make propaganda for all human ideas,"[119] in this case, National Socialism, and owed obedience to the Berlin-appointed *Volksgruppenführer*.

The Romanian ministry was supposed to supervise the ethnic German school system through a special department under the leadership of a director, but it was the ethnic group that nominated the director. Ironically, the Romanian state accepted the financial obligation to pay the teachers. Because of the expected shortage of ethnic German teachers, the law allowed the appointment of teachers from Germany. The curriculum and textbooks were to be selected by the ethnic group, and even books published in Germany were permitted if they contained no statements "or pedagogic opinions hostile to the Rumanian state and its laws."[120] The school law thus not only secured the preservation of Germandom in Romania, but also, contrary to the minority treaties, prevented assimilation at any time in the future. And it promoted the predominance of Nazi ideology. In their fight for cultural autonomy the Saxons and Swabians of Romania had hoped to preserve their unique folk culture. The "cultural autonomy" they were granted made them abandon their individuality and forced them into the Nazi mold.[121]

The attempt to remove the ethnic German group from Romanian to Reich German authority did not end with this school law. As early as October 1939 SS General Berger, whose assignment was the organization of recruitment for the Waffen SS, entrusted his son-in-law, Andreas Schmidt, with carrying out the campaign in Romania. Since according to Romanian law Romanian citizens were not permitted to serve in the formations, the first 1,000 volunteers were disguised as agricultural workers. Most of them were leaders of the ethnic group, which was in line with Berger's idea of creating "an SS-trained corps of leaders tied even stronger to the Reich, having fought side by side in the war."[122] When Antonescu became the real ruler of Romania, the recruitment campaign slowed and the ethnic Germans were encouraged to serve in the Romanian army, perhaps to show support for the new pro-German government. In a newspaper article on October 3, 1940, Andreas Schmidt reassured the Germans that they would be well treated in the Romanian army (this promise included amnesty for those who had not reported for duty) and told them that it was now their duty to serve in the Romanian army.[123]

Plans for a new SS recruitment campaign brought a warning from Ambassador Killinger that "the best German blood would be withdrawn from the ethnic German group."[124] Hitler agreed, and in February 1941 Schmidt made an even stronger statement: "On the orders of the Führer every man fit to bear arms will serve in the Rumanian armed forces."[125]

In April 1943 Marshal Antonescu authorized a large-scale SS recruitment campaign on the basis of a newly signed agreement with the Reich government.[126] According to this agreement members of the German ethnic group over the age of seventeen could volunteer to serve in either the German armed forces or the Waffen SS. The volunteers were to retain their Romanian citizenship. But those who were needed in the Romanian army because of either their high military rank or their special training were required first to obtain the approval of the Romanian general staff.

The campaign, which ended July 30, 1943, produced between 41,000 and 73,000 men for the SS.[127] A great number of them, "especially in Transylvania, volunteered quite genuinely."[128] The reason for this enthusiastic enrollment, besides admiration of the German armed forces, may be found in the conditions of the Romanian army—corruption, lack of discipline, and undeniable discrimination against the ethnic Germans in promotions to higher ranks.

On May 19, 1943, Hitler granted German citizenship to all foreigners who served in the German army, the Waffen SS, or the Organisation Todt. This created difficulties in recruitment, since volunteers were regarded from now on by the Romanian authorities "as deserters who had forfeited their Rumanian citizenship." It became necessary to apply pressure on the ethnic group, especially in the Bánát. There, to Berger's satisfaction, several of those who hesitated were punished by the ethnic group itself (their houses were burned to the ground). Not surprisingly, the Swabians of the Bánát deserted the SS in greater numbers than any other ethnic German group. Their desertion was encouraged by the Romanian authorities.[129]

Altogether some 54,000 ethnic Germans, volunteers and nonvolunteers, served in the Waffen SS, and another 15,000 served in the German army and the Organisation Todt.[130] The combined number equaled about 10 percent of the whole ethnic group. Losses (including those serving in the Romanian army) were estimated at about 9,000 dead, which was unusually high. The German folk group paid very dearly for the privileges it obtained in the Second Vienna Decision.

CHAPTER VI

Ethnic Germans of Yugoslavia

Evolution to 1934

More than sixteen national minority groups were living in Yugoslavia in 1919. Some nine different churches further divided the population according to religious affiliation.[1] The Serbs represented the state nationality and, naturally, their dream was to make the new Kingdom of Serbs, Croats, and Slovenes (called Yugoslavia after 1927) a nation-state. Considering the many different national minority groups, this was quite a task.[2]

Yugoslavia did not incorporate the minority treaty into her own laws or constitution; thus the protection of minority rights was not officially secured.[3] Ironically, however, the strongest opposition to the creation of a Serbian nation-state came not from the non-Slavic minority groups but from the 3,221,000 Croats.

Yugoslavia's foreign political aim was to maintain the status quo crated by the peace treaties.[4] This aim decided her position on the international scene: she was a member of the Little Entente and of the French security system. However, Yugoslavian foreign political designs differed from the pro–status quo group of nations in important aspects: Yugoslavia did not have a common frontier with Germany, Germany did not have revisionist claims against Yugoslavia, and revisionist Hungary sought reconciliation with Yugoslavia, toning down its claims.[5]

As the Yugoslavian leaders saw it, their state was threatened first of all by a revisionist Italy and second by a possible Habsburg restoration in Austria. Against both threats the plausible solution was rapprochement with another power that had similar interests and needed Yugoslavia's "services." This power was Germany and the services Yugoslavia was able to render were her agricultural products. (Agriculturally rich France did not need Yugoslavia's produce.) The German-Yugoslavian Economic Treaty of May 1, 1934, served mutual interests. [6] In light of the developing economic relations, as well as because she did not have common frontiers with Germany, the question of the German minority group did not represent any problem for Yugoslavia.

Associations, Religions, Culture

Yugoslavia's ethnic German population numbered 513,472 (3.9 percent of total population).[7] They lived mainly in the Vojvodina, Bánát, and Slavonia, while smaller groups lived in Croatia and Slovenia.[8] They had arrived in these territories in the eighteenth century under the Habsburg settlement programs. Their experiences with the magyarization program of pre-World War I Hungary made them hostile to the state, and upon the collapse of the Austro-Hungarian Empire, they hoped for an autonomous status within the Romanian kingdom. Frustrated in this hope, they tried to adjust to the new situation, which separated them from their brethren in Romania and Hungary. In 1920 they founded the *Schwäbisch-Deutsche Kulturbund* (referred to as the Bund),[9] with the aim of promoting culture, art, and folklore, and of preserving their German ethnicity. The *Kulturbund* had connections with the *Deutsche Auslandinstitut* (DAI) and the *Verein* (later *Volksbund*) *für das Deutschtum im Ausland* (VDA) very early on. These connections, as well as the desire to prevent assimilation, created difficulties for the Bund with the Yugoslavian state authorities. The Bund was dissolved by the state in 1924, though it was permitted to reorganize three years later.[10] By 1929, after two years of organizational work, it had 9,000 members, that is, only 1 percent of the ethnic German population of Yugoslavia.

The German political party organized in 1922 as *Partei der Deutschen im Königreich der Serben, Kroaten, und Slowenen* was short-lived: with the establishment of the royal dictatorship in 1927 it was dissolved, like every other political party. Thus the Bund remained the only organization that tried to unite the ethnic Germans in a nationwide association. The local groups, although their number was great, were either church-oriented or apolitical. It was therefore natural that the struggles of generations and ideas be fought out most bitterly within the ranks of the *Kulturbund*. The developments were similar to those in Romania, but somewhat delayed. The *Erneuerungsbewegung* gained complete control of the Yugoslav Bund only in 1939.

Yugoslavia's religious composition differed greatly from that of Romania. Here, although the religion of the state nationality, that is, of the Serbs, was Greek Orthodox, Serbs were not a majority but only 46.6 percent of the population.[11] Roman Catholics (Croats, Swabians, Hungarians, Slovenes) made up 39.4 percent and were the next most numerous religious group: the Sqiptars, the Slavic population of Albania, Macedonia, Montenegro, Bosnia, and Hercegovina, followed the Moslem faith and represented the third largest religious group with 11.1 percent.[12]

The majority of the ethnic Germans belonged to the Roman Catholic Church (76.7 percent); 20.2 percent of them were Protestants, who made up only 1.81 percent of the entire population. The religious composition suggested a cautious, tolerant policy to the Serbs, at least toward the Roman Catholics. The Greek Orthodox Church, however, was able to enjoy predominance by the simple fact that Belgrade and its vicinity—and thus the majority of government officials—were almost completely Greek Orthodox. Even officials who tried to be impartial felt the pressure of the Greek Orthodox ring.[13] In theory, state aid for the churches was provided according to the number of parishioners. In practice, for example in the year 1927–28, a Greek Orthodox priest with 1,000 church members received RM 900, while a Catholic priest with the same number of church members received only RM 544.[14]

As in Romania, the church groups were the citadel of Germandom. The Catholic parishes were usually led by priests who had been appointed before and during World War I, that is, under the Hungarian regime. Very few of them were willing to cooperate with German folkish movements. Furthermore, the ethnic German Catholics generally believed that the *Schwäbisch-Deutsche Kulturbund* was under Protestant control and spiritual influence. Since the Bund leadership—accidentally or not—did not include any prominent Catholics, although the majority of ethnic Germans were Catholic, there was no hope for reconciliation. So the religious division created a cultural division among the ethnic Germans. This division made the Bund ineffective, since the overwhelmingly peasant ethnic population was not willing to donate readily to cultural programs, bought only the cheapest books (and very few of them), and generally did not recognize the importance of culture.[15] The intellectuals who led the Bund were almost forced to turn for financial help outside the *Volksgruppe.*

Article 16 of the 1921 Yugoslav constitution established the ground rules for private schools in the country.[16] A ministerial decree of April 20, 1921, authorized private schools, but only if they were organized and run by individuals. Religious orders or other associations were not permitted to organize them. The existing German parochial schools were either closed or taken over by the state. Soon other private German schools met the same fate. The affected school properties were confiscated without compensation.

This unfavorable situation for minority education continued in Yugoslavia throughout the 1920s. In 1928 German representatives in the parliament (*Skupstina*) introduced a bill that would have ameliorated conditions, but it failed to pass. According to the 1929 school law separate German schools were not allowed, only German classes in folk schools that had at least thirty German-speaking pupils.[17] Even there the German language could be used only in the first four grades, along with instruction in a state language (Serb, Croation, or Slovenian). Because of the shortage of German teachers many "German" classes were taught by Yugoslavs who were not fluent in the language. In March 1929 there were 154 dual-language schools with 570 German classes, 38 kindergartens with 49 German classes of 3,658 German children.

The 1930s brought first slight modification, then greater improvement. The school law of 1930 allowed parents to choose the school, that is, class, for their children based on the language spoken at home. In German classes instruction in a state language would begin only in the third year. In the summer of 1933

Yugoslavia and Romania reached an agreement regarding their respective minorities in the Bánát that permitted private minority schools.[18] The German minority in Yugoslavia was understandably disappointed at this, having tried for years to get the same privilege for themselves. They hoped at least that the precedent thus set would favor them, and indeed it seems to have done so. On September 26, 1933, the Yugoslav ministry of education authorized the "School Foundation of the Germans in the Yugoslavian Kingdom," headquartered at Novi Sad.[19] At last it was possible to establish private German schools in certain areas. They were bound by numerous restrictions, such as the requirement that the state language be taught in all grades. In Slovenia German private education was still forbidden altogether.

Higher education in the German language was practically nonexistent in Yugoslavia. The *Realgymnasium* in Novi Vrbas (Neu Verbas) lost its upper classes in 1925.[20] The German teachers' academy established in Vel. Beckerek (Gross-Betschkerek) was transferred to Vrbas in 1933, and this left the Bánát with no German middle or higher school.[21]

Thus minority German parents in Yugoslavia who wanted their children to have an opportunity for a successful career had to send them to the state schools from the start to learn the state language well.

Agriculture, Trade, Commerce

In the lands added to Serbia after World War I there were many unsolved social and economic problems: illiteracy, overpopulation, land hunger, Slavic "national" rivalries. The problems were so serious that they demanded long-range planning and careful selection of priorities. In the short term, it was easier for the government to deal with two of the problems, land hunger and national rivalries, by focusing the attention of all the Slavs on a common enemy: the "foreign," that is, non-Slavic, landowner.

Preparations for land reform began in 1919. The principle on which the reform was based was "nationalization of the people's land."[22] In practice, the reform awarded land to those citizens who had no land at all or whose holdings were too small to support a family. The amount of land awarded was limited to what a given family could cultivate themselves without hiring additional help. This amount varied from province to province, from 100 to 500 yokes.[23]

This agricultural reform was embodied in Article 43 of the Vidovdan constitution of June 28, 1921, and was implemented during the next ten years.[24] Eventually, about one-fourth of the total agricultural land was redistributed. Fully confiscated were entailed estates and land that had been donated to individuals, especially by members of the Habsburg family. All Habsburg properties were, of course, included. These provisions (Paragraphs 10 and 11) revealed that the land reform served not only social and economic purposes, but also political, nationalistic ones.[25]

In the Vojvodina, Yugoslavia wanted to win over the population from Hungarian influence. Thus land reform there was directed primarily against

Hungarians, and the Germans were relatively well treated.[26] However, the goal was to populate the Vojvodina with Slavs, so the government in Belgrade did look with interest at the well-to-do Danube Swabian peasants in the Bánát and Vojvodina. Many landless Montenegrins and southern Slavs moved northward into ethnic German areas where the land was better.[27] Serb neighbors also began to look greedily at German lands.

The average size of a peasant holding between the wars was somewhat larger among the ethnic Germans than the average for all of Yugoslavia. The largest number of German holdings (36.6 percent) was in the 2.8-to-5.7-hectare category,[28] while the largest number for the country overall (34 percent) fell into the 2-to-5-hectare class.[29] Twenty-seven percent of the total agricultural area of Yugoslavia was in 5-to-10-hectare plots, while 39.7 percent of the German area was in 11.5-to-28.7-hectare tracts.[30] Thus the ethnic Germans were vulnerable to land reform, even though a minority of them had enough land to support a family.[31] Altogether some 40,000 hectares were lost by the Germans in Vojvodina and few, if any, Germans received land from the confiscated holdings, although 40 percent of them were landless workers. Various laws made the buying of real estate by non-Slavs impossible in 80 percent of the communities in Yugoslavia,[32] and the 1936 land law made even inheritance of land impossible for non-Slavs.[33]

The majority of ethnic Germans in Yugoslavia, like the great majority of their fellow countrymen, were employed in agriculture. However, certain areas had a thriving trade, commerce, and industry, and the ethnic Germans shared in these activities. Slovenia, which had a well-developed industrial life under Austria-Hungary, fared somewhat worse under Yugoslavia. Still, the Germans there were strong in industry, trade, crafts, and business.[34] The ethnic German share of Slovenian business (excluding Jews) was 3.6 percent, although they were only 2.2 percent of the population of that area.[35]

In Vojvodina some 40 percent of town dwellers and almost 30 percent of those who lived in the country worked at handicrafts. About 1930 there were 3,653 craft shops in Vojvodina, most (2,386) with no hired help and only 28 with more than five workers. There were only 15,000 industrial workers in Vojvodina,[36] about 8.6 percent of the German population,[37] while in Yugoslavia as a whole 14 percent of adult male workers were engaged in manufacturing.[38] The German population of Vojvodina, some 20 to 22 percent, controlled a disproportionate share of industry, 40 to 45 percent. Key industries were from 60 to 80 percent controlled by Germans.[39]

Ethnic German organizations in Yugoslavia developed widely in a relatively short time.[40] By 1932 there were 318 associations under five central organizations with a total of 20,228 members, mostly peasant proprietors (13,406).[41] Almost half of these groups (154) were local credit associations, which seemed to thrive despite the worldwide economic depression. The credit associations held 3.13 million Dinar investment capital in 1932, with 4.3 million Dinar reserve, 88.5 million Dinar savings, and 108 million Dinar available for loans. The most important central organization of the Germans was *Agraria*, founded in Novi Sad in 1922. It had divisions for the marketing of the different types of agricultural products (grain, hemp, etc.), and after 1927 a credit section.[42] *Selektor* was the association for livestock production, and it also had an insurance department. In Bánát *Agraria* had a virtual monopoly over grain supplies for the military.[43] Another agricultural-trade association in Bánát was *Avis*. Bánát wine growers had their own wine-marketing association.[44]

The number of German doctors, pharmacists, and other professionals increased between the wars, while the number of state employees remained low and was a cause for complaint.[45] Generally, the ethnic Germans of Yugoslavia maintained the level of agricultural and business activity that they had reached by World War I.[46]

Schwäbisch-Deutsche Kulturbund

Since with the dissolution of the political parties in 1927 the Bund remained the only nationwide organization of the ethnic Germans, it became very important to them, as well as to the Reich institutions that were trying to halt assimilation. In the 1920s and early 1930s the Bund was well taken care of by the VDA. Its representatives attended VDA meetings in Germany[47] and invited guest lecturers from German universities to Bund meetings in Yugoslavia. The Bund's annual Festival of the Folk Community was honored by the attendance of the German envoy in Belgrade, von Heeren,[48] who was celebrated as the guest of honor. Besides these events designed to raise its reputation and prestige, the Bund received material aid in the form of complete libraries. The average library contained about 3,200 books, only very few of which were VDA, that is *Volksdeutsche*, propaganda publications.[49]

Still the Bund only very slowly became a nationwide organization. One obstacle to its growth was the religious prejudice of the great majority of Catholic Swabians toward the Protestant leadership of the Bund. The second, more important obstacle was the dissolution of the Bund by the Yugoslavian authorities in 1924.[50] The membership, which in 1923 had reached 55,000, dispersed, and the 126 local organizations (*Ortsgruppen*) were dissolved. Although the Yugoslavians reissued the permit for the Bund in 1927, the organization had to start from the beginning again. The membership grew very slowly not only because of the cautiousness of the Swabians (or their fear of possible retaliation by the Yugoslavian authorities) but also because of the resistance of local police authorities. In March 1930 the Bund submitted a fifty-page memorandum to the interior ministry complaining about the refusal of local police authorities to issue it new operating permits.[51]

Even the existing, reorganized *Ortsgruppen* were passive, and the great majority of them submitted a very short and laconic report about their yearly activities: "We held our annual meeting."[52]

Only with the Yugoslavian-German trade agreement and political rapprochement in 1934 did the *Volksbund* begin to grow into a larger organization. As soon as it grew larger, new problems arose: the familiar differences of opinion between the young and old, and disagreement concerning the relationship with the Reich, and naturally with Nazism.

Representatives of the younger generation such as Dr. Nikolaus Hasslinger and Dr. Jakob Awender accused Dr. Stefan Kraft, chairman of the Bund, of financial irregularities involving Bund funds. The court of arbitration cleared Kraft of the charges. Following a meeting of the Bund leadership, both Hasslinger (1934) and Awender (1935) were excluded from membership for creating distrust and undermining the unity of the Bund.[53] This confrontation was the first clash between the younger and older leaders, and the membership divided along the same lines. Awender could appeal for the support of the younger generation with the help of Gustav Halwax, who gave him publicity in his paper, the *Volksruf.*[54] This really marked the beginning of the *Erneuerung* movement as a group separated from the Bund. The local organization of the Bund in Novi Sad became the headquarters of those young members who, under "the effects of dynamic Nazi ideas," wanted the reorganization of the Bund. In their enthusiasm for the German Reich the youth group members of the Novi Sad Bund began to wear brown uniforms and armbands and carry flags decorated with signs closely resembling the swastika. They marched on the streets of the city in closed formations singing German military songs.[55] This behavior was too much even for the Yugoslav authorities, who ordered the dissolution of the Novi Sad *Ortsgruppe*.

For the time being the old leadership seemed to regain control. In December 1936 at the annual meeting of the *Kulturbund* Johann Keks was elected chairman. The new leadership decided to reorganize the Bund to make it a community for all the ethnic Germans of Yugoslavia. They sent telegrams expressing loyalty to Prince Paul and Prime Minister Milan Stojadinović. The leaders of the youthful Bund membership were left with no other choice but to advocate a renewal movement, while Awender's small group looked for official support in the Reich—with little or no success. The unity and predominance of the Bund were saved and the Bund continued to represent the ethnic Germans of Yugoslavia without serious competition.

Developments after 1934

As the German economy began to recover from the consequences of the Great Depression, Germany tried to reestablish contact with the Successor States, which were the natural markets for her industry. Hungary, as another revisionist state, was pursuing a friendly policy and did not represent a problem.[57] The next desirable market because of its oil was Romania. Here the situation looked grim. The Germans tried for years to gain "a foothold in Rumania." Because of the anti-German policy of Titulescu, *Auswärtiges Amt* (AA) considered the situation "hopeless." During the spring of 1934 it decided to make an attempt "in Yugoslavia to strengthen a permanent interest in the German market."[58] This new direction was motivated also by the Italian and French negotiations, which were aimed at rebuilding the economy of the Danube Basin with the extension of the Rome Protocols.[59] In the face of this competition, the Germans had to move fast, and they did. On May 1, 1934, they signed a commercial treaty with Yugoslavia that promised "far-reaching possibilities" and the reorganization of Yugoslavia's agriculture according to German needs.[60]

This economic rapprochement, coupled with Yugoslavia's fear of a Habsburg restoration in Austria, brought Yugoslavian foreign policy closer to Germany's aims. Gestures such as Yugoslavia's giving asylum to the Austrian Nazis after the murder of Dollfuss,[61] the expression of sympathy by Germany upon the assassination of King Alexander, and the Yugoslavian popular reaction to Göring's personal attendance at the king's funeral[62] promoted the rapprochement. Germany gave additional proof of goodwill by withdrawing her open support of the anti-Yugoslav Croation emigrés and banning the publication of their three daily papers in Germany.[63]

With the appointment of Milan Stojadinović as prime minister, Yugoslavia's foreign policy was entrusted to a man who wanted to break away "from the overpowering influence of France's financial policy" and who was a "convinced supporter of economic cooperation between Yugoslavia and Germany."[64] The Reich naturally welcomed these changes and did its best to extend the cooperation to foreign policy. As a result, the requests and complaints of the *Volksdeutsche* in Yugoslavia fell on deaf ears in the German foreign ministry.

The Reich-Yugoslavian rapprochement, the developments within the Bund, and the changes that occurred within the Reich concerning the authority of VDA and VoMi (*Volksdeutsche Mittelstelle*) forced the Bund leadership to rethink its policy. Taking into consideration the realistic conditions of the Bund—that is, that its membership still represented only a minority of the Germans and that it was forced to rely on Reich financial support[65]—the leadership had to decide on a policy that would best serve the whole ethnic German group of Yugoslavia.

The Bund was allowed to function with the understanding that it woud deal only with cultural matters and not undermine the loyalty of the ethnic Germans toward the Yugoslav state. On this basis it was permitted to receive funds from Germany. The conservative leadership rigorously observed these conditions and, at the annual meeting, always solemnly expressed the loyalty of the Bund to the Yugoslavian kingdom. However, this policy did not produce any visible results. Although the Yugoslav government did not place difficulties in the way of Bund operations, on the local level the nationalistic Yugoslavian officials created difficulties for the *Ortsgruppen*. The Bund's aim of furthering ethnic German education through the establishment of private schools also failed because of the resistance of the Yugoslav government. Thus in the eyes of the younger generation the conservative policy did not bring the expected benefits. Although the unity of the Bund was preserved for the time being, the continuation of the traditional policy would lead to more dissatisfaction and possibly the complete alienation of the younger generation. The continuation of the old policy also seemed unrealistic because of developments in the Reich. The VDA lost authority and VoMi, under the control of Behrends, desired to see the evolution of the ethnic group along Nazi ideological lines. Failure to comply with the wishes of VoMi would have meant the forfeit of financial aid.

The rapprochement between Germany and Yugoslavia that began in 1934 developed into a closer friendship under the premiership of Stojadinović in the second half of the 1930s. However, the friendship between the two govern- ments did not bring any change in the relationship of Yugoslavia with the ethnic Germans. During the five years of Stojadinović's leadership the Yugoslav government granted neither schools nor any other significant concessions to the German minority.[66] The Yugoslavian authorities were very sensitive to any signs of nazification in the *Volksgruppe* and responded immediately with stringent measures, not hesitating even to dissolve local groups.

A close relationship with Yugoslavia was so important to Hitler because of his long-range plans against Austria and Czechoslovakia that he himself tried to bring about an understanding between Italy and Yugoslavia and between Hungary and Yugoslavia.[67] He certainly would not have tolerated a Bund policy that disturbed this relationship. On the other hand, VoMi and other Nazi party organs would have welcomed the radicalization of the ethnic German group. Still, Dr. Awender could not secure any financial support for his *Erneuerung* group from these sources, and the German finance ministry continued to send aid to the traditional ethnic German economic organizations and the Bund. Undoubtedly, the nazification of the Bund would have invited the disapproval of the older generation, on whose financial support the Bund was also dependent. The radicalization of the Bund would not have served the interest of the ethnic Germans.

Reich German party organs tried to use the Yugoslavian *Zbor*, a nationalist opposition group, as they did the Romanian Iron Guard—to promote their own foreign policy. The goal of this policy was to force Stojadinović's government to commit Yugoslavia unconditionally to the side of Germany. To promote their policy they illegally sent secret fund to the *Zbor*. Branimir Altgayer and an impatient group of ethnic Germans separated from the *Erneuerung* movement and joined the *Zbor*.[68] But the German foreign ministry demanded an end to money transfers to the *Zbor*, fearing that this activity would endanger German foreign policy. Under pressure from the embassy Altgayer terminated his connection with the *Zbor*. This alternative also seemed to be useless for the Bund.

Step by Step to the Right

The German minority group could not make a clear-cut decision on policy. The chairmanship of the Bund was in the hands of Johann Keks, a retired army captain. The honorary president was Senator Grassl. "The guiding spirit [was] the very energetic and active Dr. Kraft."[69] Thus the leadership of the Bund remained with the old conservatives and they continued the policy that had so far brought no important successes for the ethnic German group. Nor did it promise any in the future.

This was the reason that the *Erneuerung* movement, which was "not a political party in the practical sense but at best a thinking group,"[70] separated itself from the old leadership. The movement began to organize its own "cultural and economic organizations, particularly in Slavonia."[71] Naturally these activities were strongly opposed by the Bund. Within the ranks of the *Erneuerung* movement there soon developed a moderate and a radical group. The radicals, under the leadership of Dr. Awender, cooperated with the Yugoslavian group that represented the sharpest opposition to Stojadinović. The moderate group, led by Branimir Altgayer, realizing their weakness, attempted to rejoin the Bund, at least "in a working partnership."

The popularity of the radical *Erneuerung* movement in Slovenia was understandable because of the Slovene attitude toward the ethnic Germans. By 1937 they had eliminated all the German schools, and in the German classes of the state schools the instructors were mostly anti-German Slovenians. The Slovenes discriminated even against Germans who were reserve officers of the Yugoslavian army, especially in the border districts where they did not permit the ethnic Germans to buy real estate within fifty kilometers of the border.

The unsigned memorandum prepared for the upcoming visit of Stojadinović recommended that the foreign ministry use the coming negotiations to press for better conditions for the ethnic group. However, neither the officials of the German foreign ministry nor Hitler mentioned the conditions of the German minority to Stojadinović. Hitler, who in the early months of 1938 was preparing to annex Austria, was happy to hear Stojadinović's statement that "Yugoslavia welcomed a friendly Germany as her neighbor." In light of this statement, it is understandable that Hitler was not prepared to risk German-Yugoslavian friendship for the sake of betterment of ethnic German life.[72]

Stojadinović was determined to secure the support of the ethnic Germans for his own government since his popularity was slowly deteriorating in Yugoslavia. His pro-German policy was seriously questioned by those who remained faithful to the idea of French cooperation and to the idea of the Little Entente, and by those who opposed a pro-Reich policy because of Germany's Nazi system. The Croatian separatist movement joined forces with these leftist groups and thus represented an unusually strong opposition to Stojadinović.[73] Serbian intellectuals, "strongly pan-Slavic in their thinking," and nationalist Serbian groups spread the news that a German invasion was imminent, and so created a strong anti-German mood in the whole population. Among the Croatians similar anti-German sentiments were created by students returning from France after finishing their studies there.[74]

These conditions in Yugoslavia suggested to Stojadinović that he should not seek *Volksdeutsche* support too openly, and to the Reich that it should avoid overt contact with the VD. Thus the ethnic Germans of Yugoslavia were left on their own by both the Reich and the Yugoslav government. For reasons unknown Keks decided to decentralize the Bund on April 5, 1938, giving more authority to the *Ortsgruppen* leaders.[75] This decentralization weakened the old conservative leadership and gave more room to the younger generation, especially to the moderate group within the *Erneuerung* movment.

The negotiations for the restoration of unity between Johann Keks and Senator Grassl on one side and Dr. Awender on the other were successfully concluded on November 21, 1938.[76] In the meantime, the *Erneuerung* group produced a "folk political program"[77] that was to serve as a goal for all ethnic Germans. It went further in its demands than any previous program. It proposed that efforts be made for the recognition of the right of the people to self-determination and for legal recognition of the rights of the *Volksgruppe*; it demanded for the *Volksgruppe* recognition as a corporation with public rights; and finally, it demanded that the Bund and its leadership be recognized as the only legal representative of all the ethnic Germans, and as such be given the right to propagandize within the *Volksgruppe* the political view of the German people. This last demand, although carefully worded, undoubtedly referred to Nazism. These demands seemed to be too extreme even for VoMi, which decided not to interfere actively in the power struggle that now took place in the ranks of the Bund.[78]

Supporters and members of the *Erneuerung* movement increased steadily through 1938 even within the Bund, and by April 1939 Johann Keks realized that he was unable to perform his duties over the strong opposition. When he voluntarily resigned as chairman of the Bund, referring to health reasons, the threatened struggle between the old guard and the *Erneuerung* followers over the vacated Bund chairmanship convinced VoMi to interfere. It organized two meetings with the leaders of the *Volksdeutsche*, including not only the Bund leaders, but also the representatives of the moderate *Erneuerer*. At the suggestion of VoMi, a member of the *Erneuerer* group, Dr. Sepp Jankó, was proposed as next chairman of the Bund. Since Keks himself endorsed him as his successor, the Bund membership dutifully elected Jankó to the chairmanship[79] after a short election campaign in August 1939. His first order surprised everyone: he dissolved the *Erneuerung* movement and urged its members to compromise with their former opponents in order to restore the unity of the *Volksgruppe*. This restoration attempt was not completely successful since Altgayer, who was the leader of the *Erneuerer* in Croatia, did not want to lose his good connections with Stojadinović's party. So Altgayer's group remained independent in Croatia and, with the approval of VoMi, Altgayer sought to harmonize his actions with the Yugoslav government, with the different Reich organizations, and with the other ethnic German organizations.[80]

The Yugoslavian government appreciated the loyal attitude of the Bund and awarded the *volksdeutsche* leaders with the third class of the Order of the Yugoslavian Crown on September 3, 1940.[81] The decorated VD leaders were Dr. Sepp Jankó, Dr. Jakob Awender, Franz Hamm, Johann Wüscht, and

Jakob Lichtenberger. The decoration of these men proved how far Stojadinović's government had shifted to the right. While three of the honorees
could be described as pan-Germanists, Jankó and Awender clearly sympathized with Nazism. As early as March 1940 Jankó voluntarily changed the
title of his position from *chairman* to the word used in Nazi terminology,
Volksgruppenführer. At the same time he abandoned the traditional closing
for letters ("Heil Gruss") and started to use "Heil Hitler."[82]

The successes of the Nazi German Reich in domestic and foreign policy
commanded the admiration of all Germans. More and more of them accepted
without criticism the Nazi slogan: "To be a German means to be a National
Socialist."[83] After accepting the *Führerprinzip*, the leaders of the Bund
deserted democratic principles and began to transform the Bund into an
authoritarian organization. How great was their admiration for these new
principles is evidenced by the fact that Bund members accepted without
question the *Selbstbesteuerung* (self-taxation) that provided a financial basis
for future activities of the *Volksbund*. These activities, however, were not
planned and decided by the *Volksdeutsche*, nor even by the *Volksgruppenführung*. International events took a sharp turn in 1941 and the *Volksdeutsche*
found themselves in the middle of the German-Yugoslavian war.

Period of Reich-Yugoslav Cooperation

German successes during 1938, such as the annexation of Austria and the
Munich agreement, followed by the First Vienna Decision, further damaged
Stojadinović's popularity among the Yugoslav nationalists. To secure a
stronger mandate he made a pact with the ethnic German *Volksgruppenführung*. In return for their support of his party in the next elections, he
promised them more representatives and a general betterment of conditions.[84]
His pro-German foreign policy and his agreement with the ethnic Germans
antagonized Prince Paul, who was convinced that the government should
cooperate first of all with the Croats. Stojadinović, in order to prevent a
possible Serb-Croat coalition against his party, dissolved the parliament
ahead of schedule and announced elections for December 1938. Because of
the Yugoslavian electoral system, his party received 82 percent of the seats,
although its majority was only 1,643,783 votes out of 3,008,307.[85] Stojadinović realized that his remaining in power was now dependent on a successful
foreign policy and partly on his ability to prove that he had not given any real
concessions to the *Volksdeutsche*. He acceded to German wishes in leaving
the League of Nations and signing the Tripartite Pact.[86] He also conducted
negotiations with Ciano and expressed his willingness to participate in
Mussolini's plans for war against Greece, if Yugoslavia were to receive
Salonika.[87]

Stojadinović tried to force his compatriots to accept his Axis policy. In
February 1939 his government ordered a great arms shipment for the
Yugoslavian army from Germany. Unquestionably the army, once supplied

with German munitions, would become dependent on Germany. The Yugoslavian general staff was aware of this fact, and Stojadinović could not put through this arms order without first removing two generals.[88] Germany, of course, welcomed the armament order for foreign political reasons.

With this action, Stojadinović had "gone too far in both his internal and his foreign policy."[89] Prince Paul released him from office on February 4, 1939. The new government continued arms negotiations with Germany, and although the French armament industry also made an offer to Yugoslavia,[90] the government accepted a RM 200 million credit to buy armament from Germany.[91]

As Yugoslavia continued her pro-German line, Prince Paul reached an agreement with the Croats on August 25, 1939, which gave them far-reaching autonomy but left foreign affairs, defense, and communications under the control of the Yugoslav government. In the meantime, the anti-German feelings of the local population and authorities were aggravated by the agitation of Halwax and his followers in the *Erneuerung* movement. Heeren urged VoMi to stop Halwax's activities since "any unrest is at present politically undesirable."[92]

Opposition to the pro-German foreign policy continued to grow under the impact of the Polish-German war. By the spring of 1940, not only had the *Volksdeutsche* not received the promised betterment in conditions (they were actually worse off), but even Reich Germans were the victims of "ruthless proceedings." The German foreign ministry considered these proceedings a violation of Yugoslavia's neutrality,[93] which had been announced by the new government in 1939 on the eve of the Polish war.

The British and French declarations of war on Germany made it important to Germany to preserve the peace in eastern Europe and the Balkans. To secure Yugoslavia's neutral status, or if possible its active German friendship, Hitler personally held conversations with Foreign Minister Aleksander Cincar-Marković and with Minister Dragisa Cvetković during the winter of 1940–41. During these talks Hitler emphasized that a strong Yugoslavia in the Balkans was in Germany's interest. He tried to convince Yugoslavia that Germany's friendship would benefit her territorial aspirations in Greece (Salonika).[94] Furthermore, Hitler tried to frighten Yugoslavia into a German alliance by pointing to the dangers represented by Soviet ambitions and by the Communist penetration of the Balkans. Germany was taking "vigorous action" against these dangers, he said, adding "that if Germany should collapse this time, the situation would be different from what it was in 1918 when no great power at hand was oriented toward Communism-Bolshevism. This time Russia and Bolshevism would inherit the whole of Europe."[95]

The Yugoslav representatives on both occasions assured Hitler of Yugoslavia's friendly intentions, but did not reply in substance to his questions. From that time on Germany increased the pressure on Yugoslavia to move away from her neutral position. After March 1, 1941, when Bulgaria adhered to the Tripartite Pact and German troops crossed the Danube, the Yugoslav government considered it best not to resist Germany any longer. On March 25, 1941, Cvetković and Cincar-Marković signed the Tripartite Pact in Vienna. While they were out of the country, a military putsch occurred in Belgrade on March 27. The same day Hitler announced to his military staff his determination to smash Yugoslavia without waiting for any possible loyalty declaration.[96] The military preparations took only a few days and the German army, in cooperation with Hungarian and Bulgarian troops, crossed the Yugoslavian borders on April 6, 1941.

The ethnic Germans did not benefit from the election pact made by their leaders with Stojadinović. They had hoped to gain the main points in their political program of 1938, especially legal recognition as a corporate group, but they were disappointed. They were led to expect greater representation in the parliament; Dr. Grassl demanded five seats but got none.[97] In local government the situation was just as bad. In the Danube district, for example, whose population was almost one-fourth German, there were still only 3 or 4 German officials out of 760 in early 1940.

Nor were economic benefits forthcoming. The first overt indication of the legal inferiority of the ethnic group had come with the September 7, 1939, frontier zone law,[98] which strictly regulated the buying and selling (even inheritance) of property by non-Slavs in the border areas. This law continued in effect. There was also discrimination in the tests for masters and apprentices in the crafts. When applying for a charter as a corporation, a firm was required to report the number of *fremdstämmigen* (of foreign extraction) employees. As regards land reform, the governor of Slovenia reported on February 14, 1940, that between 1926 and 1938 some 1,265 hectares had been taken from Germans and Jews and given to Yugoslavs, while only 177 hectares had passed from "national" to "foreign" possession.[99] In June 1940 there was a strong economic boycott of ethnic Germans in Windisch-Graz.[100]

Discrimination against the minorities extended to the military. By order of the general staff Germans and Hungarians were removed from officers' schools. In the middle of 1940 ethnic German reserve officers were suddenly downgraded without explanation.[101]

In education likewise the situation continued unfavorable for the German minority after the 1939 elections. In Slovenia in 1940 only about seven, localities had German parallel classes. Folk Group Leader Baron called the school situation in Slovenia "hopeless."[102] In Gottschee only 1 percent of the minority pupils received any German instruction. Croatia had at the same time some 155 German classes in seventy-one localities for a German population of 171,000. Over the entire country in the school year 1939–40 only 24.8 percent of the ethnic German students in *Bürgerschule* and 2.8 percent in *Gymnasien* were receiving German instruction.[103]

The *Volksgruppe* had received no binding promises or guarantees in writing from the ruling party in the election pact of 1939. Since at that time Germany favored friendly relations with Yugoslavia, she was not willing to interfere for the benefit of the folk group, nor did she let them take more radical actions in their own behalf.[104]

The year 1939 produced the first serious shock for the *Volksgruppe* concerning German plans for their future. Hitler confidentially entrusted Lorenz, that is VoMi, in September 1939 with preparation for the repatriation of the German-speaking population from those territories that were occupied by Soviet troops.[105] On September 28 a fund of RM10 million was authorized by the finance ministry for the execution of this plan.[106] In October the assignment of resettlement was given to the SS, and according to Hitler's speech, the resettlement was to take place "among the splinters of Germandom in the east and south of Europe."[107] This statement was misunderstood, especially by the Germans of Yugoslavia, since a great many of them really lived in splinter groups. Naturally, the prospect of being forced to leave their land created such a great panic among them that by October 22, 1939, the German envoy in Belgrade, Heeren, requested the German foreign ministry to make a statement in order to quiet the unrest among the *Volksdeutsche*.[108]

The nationalist Yugoslavian press welcomed the news, of course, and urged the resettlement of the German group as soon as possible. The press even volunteered the number of Germans who should be evacuated from Yugoslavia: 450,000.[109] On October 27, 1939, Weizsäcker replied to Heeren's telegram, stating that "the question of repatriating the German communities in Yugoslavia is by no means acute at the present time." The reply recommended that Heeren avoid the question altogether, but if he had to give an answer, to emphasize that "such an action would naturally be undertaken only with the agreement of the government and German community," since Germany needed only volunteers for repatriation.[110]

The dismissal of Stojadinović on February 4, 1940, and the appointment of the new government of Cvetković encouraged the anti-German circles in Yugoslavia and created a new panic among the ethnic Germans. They flooded the German legation with applications to immigrate to Germany. The foreign ministry interpreted this increase in requests as a result of the general war psychosis in southeastern Europe. Therefore it permitted only the evacuation of German citizens from Yugoslavia. Ribbentrop personally forbade any measures for the evacuation of *Volksdeutsche*.[111] Although the question of resettlement died down, it kept the *Volksdeutsche* in great suspense throughout the year and into 1941.[112]

The relationship between the ethnic Germans and the Serbs deteriorated even further by the end of 1940. Serbs and Romanians attacked the participants in *Kulturbund* meetings, and only the police could stop the fighting.[113] These incidents indicated that the members of the German ethnic group had to face a natural front of Serbs and Romanians in the Bánát. Gendarmes took up weapons against the ethnic Germans in Ljubljana (Laibach) on April 26, 1940. Flyers were distributed in March in Slovenia, calling for the death of all ethnic Germans. By June 1940 the flyers were warning the population that the ethnic Germans were a fifth column. Aid packages sent from Germans to *Volksdeutsche* were confiscated by the police and those to whom they were addressed were charged with cooperation with the Reich.[114] At the same time there were instances of friendly gestures toward the VD by those Yugoslavs who feared bolshevism. To this group belonged the minister of education, Dr. Anton Korosec. Thanks to his sympathy, the ethnic Germans received favorable treatment—for example, the opening of a German gymnasium in Novi Vrbas in September 1940.[115]

As relations between the German and Yugoslav governments deteriorated, tensions between the Yugoslav government and the ethnic Germans increased. On the day of the military putsch in Belgrade (March 27, 1941) the Yugoslavian authorities arrested the entire ethnic German leadership. Although they were released shortly afterward, they were warned about the possible consequences of any disloyalty. The *Volksgruppenführung* (VGF: leaders of the ethnic group) hurried to send assurances of loyalty to young King Michael.[116] However, since the new military government was made up of strong Serb nationalists, the *Volksgruppe* knew that its fate depended upon the outcome of the seemingly inevitable war.

Volksdeutsche *Participation in the War*

The German security police under Himmler's leadership looked on Yugoslavia with suspicion after the dismissal of Stojadinović. On August 18, 1940, a new "police attaché" was added to the German legation in Belgrade in the person of SS-*Sturmbahnführer* Hans Helm. Because of increasing sabotage and espionage activity by British and French agents against the Germans in the Balkans, on November 4, 1940, the police attaché's office was strengthened with two "criminal" inspectors.[117] These three police officers at the German legation were helped by undercover police agents who arrived from Germany as clerks, officials, and employees of different German firms in Yugoslavia. One of their assignments was to put into operation secret radio stations. Until March 27, 1941, there was only one station operated in Belgrade (by Hans Bock). After that date many more secret radio stations were installed in Yugoslavia. All of them were operated by the undercover agents, who were without exception Reich Germans. The existence of these radio stations was kept secret not only from the *Volksdeutsche* but even from the German diplomats serving in Yugoslavia.[118]

The simple *Volksdeutsche* were kept uninformed concerning the possibility of a German-Yugoslav war. Thus they had to prepare for this possibility on the basis of gossip and rumors concerning the evacuation of Reich German families. Although the Belgrade police attaché's office worked out directives for the organization of an auxiliary police force from among the folk Germans in Yugoslavia as early as March 5, 1941, these directives were never implemented.[119]

The new Yugoslavian government ordered general mobilization on March 28, 1941. The order for general mobilization crossed the order for partial mobilization, which had already been secretly issued in the first days of March. This mixup in orders created such confusion in the Yugoslavian army that units were not in their assigned positions on April 6, 1941, when the war began.[120]

The folk Germans were equally confused. The majority obeyed their mobilization orders.[121] Some went into hiding. Those who were fortunate enough to live near the Romanian border escaped to Romania.[122] The *Volksdeutsche* leadership was also divided as to how to react to the events. Some of them recommended that *Volksdeutsche* who were subject to the mobilization orders escape over the border or fight their way to Croatia, but Jankó opposed this idea and considered it dangerous for ethnic Germans to disobey the mobilization orders.[123] Actually, these mobilization orders affected only a small minority of the *Volksdeutsche* in reserve since the Yugoslavian military authorities had declared the ethnic Germans untrustworthy. Therefore, with the exception of some reserve officers, they were not drafted for combat duty.[124]

The Reich authorities anticipated hostile actions against the *Volksdeutsche*, especially on the part of Serb nationalist organizations such as the *Chetniks* and the *Sokols*.[125] The *Abwehr* (the military intelligence department), which in May 1940 had refused to fulfill the request of the VD organizations for arms,[126] now considered their arming for self-defense an absolute necessity. From March 28 to April 1, 1941, General Erwin Lahousen, chief of Department II of the *Abwehr*, personally directed the smuggling of weapons through the Hungarian-Yugoslavian border.[127] On March 28, 1941, Hitler advised the *Volksdeutsche* through VoMi channels to avoid obeying the Yugoslav mobilization order. However, VoMi was unable to transmit this message in time to affect the mobilization since the Yugoslav authorities held the leadership of the ethnic Germans in "protective custody" and thus incommunicado.[128]

Deprived of its leadership, the *Volksgruppe* in general remained passive, and the partisan and fifth column activities of a few overzealous young men did not have a significant effect on the outcome of the military operations.[129] The *Abwehr* had installed a secret radio station in Novi Sad, which was supposed to be used by ethnic German leaders, but because of their detention, and later because of the danger created by the march of the Yugoslavian army, it was not used for VD messages until after the Yugoslavian army had evacuated the territory. The first message was broadcast by Sepp Jankó. Because the activities of groups such as the *Chetniks*, he was concerned for the well-being of the ethnic Germans. The message was: "The situation is extremely critical. Expecting catastrophe any minute. Send German troops at once."[130] These sentences, in light of the existing situation, can hardly be interpreted as a spy report. Sabotage actions and fifth column activities could not be executed;

spy reports, if any were made, quickly became obsolete because of the swift advance of the German troops.

Hitler intended to connect the strategic operations in Yugoslavia with his plan to occupy Greece, and at the same time relieve the Italian forces, which had withdrawn their defenses to Albania. To carry out the plan he issued the following directive:

1. Beginning of Operation *Marita* as early as possible with the limited objective of capturing Greek Thrace and the basin of Salonika and to win the high ground of Edessa.
2. Thrust from the region south of Sofia in the direction of Skoplje in order to relieve the flank of the Italian front in Albania.
3. Thrust with stronger forces from the area around Sofia in the direction of Nis, then of Belgrade, in cooperation with
4. stronger German forces penetrating from the area around Graz and Klagenfurt in a southeastern direction with the aim of destroying the Yugoslav Army.[131]

The Yugoslavian general staff realized that its army alone was no match for the German forces. Therefore they saw as their primary duty the defense of the main valley leading to Salonika in order to secure a channel for reinforcements from Greek and British forces. The strategic plan for the northern defenses was conceived as a delaying operation in which forces would be withdrawn step by step from the Drava-Danube line to the Sava-Danube line.

When the German attack began, the mobilization and deployment of the Yugoslavian forces had not yet been completed. This unpreparedness, coupled with the disruption of communications by the German air force, caused a panic in the Yugoslavian army leadership. Although individual units fought bravely, a mood of hopelessness permeated the army and the defense lines melted away.[132] The German column penetrating Yugoslavia from the direction of Graz, Austria, found no measurable resistance because the Croatian units laid down their weapons without a fight—some even joining the Germans against the Serbs.[133] The behavior of the Croats is understandable in light of Ribbentrop's message to the nationalist leaders on March 31, 1941, promising them independence if they would "promote" the collapse of Yugoslavia.[134] On April 10, 1941, General Slavko Kvaternik, the leader of the nationalist Croats, proclaimed the Independent State of Croatia.[135]

The formation of independent Croatia gave an excuse to the Hungarian government to regard the Hungarian-Yugoslavian "eternal friendship" pact as invalid, since Yugoslavia had ceased to exist. On April 11, 1941, Hungarian troops invaded Baranya and Vojvodina (Bácska). Encountering no significant resistance, they reached the Danube River a few days later.

The political reorganization of defeated Yugoslavia recognized the independent state of Croatia. Hungary incorporated Bácska and the Baranya triangle. Italy received the southern corner of Slovenia and islands along the Dalmatian coast as well as the area bordering Albania. Bulgaria moved into Macedonia. The Bánát remained under German military administration.

Serbia as an independent state was restored to its pre-World War I boundaries, naturally as a satellite of Germany.[136]

Reorganization of the Volksgruppe

The arrangements made by Hitler for the former Yugoslavian territories brought a certain degree of disappointment to all parties concerned. Germany expected independent Croatia to become a fascist state. Instead, Ante Pavelić planned to establish a Croatian dynasty and offered the Croatian throne to the prince of Spoleto.[137] Croatia, which hoped to establish itself as a nation-state, had to comply with German wishes and make room for *Volksdeutsche* who were to be evacuated from the Serbian kingdom and settled in Croatia. Hungary hoped to reincorporate not only the Bácska but also the Bánát, as well as the area between the Drava and Sava rivers.[138] Germany, however, limited the realization of Hungary's hope to the territories of Bácska and Baranya.

The *Volksdeutsche* hoped to join the "great German community" of three million Germans in southeastern Europe "according to the will of the Führer.[139] However, they had miscalculated the Führer's will. Those *Volksdeutsche* who lived in German-occupied territories could consider themselves fortunate. Undoubtedly, they became the favored group in these territories, and their leaders received broad authority. Administration of the Bánát was placed in the hands of ethnic Germans. This privilege caused numerous problems. The majority of *Volksdeutsche* had neither training nor experience in administration. In certain cases they misused their power against the local Serb population, creating obstacles for peaceful cooperation.[140] After the first days of occupation the *Volksdeutsche* organized an auxiliary police force to take over the duties of the former Yugoslavian gendarmerie.[141] Relations between ethnic Germans and Serbians were generally friendly. The few cases in which the Serbian population turned against the ethnic Germans during the war were the result of the "extreme propaganda agitation of the Yugoslavian state radio and press, and were soon forgotten."[142] The only anxiety of the ethnic German group was caused by talk of their resettlement coming from the Reich.[143] Although this resettlement was postponed "for the duration of the war," the planning went on and caused a certain alienation of the *Volksgruppe*.[144] A disagreement occurred concerning the organization of the folk group. While Jankó regarded it as his duty to protect the interests of the ethnic Germans, the Reich German authorities wanted to use them to further the interests of the Reich. Furthermore, the *Volksdeutsche* were regarded, especially by lower-ranking Reich officials in Serbia, as second-class Germans; some did not even consider them "real" Germans.[145] Requisitioning conducted by appointed Reich German officials embittered the ethnic German farmers and increased the tension.[146]

When the auxiliary police forces were placed under the supervision and authority of the SS, ethnic Germans were subjected to draft for police duties.

They were to be placed under military disciplinary laws and dismissal from the units was to be permitted only in especially well founded cases. These developments caused dissatisfaction among the ethnic Germans and, when the auxiliary police units were deployed by the SS against the Serbian population and partisans, the *Volksdeutsche* almost completely ceased volunteering for service in them.[147]

In Croatia the German ethnic group was recognized as a corporate body and given far-reaching privileges, especially in the field of education. Their old leader, Altgayer, received every cooperation from the new Croatian government.[148]

Volksbund organizations mushroomed in the most remote villages. The leadership naturally welcomed this development, hoping that all the ethnic Germans would "obey the order of time" and "continue to be a powerful and a proud" supporter of the Bund leadership.[149] The joy of the *Volksdeutsche* did not last long. In the spring of 1942 the Waffen SS began its recruitment campaigns among the ethnic Germans in southeastern Europe, and what Dr. Sepp Jankó visualized as a self-defense regiment for the *Volksdeutsche* was transformed into SS-Division Prinz Eugen.[150]

The Prinz Eugen Division

During the summer of 1942 unofficial conscription for the Waffen SS began. Gottlob Berger, who organized the SS recruitment campaign in Romania, believed he would be able to create an entire SS division composed of ethnic Germans from former Yugoslavian territories. However, very few *Volksdeutsche* volunteered during the recruitment campaign of 1942.[151] The leaders of the folk group opposed the SS recruitment, and the Reich had to order Jankó to supply 20,000 "volunteers." Still the necessary number of men was not produced. The SS and the ethnic German leaders began to use "public pressure" and stronger measures. Jankó stated that "from this service nobody who is healthy can exempt himself" between the ages of seventeen and fifty.[152]

When "public pressure" proved insufficient, the SS, under the instructions of General Rudolf Phelps, began conscripting the *Volksdeutsche*.[153] Jankó protested to VoMi the drafting of his men without his knowledge. His worry was that the indiscriminate drafting would weaken the leadership and the work would suffer.[154] On the other hand, he did not show any concern for the common people; in fact, he threatened with arrest, even locked up, those men who had German names and refused to join the SS.[155]

The SS recruitment committees used even stronger methods and on occasion, with the help of the German security police and local "self-defense" units, actually beat those men who did not answer their call and carried them away by force. They forced the wives and mothers of such "draft dodgers" to march through the village with signs around their necks which read: "I am a folk German swine."[156]

In November 1942 Jankó resigned in protest against the indiscriminate conscription of the *Volksdeutsche* and began to organize a labor service in order to save the very young ethnic German boys from SS conscription. He warned VoMi about the growing anti-Reich German attitude. Similar warnings against SS conscription were sent by Altgayer, the leader in Croatia.[157] Nevertheless, the SS draft continued and by the end of 1943 the folk Germans serving in the SS from Serbia numbered 21,516, and from Croatia 17,538.[158] Not all the *Volksdeutsche* were forced into the SS. SS propaganda used both the carrot and the stick in its recruitment campaigns. It offered Reich citizenship to those who served in the SS, and promised them good pay and care for dependents.[159]

The repeated "recruitments" (April 1942, October 1943, March 1944) produced a body of ethnic Germans in the Waffen SS well above the expected capacity of a group of that size—12.5 percent of the entire ethnic German population. With the exception of the very old, the very young, and the disabled, almost the entire male population served in the Waffen SS (the majority in the Prinz Eugen Division). Since during its entire existence the Prinz Eugen Division operated in the Balkans against Serbian as well as Greek partisans with the usual SS methods, its activities turned the non-German population of this territory hostile to the *Volksdeutsche* in general. Even if the majority of the *Volksdeutsche* were not Nazi in their convictions, the fact that they did not feel compelled to turn against the Reich, despite the exploitation they suffered at German hands, seems to justify the Serbian feeling against them.

CHAPTER VII

Ethnic Germans in Hungary after 1938

Consequences of the First Vienna Decision

In August 1938 the ethnic Germans of Hungary still belonged to the *Ungarländisch-Deutscher Volksbindungsverein* (UDV) "were completely loyal in their thinking and entertained no separatist ideas. What the *Volksgruppe* wanted was the evolution of its national individuality in the cultural field *within the Hungarian state*"[1] (italics added). However, the German government distrusted the old leaders of the UDV, such as "former Hungarian foreign minister [*sic*] Gratz, an enemy of anti-Semitism," and Canon Pintér, who was completely under the government's influence. Dr. Basch and his *Volksdeutsche Kameradschaft* operated undercover without Hungarian permission, but enjoyed the unconditional support of the Reich, which regarded the group as an assembly of the most self-conscious ethnic Germans. Since the Hungarian government was ready to "stand up with all its energy" against the *Volksgruppe* that entertained hostile ideas "under the disguise of the minority treaties," the *Kameradschaft*'s and the Reich's goals seemed unreachable for the time being.[2]

The Reich had its first opportunity to help the Basch group openly at the time of the First Vienna Decision. It urged the Hungarian government to grant autonomy to the ethnic Germans under the exclusive leadership of Basch's group and demanded that Basch be appointed undersecretary of state for German affairs.[3]

On November 26, 1938, the *Volksbund* was legally founded under the presidency of Basch. It claimed the right to be the exclusive representative of the *Volksgruppe* and demanded from the Hungarian government recognition of the *Volksgruppe* as a corporate body. This demand created such a hostile mood in Hungary that Prime Minister Béla Imrédy felt it necessary to quiet the popular uproar with an article in which he announced that the Hungarian government could not recognize the ethnic Germans as a folk group of the German Reich because such recognition would make them a part of the Reich living in Hungary. For the same reason he refused to appoint Basch as undersecretary of state for German affairs.[4] The elections of May 28–29, 1939, showed a sudden surge of strength for the Hungarian national socialist parties. They had received secretly from the Reich authorities through Switzerland 500,000 Pengö for election expenses.[5] This support indicates that the Reich pursued the same double foreign policy in Hungary as it did in the other East European countries. While the foreign ministry preferred to deal directly with the Hungarian government, the Nazi party and its *Volksdeutsche Mittelstelle* (VoMi) tried to influence Hungarian foreign and domestic policy through the support of native Nazis. When this approach promised success, the *Volksdeutsche* were ordered by the Reich authorities to remain quiet. Thus Basch toned down his antigovernment speeches in 1939.

By October 1939 Hitler's speech concerning the probable resettlement of Germans from southeastern Europe had created such a panic among the ethnic Germans in Hungary that Basch hurried to ask the help of the Hungarian government. He wanted the government to make a statement that it did not want the ethnic Germans resettled outside Hungary. The government refused his request on the basis that the question had been raised by Hitler and not by the Hungarians.[6]

The Bund expected help from Germany now, but Hitler's plans for 1940 demanded quiet in southeastern Europe. Only in the fall of 1940 did the Bund and its German patrons have a chance to further the cause of the ethnic Germans in Hungary. The Second Vienna Decision included a German-Hungarian protocol that, theoretically at least (as in Romania), secured far-reaching privileges for the ethnic German group.

The Second Vienna Decision

The Second Vienna Decision of August 30, 1940, included German-Hungarian and German-Romanian protocols that regulated the conditions of the *Volksgruppe* and their relationship to their respective governments.[7] In the German-Hungarian protocol the Hungarian government, which up to now had opposed granting a privileged status to the *Volksdeutsche*, gave in to the demand of the German government. Afraid that the Romanian government would win the sympathy of the Reich by granting the greatest possible freedom to their ethnic Germans, the Hungarians granted very similar rights to the Hungarian *Volksdeutsche*.[8]

According to the protocol, the Hungarian government recognized this new definition of an ethnic German: one "who identified himself as a German and was recognized as a folk German by the leadership of the *Volksbund* of Germans in Hungary."[9] The *Volksbund* was reorganized as the sole representative of the ethnic Germans and received the status of a corporate body under Hungarian law. The Hungarian government accepted the obligation to allow complete freedom of organization to the *Volksgruppe*, if these organizations sponsored youth, sport, or artistic activity. It granted the Germans equality in every field of life. It promised to transfer *Volksdeutsche* officials to counties where the majority of the ethnic Germans lived. The protocol entitled the German group to maintain schools, and the Hungarian government promised to help with teacher education. To wipe out the effects of forced magyarization, the members of the *Volksgruppe* received the right to change their magyarized names back to German. The Hungarian government succeeded in closing the protocol with the following sentence: "The above principles should not in any way affect the duty of the members of the *Volksgruppe* to remain loyal to the Hungarian state."[10]

The ethnic German leadership, disregarding the last point, interpreted the agreement differently. Basch announced that "on August 30, 1940, Adolf Hitler, Führer of every German in the world, became the overlord and protector of the *Volksgruppe* in Hungary." He expressed gratitude to the Führer for guaranteeing "the rights of the *more than 800,000 Germans* in Hungary"[11] (italics added). According to the 1930 census, Hungary had 479,000 ethnic Germans.[12] Including the territories attached to Hungary by the First Vienna Decision, the number of Germans increased by 13,875. The Second Vienna Decision added another 57,010 ethnic Germans. This totaled 549,885. Though Basch greatly exaggerated the number of Germans, this was no exaggeration in his mind, since the aim of the Bund after the Second Vienna Decision was not only the preservation of Germandom, but, in complete contradiction of the minority treaties, the "regermanization" of the already assimilated *Volksdeutsche*. To reach this goal the Bund listed in its national register not only those who professed to be Germans but also those who professed to be Hungarians but had German ancestry.[13] The number of such Germans was significant. For example, in Szatmár County alone the Bund wanted to "reintroduce 45,000 Swabians to their German mother tongue since, due to the magyarization campaigns of Hungary *before the First World War*, they had no knowledge of the German language" (italics added). But the Bund wanted more than to teach the German language. It wanted to reawaken German self-consciousness and, after that, incorporate the "Szathmár lands in the great German folk community."[14]

The Hungarian government, referring to technical and financial difficulties, postponed the implementation of the Vienna protocol. To the Reich authorities Basch accused the government of sabotaging obligations accepted in the Vienna Decision.[15] However, the Reich authorities again considered Germany's good relationship with Hungary to be more important than the ethnic Germans and ordered Basch to restrain the more impatient members of the *Volksgruppe*. Basch did not seem to be willing to do that. During Bund meetings he viciously attacked the Hungarians in his speeches; for example: "first comes the German folk, then a pile of manure, then one more pile of manure, and then come the Hungarian lords."[16] The Bund forbade the members of the newly organized youth group to sing Hungarian folk songs, dance Hungarian dances, or wear Hungarian costumes. The lecturers emphasized that Hitler was the only Führer of the German *Herrenvolk* and therefore Germans should not marry those of other nations.[17]

Besides having difficulties with the Hungarian government, the *Volksbund* and Basch had problems created by the inclusion of 57,010 ethnic Germans of North Transylvania. This *Volksgruppe* was made up mostly of Saxons who had played a leading role in ethnic German affairs while they lived in Romania. Their annexation by Hungary, ordered by the Second Vienna Decision, caused a mixed reaction among them. The leaders were generally hostile to Hungarian rule and even requested of the Führer before the decision was made that he not award their territory to Hungary.[18] Among the common *Volks-deutsche* the older generation who had served in the *Kaiserliche und Königliche* (Imperial and Royal) army felt nostalgia for the good old days and hoped for their return with the Hungarian occupation. The younger generation, educated by the *Erneuerungsbewegung*, "knew about the magyarization methods and therefore received the Hungarians with hostility."[19]

The Hungarian troops and administrators, however, behaved very tolerantly. Vacant positions in local administrations (vacated because of the Romanian officials' departure for Romania) were divided equally between Hungarians and Saxons. The official language was Hungarian but the population was free to use its mother tongue in public offices.[20] Against the pessimistic expectations of some Saxons, the Hungarian authorities did not assemble secret lists of active *Volksbund* members.[21] What impressed the Saxons most was that the Hungarian officials treated them in "West European style."[22]

Right after the return of North Transylvania to Hungary a Saxon delegation visited Budapest and was received by Minister President Pál Teleki. The members came away with the best of impressions. They then made contact with the *Volksbund* leaders of Hungary,[23] who received them with suspicion because of their visit to Teleki. The Bund leadership told the Saxons that they were now subordinated to the Bund and should not circumvent it by making direct contact with the government. The Saxons regarded this attitude as very strange, determined that the thinking of the Bund leaders was quite different from their own, and became pessimistic about future cooperation. When the *Volksbund der Deutschen in Ungarn* (VDU) attempted to "streamline" the Saxon group, the Saxons fought against these attempts just as hard as they did against the magyarization attempts of some overzealous local Hungarian officials.[24] They regarded Basch as a man who had no personal freedom but was bound to obey every directive from Berlin.[25]

Bácska Swabians Join the Hungarian Volksbund

In the spring of 1941 the Bund was again forced to slow down its activities in Hungary. Hitler anticipated the participation of Hungarian troops in the destruction of Yugoslavia and therefore warned Basch to calm the more impatient members of the *Volksgruppe*. The suicide of Count Teleki and the appointment of László Bárdossy as prime minister gave the *Volksbund* new hope of realizing its aim, which was now nothing less than a state within the state.

The leaders of the Bácska Swabians, however, were shocked to learn that their territories would be occupied not by German but by Hungarian troops. During the military operations they sent the following radio message to the Reich: "We are just as embittered as shocked. What are the Hungarians doing here? Better a whole lifetime under the Hottentots than one single day again exposed to the blessings of St. Stephen's crown."[26] The hysteria of the leaders spread to the population. No one welcomed the Hungarian army units into the Swabian villages.[27] The *Volksdeutsche* were so hostile, in fact, that the Hungarians were more successful in cooperating with the Serbs than with the Swabians. The Hungarian authorities, of course, reacted to this hostility with a similar attitude. The German language was barely tolerated and in some cases completely forbidden as an official language.[28]

The anti-Hungarian attitude of the *Volksdeutsche* leadership was based more on personal reasons than fear of magyarization. Dr. Jankó, and through him the whole leadership, learned during the summer of 1941 from VoMi in Berlin that Dr. Basch would take over the leadership in the Bánát, Bácska, and Baranya. "Jankó and his comrades were not prepared for such a decision."[29] The leaders of the Yugoslavian ethnic Germans considered themselves better and more useful members of the German community than the Hungarian *Volksdeutsche* were. After all, by 1941 a great number of volunteers were serving in the Waffen SS, and only a negligible number were from Hungary.

Basch and the Hungarian leaders were naturally delighted when they heard the decision of VoMi and received the draft of the new agreement the Reich wanted to negotiate with the Hungarian government.[30] According to this new proposal, the ethnic German group in Hungary was to be represented before the government by the *Volksgruppenführer*. The VGF would retain his privilege of accepting or rejecting an individual as an ethnic German, but now he would screen not only those who considered themselves Germans but also those whose physical features clearly showed German characteristics.

In the field of commerce the proposal suggested the direct linking of the *Volksdeutsche* economy with that of Germany. The first step toward the realization of this aim seemed to benefit only the *Volksdeutsche*. On October 30, 1941, the *Deutsche Volkshilfe* began to send through the *Volksbund* winter help, accident and unemployment aid, and provided free medical and hospital services. Basch promised that the Reich would take care of the social needs of ethnic Germans from birth to death. The wealthier *Volksdeutsche* farmers received financial aid to organize marketing cooperatives, which enabled them to increase their profits. They exported directly to Germany, circumventing the Hungarian commercial authorities. With the help of the *Kreditanstalt Bankverein*, the Bund bought up the stocks of a savings and loan association and propagandized among the Germans to deposit their savings with this bank.[31] Only a few of the ethnic Germans knew that the Bund leadership had researched and reported, at the demand of the Reich, the economic capacity of the folk group. Since the war demanded great economic sacrifices, Germany wanted the *Volksgruppe* to carry a proportionate share of this burden and so needed these data.

In the field of justice the proposal foresaw the organization of German sections at every level of the court system for the members of the *Volksgruppe*. In the cultural area the ethnic Germans were to receive complete autonomy. The Hungarian government was to hand over control of all the schools in which the majority of students were German. It was also to secure the right of the ethnic Germans to fulfill their military duties in the German army or in the Waffen SS. In addition, the Bund was to have a youth organization and membership in it would exempt the ethnic German youngsters from participation in the required *Levente* training.[32] What was to make the German folk group really a state within the state was the suggestion in Article 33 that different questions between the group and the Hungarian government be settled through diplomatic channels.

Basch and the Bund welcomed the appointment of Bárdossy as minister since he had the reputation of being pro-German. No wonder they believed that VoMi's proposal would be implemented at once. They soon were disappointed. Bárdossy not only rejected the new proposal, he even postponed the implementation of the Vienna Decision. His attitude outraged the radical members of the *Volksgruppe* so much that Ambassador Jagow felt it necessary to instruct Basch personally to restrain the folk group with strong measures in order not to endanger German-Hungarian relations.[33]

Jagow's warnings were not heeded by Basch. Instead, he made a speech in which he sharply attacked the Bárdossy government, and his attacks were received by his audience with delight (and boos against the Hungarian government). As a result Bárdossy summoned Jagow to his office where the ambassador experienced what he later described as "the most painful hour of my life."[34] Bárdossy skillfully argued that if the Hungarian government's authority was undermined, it would not be able to fulfill its trade obligations toward the Reich. He characterized Basch's attitude as similar to that of Henlein and warned the German ambassador that he would not succeed with these methods in Hungary. Finally, Bárdossy suggested to Jagow that he make the Bund understand that such behavior did the "worst possible service to German-Hungarian friendly relations."[35] The German government instructed Basch accordingly. Basch's attacks on Hungary had come at an inopportune moment for the Reich, which was counting on Hungarian economic and military help in the campaign against the Soviet Union.

The military operations on the Soviet front in late 1941 and early 1942 resulted in greater losses than Hitler had anticipated. It was time to request the Germans of Hungary to pay for his past support. As a result of a direct agreement with the Hungarian government in the spring of 1942, the

Volksbund was instructed to support the recruitment of the *Volksdeutsche* for the Waffen SS.

Hungarian Volksdeutsche in the SS

The Waffen SS began to recruit secretly young Hungarian *Volksdeutsche* who were members of the *Volksbund* as early as 1940. These young men were lured into the SS with the promise that they would participate in only a two-to-three-month-long "sport course," and that completion of the course would secure great advantages for them in the Bund. This secret SS operation came to light when at the end of the three months they failed to return home and, instead, sent letters explaining that they had become volunteer soldiers of the Waffen SS. Since the majority of them were underage, the desperate parents bombarded the Hungarian and German authorities with requests that their teenage sons be returned immediately.[36] This recruitment had occurred without the knowledge of the German foreign ministry, and Hitler himself considered it damaging to Hungarian-German relations.[37]

Until the end of 1941 only 1,500 *Volksdeutsche* volunteered for the *Wehrmacht*, all of them from the territory of Bácska and all of them before the Hungarian occupation of that area.[38] Those who volunteered for the SS, even though the recruitment went on with the permission of the Hungarian government after April 1942, had to face severe consequences. The Hungarian government excluded them from Hungarian citizenship. Since this recruitment was restricted to *Volksbund* members, it was relatively successful (25,709 reported; 7,566 accepted in the SS; 10,294 accepted in the Wehrmacht). The German ambassador to Hungary pointed out the disproportion between the numbers coming from the original Hungarian territories (5,793) and from the annexed territories. Bácska alone had provided 9,446 volunteers.[39]

To make the recruitment more successful, the SS promised the volunteers better pay than the Hungarian army offered, and also better care for their families.[40] The SS also used scare tactics, spreading rumors that the Hungarian army organized the *Volksdeutsche* into special units and always used them for the most dangerous assignments.[41] Those *Volksbund* members who refused to volunteer were threatened, beaten, and their property damaged or destroyed.[42]

The reaction of the *Volksdeutsche* to these tactics was mixed. Their original enthusiasm for the Reich declined. The great majority of the assimilated *Volksdeutsche* refused to identify themselves as German. The Bund membership also suffered losses.[43] Others were more active and in the second half of 1941 organized the Fidelity Movement (*Hüség Mozgalom*) with the tacit, unofficial, "but nevertheless strong encouragement of Budapest."[44] Basch and the Bund leadership were naturally outraged by the Fidelity Movement's success. Its successful counterpropaganda deprived the Bund of thousands of members.[45] Dr. Franz Kussbach, whose name undoubtedly attracted many *Volksdeutsche*, participated in the campaigns for the Fidelity Movement. Although the Fidelity Movement was not very effective, it did dampen the desire of the *Volksdeutsche* to volunteer for the Waffen SS so much that Basch recommended the introduction of forced conscription.

The *Volksbund* tried to counterbalance the reactions of the Swabians by professing to be good Hungarian patriots. Basch ordered the local organizations to display Horthy's picture beside the picture of Hitler in their offices, and to use the Hungarian tricolor in addition to the swastika in their parades. These measures came too late. The military situation of Germany deteriorated during the fall of 1942 and in early 1943. VoMi now wanted Basch to set a good example for the *Volksdeutsche* in Hungary by enlisting in the SS himself. Fortunately for him, the foreign ministry was able to prevent this with the argument that the ethnic Germans would lose their leadership if Basch and his comrades were conscripted, since they would be deprived of their Hungarian citizenship.[46]

Financial problems also had far-reaching consequences. The sum needed for the support of families of SS volunteers in Hungary was thirty million Pengö per year, while the Reich provided the embassy there with only five million Pengö for this purpose.

The Hungarian authorities were less than cooperative. Basch still complained about the Hungarian school policy in 1942, but this was not his largest problem. When the *Volksbund*, in order to send Christmas packages to the Hungarian *Volksdeutsche* serving in the Waffen SS, began to collect their names, Basch and his comrades were interrogated by the Hungarian counterintelligence agencies. They hinted to Basch that this activity fit the definition of spying and high treason. Although the investigation was dropped through the intervention of the German ambassador, it created great tension for Basch during the last five months of 1942.[47]

In April 1943 a new agreement between the Hungarian and German governments made the next SS recruitment possible. According to this agreement the recruitment, which was formerly restricted to *Volksbund* members, was extended to all *Volksdeutsche*. The Hungarian government promised to dismiss from the Hungarian army those who wanted to volunteer for the Waffen SS, but the Reich still could not convince the government not to deprive these volunteers of their Hungarian citizenship.

This new recruitment also was unsuccessful because of the counteractions of the Hungarian government and *Volksdeutsche* parents. Although the Hungarian authorities gave their consent to the recruitment, they demanded the presence of a Hungarian army officer, who advised the prospective volunteers of their rights and the consequences of joining the SS.[48] The advice of these army officers made many volunteers change their minds. *Volksdeutsche* members of the Hungarian Second Army, which was destroyed on the Don front in 1943, spread defeatist propaganda in the villages and greatly contributed to the decline of volunteers.[49] Finally, *Volksdeutsche* parents, whose consent was required for the enlistment of their underage sons in the SS, denied their signature in the overwhelming majority.

The upshot was that ethnic Germans tried to avoid this draft, hid from the recruitment commissions of the SS, and sought the protection of their Hungarian neighbors. In the last they were not disappointed. Hungarian peasants fed and sheltered their unfortunate ethnic German neighbors, proving that a community spirit based on centuries of common experience had survived the impact of Nazism.[50]

The SS recruitment was not a success. The SS had estimated that some 30,000 men would be available for recruitment,[51] but only 20,000 were found.[52] According to the official figures of December 28, 1943, 22,125 men served in the Waffen SS (Bácska and North Transylvania included), 1,729 served in the German armed forces, while 35,000 chose to remain in the Hungarian army. These numbers clearly support the statement that the recruitment campaign of 1943 failed. After March 15, 1944, when German troops occupied Hungary, the SS recruitment campaigns became unnecessary because the *Volksdeutsche* were drafted into Waffen SS units with the active cooperation of the *Volksbund.*

The Volksbund Turns against Hungary

By 1943 the *Volksbund* in Hungary had grown into a huge organization. Although exact figures are not available after 1941, at that time the Bund had 473 local organizations and more than 50,000 members.[53] This number must have increased between 1942 and 1944 even though the Fidelity Movement cut into the membership somewhat. A further proof that the organization increased is the financial projection of the *Volksgruppe* for 1942–43. They foresaw subsidies in the amount of 28,000,000 Pengö.[54] VoMi intended to provide 17,000,000 Pengö. Of this amount only 2,500,000 Pengö was projected for expenses concerning economic transactions, such as loans for *Volksdeutsche* peasants to buy land and aid to VD businessmen. Thus the remainder was spent for administrative and "other" expenses. The *Volksbund* really needed the money. Its organization now included such units as the Investigative Department, and a very large sum was needed for the organization and training of the units of the *Deutsche Mannschaft* (DM).

As early as August 1943 the Hungarian government judged the military situation hopeless and began to explore the possibility of signing a separate peace treaty with the Allies.[55] The Hungarian crown council explored the possibility that the Allies might be willing to discriminate between Hungary's and Germany's responsibility in the war. For that purpose the strictest orders were issued to the Hungarian army as to how to behave in occupied territories against the hostile population. Even the 1941 Bácska massacre was investigated and the commander of the troops, General Feketehalmy-Czeydner, was to be court-martialed. (He avoided arrest by fleeing to Germany.) Furthermore, the Hungarian government showed less and less willingness to engage additional Hungarian troops in the war. On the contrary, Horthy asked the German general staff to send home all the Hungarian troops from the Soviet front. Even before the arrival of the German reply he sent orders in this spirit to the two army corps deployed on Soviet territories.[56]

The *Volksbund* watched these events with more and more anxiety. It began spontaneously to collect intelligence information about persons with anti-German or anti-*Volksbund* leanings. This was relatively easy since the *Volksbund* had many members in important government and army positions.[57] The Bund members never hesitated to inform German authorities about the secret plans of the Hungarian government.[58] These activities of the Hungarian *Volksdeutsche* were especially appreciated by VoMi, SS, and SD, which gave aid in case of trouble with the Hungarian authorities.[59]

The *Volksbund* did not stop at the collection and reporting of information about anti-Nazis. Early in 1944 the Bund sent VoMi "Suggestions for Solutions" (*Lösungsvorschläge*) concerning the necessary German reactions, and the role of the Bund, in various hypothetical situations.[60] They went even further: in case Hungary's occupation by German troops became necessary, they planned to form a new Hungarian government.[61]

Hungary's occupation became a reality on March 19, 1944, but the Germans, in order not to create additional problems, left Horthy in office. Horthy appointed Sztójay, a well-known German sympathizer, as minister president. Basch had only one course left—to present his demands to Sztójay. These demands were:[62] (1) dismissal of anti-German state employees; (2) dissolution of the Fidelity Movement; (3) an end to the draft to the Hungarian Army as punishment; (4) complete freedom of activities for Bund members; (5) solution of the school question; (6) permission to publish a morning edition of the *Volksdeutsche Zeitung*; (7) a German program of thirty-five minutes three times weekly on Hungarian radio; (8) the right of *Volksbund* to requisition cars for political activities; (9) a government declaration over the press and radio promising the prompt fulfillment of the Bund demands. Sztójay did not answer these demands.

On March 19 the *Deutsche Mannschaft* actively helped the German troops in the occupation of Hungary by attacking railroad stations, occupying post and telegraph offices, and disarming gendarme and police patrols.[63] During the period between March 1944 and the end of the war Basch and the *Volksbund* considered themselves (correctly) the overlords of Hungary. They even rejected the suggestions of the German ambassador and were willing to cooperate only with Otto Winkelmann, the chief of the SS and security police forces in Hungary. This German occupation of Hungary changed the relationship between the *Volksbund* and the leaders of the formerly uncooperative Transylvanian Saxon and Bácska-Swabian leadership. With the support of Winkelmann, Basch became the undisputed commander of the *Volksgruppe*, which willingly and (more often) unwillingly served the interest of the Reich.

Conclusion

Czechoslovakia

After reviewing the course of events, we may answer with more certainty the questions raised in our introduction.

Did German policy promote the interest of ethnic Germans living in Czechoslovakia? If we are willing to accept the Reich German interpretation of ethnic German interest, then the answer must be positive. But can the interpretation that the annexation of ethnic German territories provided the greatest good for the ethnic Germans be accepted at face value? Definitely not!

The Reich brought continuous economic hardship to the Sudeten Germans; put an end to their ethnic character; "gleichsgeschalted" their educational, cultural, and social institutions, replaced their lively political individualism with a totalitarian one-party system. Were these changes brought about by Munich desired by the Sudeten Germans? The reply again is a definite no!

For two years after the election victory in 1935 the moderate majority, not only of the ethnic group but also of the Sudeten Germany party (SDP) leaders and membership, sought solutions for their problems *within* the framework of the Czechoslovak republic. While their pan-Germanism certainly did not prepare them to accept Czech supremacy unconditionally, the Sudeten German masses were willing to adjust to the new situation created by the Versailles Treaty even so far as slowly to assimilate. The best proof of this is the fact that every fourth German woman married a non-German man. If we add to that the declining birth rate among the Sudeten Germans,[1] we may say that the German minority problem of Czechoslovakia would have been solved according to the concepts of the minority treaties within the next two or three generations. The Reich, referring constantly in its propaganda to the right of people to national self-determination, denied this same right to the Sudeten German masses by its constant interference, and finally by its decision to annex their territory to "Greater Germany." It did not occur to the Reich Germans to ask the Sudeten German population how they would like to manage their own affairs because the Reich Germans were not concerned about the interests of Sudeten Germans. They used them as pawns for one purpose only: to serve the foreign political designs of the Third Reich.

The Czechoslovak government's minority policy was not consistent. Right after the creation of Czechoslovakia Masaryk's enlightened and liberal policy secured the cooperation of the Sudeten Germans. By giving their votes and confidence to the leftist, activist German parties, they demonstrated their willingness to cooperate. Partly because of economic problems, and partly because of the impatient and intolerant attitudes and actions of lower government officials, militant Czech nationalist politicians, and leaders, Masaryk's intentions were circumvented. Under the influence of Nazi propaganda and the impact of international developments, accumulated small personal grievances grew into a big issue during the election campaign in 1934.

Still the Sudeten German electorate did not make a complete about-face. Only two-thirds of them deserted the traditional leftist parties, and even this two-thirds voted for the moderates, who were ready to cooperate with SDP representatives. With Masaryk's death and the election of Beneš, this opportunity for cooperation was missed. Instead, there followed a time of confusion, controversies between Beneš and Hodža, more and more international political victories for Hitler, and finally Munich. The Czech attempt at reconciliation came too late. Czech minority policy failed its great test: it did not assimilate the minority by peaceful means. It alienated them by using authority and it proved unable to force them to remain loyal.

The policy of Sudeten Germans testifies to their political maturity. Up to 1935, in every election the Sudeten Germans awarded their votes to the activist parties. Even in 1935, one-third of them chose to remain faithful to these parties, though their inability to solve Sudeten German problems was already clear. An important factor, which may have been primary, was the economic condition of the Sudeten Germans. The economic crisis, which hit them especially hard, caused them to reorder their priorities and place their economic well-being above their political convictions. Under the influence of such economic distress and disappointment, one might expect the entire group to have turned opportunistic and lent their support to the Nazis, who seemed to be successful. However, a comparison of the size of the ethnic group and of the members registered by the Nazis shows a relatively low percentage of actual Nazi party members. In the Czech and Sudeten territories proper the German population numbered 3,460,000;[2] Nazi party members numbered 61,000,[3] that is, 1.76 percent of the German minority. In Slovakia the number of Germans was 140,000; membership in the party had hardly reached 11,000 (7.8 percent of the German population) by March 1938.[4] It is probable that these numbers would have been even lower if the Reich had not made an international issue of Czechoslovak-German relations. The condemnation of the entire Sudeten German group woud hardly be an objective interpretation of these facts.

Poland

In the absence of a unified and centralized minority organization, one cannot talk about a German minority group policy in Poland. There were groups that advocated cooperation with Poland (Senator Pant) and lost support when they could not improve the conditions of the minority. There were pro-Nazi elements, which advocated revisionism and promoted German imperialism, but they did not gain the support of the majority of Germans. It seems to these authors that the great majority of the *Volksdeutsche* were disinterested in the arguments of nationalists on both sides. Their only concern was survival under German or Polish rule, keeping their traditional customs, preserving their language and way of life, and securing the best possible economic conditions for themselves. They were even ready to assimilate. What made them conscious of their Germanness was the "polonization" effort of the Poles, the pan-German and, later, Nazi propaganda of the Reich Germans, and most of all the economic hardship they suffered or the advantages they received simply because of their nationality. As events led up to the war, their attitude did not change much, though the younger generation placed their hopes more and more in Germany. Perhaps the older generation's traditional suspicion of politics and their centuries-old experiences with great power politics prevented them from active participation in great numbers in the events of August and September 1939.

The German archives were destroyed; thus a documentary and numerical reconstruction of *Volksdeutsche* participation on the side of German troops is impossible. German and Polish sources naturally contradict each other. However, the Polish document collection, which attempts to prove that the ethnic Germans in their entirety acted as a fifth column, seems to be less than trustworthy. Some of its statements reflect the Polish fear. Mader estimates the number of people in "Hitler's underground divisions" at 25,000, but at the beginning of the war, at only 4,000.[5] If all 4,000 of them had been *Volksdeutsche*, this number would have represented only 0.004 percent of the ethnic German population. But the fact is that very few of these agents were *Volksdeutsche*, even those who were considered Germans. There is no doubt that there was a special force in the German armed forces, directed by the Intelligence Service. It operated in civilian clothes, often in Polish uniforms. It staged border incidents, performed sabotage actions, occupied strategically important points at the rear of the Polish army and held them until the arrival of the advancing regular army units. Since the majority of its members were Reich Germans, they could not be considered fifth columnists in the classical definition.

There is also no doubt that armed *Volksdeutsche* individually or in small groups interfered with the operations of the Polish army. Their number in the best-known Blomberg incident amounted—according to East German sources—only to two or three, with *Reichdeutsche* from Berlin and Danzig making up the rest of the 600-man group.[6]

Romania

The ethnic Germans of Romania were old favorites of Reich organizations dealing with the *Volksdeutsche*. OSSA and its successor, the *Vereinigte Finanzkontore* (whose cover name in Romania was Excelsior), as well as the foreign ministry, granted large amounts of money to folk German banks,[7] agricultural cooperatives, and building associations in Transylvania and the Bánát when they encountered financial difficulties not surmountable with their own resources. They also helped to found new companies. Besides this open economic help, the foreign ministry's secret fund was used for furthering German economic interests in minority areas. Naturally, VoMi also poured money into the folk German economy. All of these funds were used for cultural purposes—schools, libraries, and so on. There is no evidence that the funds were used for setting up secret fifth column *Volksdeutsche* organizations in Romania.

The finance ministry, conscious of the great shortage of foreign currency, advocated "the development and strengthening of National powers of resistance through self-help." The foreign ministry was convinced that in many instances self-help would be insufficient; therefore it advocated the revival of "economic activities by fresh credits" and sought to provide "the younger German generation with the means of acquiring land."[8] VoMi and the Nazi party wanted to use this money more directly for the realization of foreign political aims,[9] as well as for the strengthening of rightist groups within the *Volksdeutsche* population.

As a result of this divided opinion among the Reich German institutions, the folk Germans were partly encouraged and partly forced to cover their expenses from their own resources. The *Erneuerung* movement in Romania solved this problem by demanding from its members 4 percent of their yearly income as membership fees.[10]

Until 1937 the NSDAP did not participate in the financing of the *Volksgruppe*. Up to that time, even Fabritius had to pay for his trips to Berlin when he went there to give reports or receive information.[11] After 1938, when Fabritius lost party support, the foreign ministry provided him with financial aid of an uncertain amount.[12] There are indications that the *Volksdeutsche* of Romania also received financial support from Admiral Canaris,[13] but this money did not further ethnic German goals. It was used, for example, for the organization of folk German units for the defense of the Romanian oil fields.[14]

It seems that Reich institutions generally found it more convenient to provide money to the Iron Guard and Romanian politicians to promote German foreign political aims than to support the *Volksgruppe*. Events proved that their judgment was correct. Both the Iron Guard and Antonescu's government tried to satisfy Germany's needs for the war against the Soviet Union. They served the German side by furnishing the greatest possible amount of resources to the German war machine, and also through the active participation of the Romanian army in the war. The German high command looked upon Antonescu's Romania "as the most loyal and reliable ally of the National Socialist German Reich."[15] The German ethnic group, therefore, could not better serve the German Reich than by supporting and collaborating with the Antonescu government. Because of the close cooperation between the two governments there was no reason for fifth column activities by the ethnic

Germans of Romania. Certainly if the need for such activities had arisen, many fanatical Nazis would have been willing to perform them.

Andreas Schmidt put the most trustworthy Nazis in control of the ethnic German organization. Under his pressure these cadres of the *Volksgruppe* were among the first to volunteer for the Waffen SS. Their number, between 1,000 and 1,500, represented 0.01 percent of the ethnic group—a negligible number. The ethnic Germans of Romania never became a fifth column because the German Reich did not need such activities in Romania.

Yugoslavia

The ethnic Germans of Yugoslavia adjusted very quickly to their new minority status after World War I. Their leadership attempted to secure minority rights through legal means. The Yugoslavian state, desiring to become a Serbian nation-state, used economic and educational measures to force the national minorities into obedience. Ironically, not the Germans but the Croats were the strongest opponents of these measures. Still, the German minority group, with the help of the VDA, was able to avoid losing too many members.

The great changes in the behavior of a small number of ethnic Germans (*Erneuerungsbewegung*) occurred under the impact of Nazi Germany. At the same time, 1934, a rapprochement between the Reich and Yugoslavia began. As long as this cooperation lasted, the Reich government tried to prevent any disturbance. The swift reaction of Hitler and the surprisingly rapid collapse of the Yugoslavian army made a fifth column unnecessary. Therefore, very few sabotage acts or other fifth column activities were carried out by the *Volksdeutsche*. This passivity of the ethnic Germans of Yugoslavia is interpreted by writers from the minority group as a sign of loyalty to Yugoslavia. In light of later developments and the *Volksdeutsche* participation in the Waffen SS, this interpretation seems to be biased. Although the *Volksgruppe* was not Nazi in its entirety, its alternate solution, complete autonomy in a state based on the cooperation of different nationalities,[16] was no less disloyal, for it would have led to the dissolution of Yugoslavia. Very few of the ethnic Germans actively turned against the Nazi war machine. On August 15, 1943, the number of active anti-Nazi ethnic Germans fighting in the ranks of the Yugoslav National Liberation Army reached the size of a company: "right up to the end of the war, the major part of the German national minority remained on the side of Hitler..."[17]

Hungary

To evaluate the attitude, loyal or disloyal, of the ethnic Germans of Hungary is a complicated task. In order to avoid the trap of generalization, it is necessary to analyze the leaders and membership of the *Volksbund* of Hungary separately.

In 1934 Dr. Franz Anton Basch wrote a pamphlet[18] about the Germans living in Hungary and for an introduction he quoted the little poem of Jacob Bleyer, who was the founder of the *Ungarländish-Deutschen Volksbindung-verein.* It is worth quoting the last stanza of this Swabian song:

> Gott segne Ungarn, dich o Heimatland!
> Der Heldenwall der Christenheit
> Mit deutschen Herzen, treuer Schwabenhand
> Steh'n fest zu dir wir alle Zeit.

Anton Basch separated himself completely from Bleyer's convictions, expressed in this poem. Basch ended his career as a zealous servant of Nazi Germany.

Basch had become the leader of the radical Swabians in 1934. He rose to prominence because he was the personal secretary of Bleyer and received support from the German Reich. His pamphlet *Der Deutsche in Ungarn* was published in Berlin, but did not concern itself with controversial political issues. Within a year Basch had a head-on collision with the successor of Jacob Bleyer, Dr. Franz Kussbach. In their struggle for control of the UDV, both sought help from the German embassy and from Reich German institutions. Then Basch organized his own Bund and separated himself from the moderate Swabians, who remained faithful to the principles of Gratz. After the separation Basch played a tragicomic role. He firmly believed that the only hope of the German minorities lay in the Nazi party and in the government of the Third Reich. He was constantly double-crossed and used by both of them. His "victory," which seemingly secured almost complete autonomy for the VDU, was a Pyrrhic one that caused the deaths of 20,000 Swabians serving in the Waffen SS, and provided the excuse for the postwar Hungarian government to expel 240,000 ethnic Germans from Hungary.

Although in front of the People's Court during his war crimes trial,[19] Basch denied the charges and defended himself with his naiveté, the fact remained that his activities were treacherous, not only in the eyes of the Hungarian public, but also in the light of the international laws incorporated in the minority treaties. It is regrettable that some of his followers and admirers even today look upon him and his close associates as martyrs of the ethnic German cause. They were not martyrs, only willing puppets of the Third Reich.

Basch boasted that the membership of the *Volksbund* at the end of 1940 was near 50,000. If we accept 533,021 as the actual number of ethnic Germans in Hungary, the *Volksbund* membership represented only a small (9 percent) minority. If we take the number based on using the mother tongue (719,749), the *Volksbund* members made up only 6 percent of the ethnic German population. The *Volksbund* claimed that the Second Vienna Decision placed the protection of the Hungarian ethnic Germans in the hands of Adolf Hitler. There was no doubt about their attitude: the *Volksbund* leaders abandoned their loyalty to Hungary and became the obedient followers of Nazi Germany.

But this does not mean that the membership also became disloyal. The Fidelity Movement launched, with the tacit support of the Hungarian government, a campaign to enlist the participation of ethnic Germans of Hungary. After a year of organized work it had recruited 2,000 Swabian members in Tolna County and 8,500 in Baranya County, out of a Swabian population of 66,646 and 86,481, respectively.[20] In percentages, this was 3 percent and 9 percent. Thus the majority of ethnic Germans tried to remain neutral. The above calculation proves that the *Volksbund* did not represent the majority of ethnic Germans in Hungary. The great majority tried to stay away from politics. This attitude does not prove that they were disloyal.

There are two even more important facts that support our statement. In 1935 the Minority Educational Order in Council gave the right to the parent association to decide the language of their school. The VDU in 1941 started a campaign demanding that the Hungarian government rescind this right. Why was this necessary? Because the Bund did not command the loyalty of Swabian parents, who in 1941 still preferred to send their children to Hungarian schools. Is this fact not a clear declaration of loyalty to the Hungarian state?

The total number of ethnic Germans fit for military service was about 100,000. One-fifth of them served in formations of the German Reich (Waffen SS, Wehrmacht, Todt Organization). (The majority of these came from the Bácska Swabians and Transylvanian Saxons, that is, not from the *Volksdeutsche* of Trianon Hungary.) Four-fifths served in the Hungarian army and in paramilitary formations (civil air defense, and so forth). This number again indicates clearly that the majority of ethnic Germans remained loyal.

Finally, the number of expelled Germans seems also to prove our statement. The Hungarian government in 1945 estimated the number of Swabians who were to be expelled at 250,000. The final number of ethnic Germans actually expelled was 240,000,[21] of whom 228,000 migrated to East and West Germany and 12,000 to Austria. These numbers include whole families. Since Swabian families averaged four members and whole families were expelled if one or two members had been members of the *Volksbund* or of the Waffen SS,[22] the membership in these organizations could not have exceeded 60,000, which was only 12 percent of the German minority.[23] Some 424,540 ethnic Germans remained, if not positively loyal to Hungary by joining anti-Bund groups, then at least negatively loyal by *not joining* the Bund or the Waffen SS.

The aim of our study was to investigate the relationship between the German minority groups living in the different East Central European countries and the Third Reich. Although it is impossible to produce a detailed account of this relationship within the framework of a short study, we hope that our work has contributed to the better understanding not only of the German minority problem but also of minority problems in general.

It is clear to us that any judgment that regards the German minority groups either as conscious fifth columnists or as unconscious instruments of the Third Reich's imperialist designs is oversimplified and misleading. The German minority groups living in East Central Europe were not all educated (or, if you prefer, indoctrinated) with the same philosophy or ideology. Their differences in historical experiences, religion, lifestyle, and hopes for the future divided them. Their relationship to the Third Reich varied according to their different individual beliefs. The same individual beliefs influenced their attitude toward their respective state governments. Thus we found conservative, liberal, Marxist, and Nazi elements and organizations within the same German minority group in each of the countries discussed.

One characteristic that might have been common in all the German minority groups was their desire to preserve their Germanness. This was not the product of Nazi influences, nor was it a special quality of German minorities. All the minority groups in East Central Europe desired to preserve their ethnic distinctiveness, and their right to do so was recognized by the minority treaties. Of course the liberal-minded dreamers who drew up the treaties hoped for the gradual disappearance of the entire minority problem through a process of natural assimilation. Just the opposite happened. Instead of speeding up assimilation, the minority treaties actually slowed down the process because some of their consequences were unforeseen by their authors.

Natural assimilation is necessarily a slow process. The nationalistic spirit of the post-World War period makes it understandable why all the governments tried to speed up this process. In most cases, their attempts to do this worked in an opposite direction and actually strengthened the consciousness and resistance to assimilation of the ethnic groups. It was a genuinely democratic minority policy that promoted natural assimilation (intermarriages, for example, caused the Reich German authorities quite a problem).

The treaties secured for the minorities the right to organize their own cultural and other associations, maintain their own schools, and use their own language—even in addressing administrative and judicial authorities. The unforeseen difficulty created by these privileges lay in the fact that language is more than an instrument of communication; it is the vehicle of national culture and national spirit. How could folk German boys and girls become loyal Polish, Czech, or Romanian citizens when both at school and at home they used only German, had no contact and experiences with non-German speaking boys and girls, and instead of learning about Chopin or Smetana learned only about Goethe and Wagner? It was inevitable that the ethnic Germans educated in the German spirit, using the German language, would be regarded by German leaders already in the time of Stresemann as outposts of Germandom. It was also inevitable that these folk German groups would develop a divided loyalty between the state they lived in and the Reich, which remained their cultural motherland, and that in a conflict between their state and Germany their practical German culture and consciousness would influence them to side with Germany, no matter what the form of government there.

There was another, perhaps even more important, consequence of the right of minorities to use their language in the schools and learn the German cultural heritage. Because the folk German youngsters learned the state language only superficially or not at all, their career opportunities were restricted to the German communities. Since higher intellectual and professional positions were very limited within the ethnic community, the young ethnic German intellectuals who spoke only German were forced to accept positions and jobs below the level of their education.

Therefore the right to maintain German schools had a double negative effect. It prevented assimilation by restricting job opportunities, and at the same time produced half-educated intellectuals who were frustrated because they had to work in jobs below their expectations. The young intellectuals had three choices: they could learn the state language fast, take the language examinations, and seek employment outside the German community; they could look for some other way to make themselves more important and thus increase self-esteem; or they could escape to Germany and make a career for themselves within the German Reich.

The first choice was hard because the language examination required long and arduous preparation. The third required a certain adventurous spirit and willingness to face the unknown. The second choice seemed the most inviting: a leadership position within the political/social/cultural organizations of the folk groups compensated the ethnic German intellectuals for the relatively low positions they held in everyday life. (There is here a striking similarity with many of the ethnic group leaders of European origin in the United States.) Those who made this choice (the majority) now had a personal interest in preventing the decline of the number of Germans, that is, in preventing assimilation or even conciliation between the minority group and the state. At the same time, although it sounds contradictory, many of them honestly tried to serve the interests of their compatriots. Their method of rendering this service depended on personal convictions and the age group to which they belonged. Our study shows that generally the older generation served the folk group by seeking a *modus vivendi* with the government, while the younger ones placed their hopes in Germany and in Nazism. We also found examples of pro-Nazi folk group leaders who turned against the wishes of their Nazi patrons in an effort to serve their folk group honestly.

The simple, uneducated members of the different minority groups usually followed their leaders' policy, but the rise of Nazism caused confusion in their ranks. Economic hardship, unemployment, Reich German financial aid, and in many cases simple opportunism drove the less educated folk Germans into the Nazi-controlled or Nazi-oriented organizations. Those who volunteered for the Waffen SS represented only a minority of the *Volksgruppe*. As Germany gained control over the folk Germans through occupation of the countries or through special agreements with the respective governments, the male ethnic German population was drafted into the Waffen SS. Thus service in the SS did not necessarily mean Nazi party membership, though some folk Germans did commit atrocities as members of the Waffen SS.

Our study shows a fifth column did exist in the various countries, but its numbers were insignificant. Fifth columnists caused some local damage and confusion with their sabotage and terrorism, but to attribute the defeat of the Polish and Yugoslavian armies to their activities is to overestimate their importance. Such a judgment underestimates the capacity of the two armies. Their valiant fight ended in defeat because of overwhelming numbers and technical superiority of the German Wehrmacht, and not because of isolated incidents created by folk German armed saboteurs.

A special case are the Jews. Although the Successor States attempted to create a separate ethnic minority group by recording the Jews separately in their census, the great majority of assimilated ethnic German Jews (and to a lesser extent the ethnic Hungarian Jews) remained loyal to their chosen nationality. They continued to register as Germans, participated in the life of the ethnic groups (in many instances as leaders), and worked to preserve the German language, culture, and tradition. Naturally the triumph of Nazism forced them to withdraw from the ethnic group. Still, they did not altogether reject the Germany with which they had identified. Even many of those who migrated to the United States after World War II kept their German consciousness and became active in German ethnic life in their new home.

The history of the German minority groups' relationship with the Third Reich is a tragic story for which the minority treaties provided the preconditions. The folk Germans wanted to preserve their German identity. In order to do so, they asked for help from the Reich. The Reich government gave them the help they requested, while using them to promote German foreign political aims. The respective state governments came to consider the German minority groups as villains because they provided an excuse for the Reich to intervene in their domestic political affairs. The governments could not implement countermeasures against the Reich; they could and did against the divided folk Germans. War psychosis, and then the war itself, sharpened the conflict to the point where reconciliation was impossible. After the defeat of Germany most of the ethnic Germans were expelled from East Central Europe.

The postwar expulsions caused hardship and, in many cases, punished the innocent. None of the expelled ethnic Germans we interviewed, however, want to go back to the territories in which they lived before the war. They have found new homes, new friends, and a higher living standard. Those who migrated to Austria and Germany are content with their new life in the home their ancestors left centuries before. Those who migrated overseas have tried to forget the past and have created a new life for themselves. They have lost whatever desire they may have had to remain Germans forever. Our questionnaires show that only one out of every ten German families living in Canada or the United States wants its children to retain a German identity. Nine out of ten want them to assimilate. They could—as other minority groups do—organize their own schools, nurture their ethnic heritage, and isolate themselves from the rest of the population. But they do not. The members of their associations are mostly old people, and the readership of German-language papers is dwindling. From their bitter experience they have learned that loyalty is indivisible.

NOTES

Introduction

1. Although this fantastic image of the German has begun to fade, it is still very much alive in the minds of ethnic Germans who suffered because of it. Many ethnic Germans, particularly the less educated ones, refused to be interviewed for this study or to fill out questionnaires because they suspected that we wanted to resurrect this stereotype. The number expelled was approximately 5,500,000 (calculated from data in Joseph B. Schechtman, *Postwar Population Transfers in Europe, 1945–1955 [Philadelphia: University of Pennsylvania, 1962], pp. 93, 206–208, 270, 272, 274, 282).

2. Prominent among these studies are Bohumil Bilek, *Fifth Column at Work* (London, 1945); Louis De Jong, *The German Fifth Column in the Second World War* (Chicago, 1956); M. Wojciechowski and R. Breyer, *Das Deutsche Reich und Polen 1932–1937: Aussenpolitik und Volksgruppenfragen* (Würzburg, 1955); and Endre Arató, "A Volksbund és a Harmadik Birodalom" [The Volksbund and the Third Reich], *Valóság*, IV, No. 1 (1961), pp. 88–90. For further titles see Bibliography.

3. Ten treaties were drawn up in the years 1919–21 between the five Principal Allied and Associated Powers on the one hand, and Poland, Czechoslovakia, Yugoslavia, Romania, Greece, Armenia, Austria, Bulgaria, Hungary, and Turkey on the other. The treaties were placed under the guarantee of the League of Nations. Cf. *The League of Nations and Minorities*, Information Section (League of Nations Secretariat, 1923), pp. 13–14.

4. William E. Rappard, "Minorities and the League," in Carnegie Endowment for International Peace, *International Conciliation* (New York, 1926), No. 222, p. 20.

5. Revision of the treaties could be implemented with the unanimous vote of the General Assemby of the League of Nations according to Article XIX of its basic charter.

6. "Successors" of the Austro-Hungarian Empire.

7. Cf. N. Gordon Levin, Jr., ed., *The Zionist Movement in Palestine and World Politics, 1880–1918* (Lexington, Mass.: Heath, 1974), p. ix. (Hereinafter referred to as *Zionist Movement*).

8. Radomír Luža, *The Transfer of the Sudeten Germans* (New York: New York University Press, 1964), p. 36. (Hereinafter referred to as Luža, *Transfer*.) See also Peter Meier, Bernard D. Weinryb, Eugene Duschinsky and Nicholas Sylvania, *The Jews in the Soviet Sattelites* (Syracuse, N.Y.: Syracuse University Press, 1953), p. 53.

9. We shall name these assimilated Jews in our study wherever appropriate.

Chapter I: Germany's Concern for Germans Abroad

1. For a short account of the history of these German migrations see G. C. Paikert, *The Danube Swabians* (The Hague: Martinus Nijhoff, 1967), pp. 7–42.

2. Louis de Jong, *The German Fifth Column in the Second World War* (Chicago: University of Chicago Press, 1956), p. 268.

3. Paikert, *Danube Swabians*, p. 23, 3n; Viktor Vajna-István Nádai, *Hadtörténelem* [War History] (Budapest: Stádium, 1935), p. 279.

168   *Notes*

4. Hugh Seton-Watson, *Eastern Europe between the Wars, 1918–1941* (New York: Harper Torch, 1967), 3rd rev. ed., p. 66.

5. Paikert, *Danube Swabians*, p. 98.

6. *France* received Alsace and Lorraine; the Saar Valley was placed under the care of the League of Nations and the Rhineland was placed under French military occupation. *Denmark* was awarded the territory of Schleswig. *Belgium* received a narrow strip of land along the German frontier. *Poland* obtained an outlet to the Baltic Sea through the Danzig Corridor (Danzig itself was placed under the League of Nations' supervision) and took control of the eastern part of Silesia after the plebiscite of March 1921.

7. For example, there were about 200,000 Germans who emigrated from Czechoslovakia alone. Österreichisches Staatsarchiv, *Prague Berichte*, 1937, Judmeier to Schmidt, Prague, November 17, 1937, fol. 809. (Hereinafter referred to as *RAA* [for *Reports of the Austrian Ambassadors*].)

8. *R 57 neu*/1009-2, p. 1. The VDA was the successor of the *Allgemeiner Deutscher Schulverein zur Erhaltung des Deutschtums im Ausland* (Universal German School Association for the Preservation of Germandom Abroad), founded in 1881 as a branch of the *Deutsche Schulverein* of Vienna.

9. Alfred Kruck, *Geschichte des Alldeutschen Verbandes, 1890–1939* (Wiesbaden: Franz Steiner Verlag, 1954) Veröffentlichungen des Instituts für Europäische Geschichte, Mainz. Vol. 3., p. 216. (Hereinafter referred to as Kruck, *Alldeutscher Verband*.)

10. *R 57 neu*/1009-2, No. 15016. Yearly report of VDA. 1926. For a detailed analysis of the problems of pan-Germans see George L. Mosse, *The Crisis of German Ideology* (New York: Grosset & Dunlap, 1964), pp. 218–233.

11. Mosse, *German Ideology*, p. 220.

12. *R 57 neu*/1009-1. Reported in the *Bergische Zeitung*, Wald, December 24, 1928.

13. Paikert, *Danube Swabians*, p. 103, ln. For some of the transactions of OSSA see *Inland II* g, 241.

14. Hans-Adolf Jacobsen, ed., *Hans Steinacher, Bundesleiter des VDA, 1933–1937: Erinnerungen und Dokumente* (Boppard: Harald Boldt Verlag, 1970), Schriften des Bundesarchivs, No. 19, p. xxxviii. (Hereinafter referred to as Jacobsen, *Steinacher*.) The VDA budget exceeded RM2,000,000 in 1926. *R 57 neu*/1009–2, No. 15016, yearly report of VDA, 1926.

15. Data for the year 1933 are in Jacobsen, *Steinacher*, p. 29.

16. *R 57 neu*/1009-2, No. 18585.

17. *R 57 neu*/1009-2, No. 16216, resolution of the Czechoslovak government, Prague, May 25, 1927.

18. See, for example, the attitude of the Hungarian government toward the *Wandervögel* movement. *Wandervögel*, which means "birds of passage," was the romantic name of a hiking association whose members visited ethnic German territories and tried to spread German culture and German self-consciousness among the minority group members. For further details see Gerhard Ziemer and Hans Wolf, *Wandervögel und Freideutsche Jugend* (Bad Godesberg: Voggenreiter Verlag, 1962). Activities in Czechoslovakia described in *Ost Dok. 20*/I-B3 No. 6; in Hungary, Paikert, *Danube Swabians*, pp. 104–106.

19. *R 57 neu*/1009-3, *Berliner Tribune*, November 1, 1930.

20. Mosse, *German Ideology*, Chapters 10 and 15.

21. *R 57 neu*/1014-1.

22. *R 57 neu*/1009-2, No. 15016, p. 3.

23. *R 57 neu*/1014-1.

24. Gustav Stresemann was only one of a long list of assimilated German Jews whose contributions to German culture, art, literature, poetry, music, and so on, are undeniable. Stresemann's political credo, his support of pan-Germanism, his efforts to preserve Germandom

outside the frontiers of the German republic, are especially interesting from the point of view of our study, since the organizations that became predominant under his administration were useful instruments of the Nazi imperialistic foreign policy. See Henry B. Bretton, *Stresemann and the Revision of Versailles* (Stanford, Cal.: Stanford University Press, 1953); Hans W. Gatzke, *Stresemann and the Rearmament of Germany, 1924–1928* (New York: Bookman, 1963); Annelise Thimme, *Gustav Stresemann* (Hannover, 1957); Henry Ashby Turner, Jr., *Stresemann and the Politics of the Weimar Republic* (Princeton, N.J.: Princeton University, 1963).

25. *R 57 neu*/1009-3, *Berliner Tribune*, November 1, 1930; *R 57 neu*/1009–2.

26. Unemployment passed the five-million mark in 1931. Alan Bullock, *Hitler: A Study in Tyranny* (New York: Harper Torch, 1964), p. 189.

27. Calculated on the basis of the 1933 budget. Jacobsen, *Steinacher*, p. 30.

28. *Ibid.*, p. xii, 37–38.

29. Bullock, *Hitler*, p. 278.

30. *Ibid.*, p. 189.

31. *Ibid.*, p. 278.

32. Wertheimer is another example of how strongly Jewish people assimilated in imperial and republican Germany to the German nation and ideology.

33. Dr. Wilhelm Frick was appointed minister of interior of January 30, 1933. He was one of the original followers of Hitler and had taken part in the 1923 Nazi putsch attempt. In 1929 he became the first Nazi who assumed a state office, as Thüringian minister of interior. Bullock, *Hitler*, p. 150.

34. Office of the United States Chief Counsel for Prosecution of Axis Criminality, *Nazi Conspiracy and Aggression*, 11 vols. (Washington D.C.: U.S. Government Printing Office, 1948), Supplement B, p. 1490 (hereinafter referred to as *Nazi Conspiracy*).

35. Jacobsen, *Steinacher*, p. 27. Although the doorman acted on his own initiative, his action was unquestionably regarded by Frick as a wonderful opportunity and excuse to remove Jewish leaders from the DAI. In any system other than Nazism the affair would have ended with the prompt firing of the impertinent doorman and not with the firing of the leader of the DAI.

36. *Ibid.*, p. 28. For a short review of the convictions and activities of Csáki as secretary general of the DAI see Paikert, *Danube Swabians*, p. 110, ln.

37. Gessler was already an antagonist of Hitler during the 1923 Nazi putsch attempts. Bullock, *Hitler*, pp. 100–120.

38. Jacobesen, *Steinacher*, p. xxi. See also pp. 1–3.

39. *Ibid.*, p. 4, 3n, presents the supporting arguments for this assumption.

40. Neurath testified to Hitler's feeling against Rosenberg. *Nazi Conspiracy*, Supp. B, p. 1490.

41. On May 2, only two days after the VDA elections, the trade unions were dissolved. This was certainly a major political operation requiring enormous preparation, and it could have diverted the party's attention from the VDA election.

42. For Steinacher's philosophy, see Jacobsen, *Steinacher*, pp. xxix–xxxi.

43. *Ibid.*, pp. 9–11

44. *Ibid.*, pp. 59–61. The implementation of the "leadership principle" meant the transformation of the VDA organization from an elected democratic hierarchy into an authoritarian hierarchy in which the lower officials were appointed by superiors.

45. Hans Otto Roth was one of the conservative leaders of the *Volksdeutsche* in Romania, *Ost DOK. 16 Rum.*/90, interview by Hans Wüscht of Gerhard Fabritius, p. 5. Also see p. 107 of this study.

46. Jacobsen, *Steinacher*, p. 20, 9n.

47. *Ibid.*, pp. 101–103.

48. Kruck, *Aldeutscher Verband*, p. 216.

49. Bullock, *Hitler*, p. 246.

50. Kruck, *Alldeutscher Verband*, p. 193.

51. *Ibid.*, p. 211.

52. Bullock, *Hitler*, p. 255

53. Kruck, *Alldeutscher Verband*, p. 216. One of the members of the League who became well known in the anti-Nazi resistance was Fabian von Schlabrendorf. His book, *The Secret War against Hitler* (New York: Pitman, 1965), gives insights into the personalities in the anti-Nazi movement and their activities.

54. Gerhard L. Weinberg, *The Foreign Policy of Hitler's Germany* (Chicago: University of Chicago Press, 1970), p. 33.

55. *Nazi Conspiracy*, Supp. B, p. 337.

56. Such as the preparation for the putsch against Dollfuss in Austria. Weinberg, *Hitler's Germany*, p. 94.

57. International Military Tribunal, *Trial of the Major War Criminals before the International Military Tribunal*, 42 vols. (Nuremberg, 1945–46), X, 12–13. (Hereinafter referred to as *Nuremberg Trials.*)

58. For details see the chapters dealing with individual countries.

59. Paikert, *Danube Swabians*, p. 110

60. *Nuremberg Trials*, X, 62

61. Jacobsen, *Steinacher*, p. 16, Doc. No. 4. *Auslandsdeutsche* in Steinacher's definition included *all* Germans living abroad, that is, both citizens of the Reich and ethnic Germans who were citizens of the countries they lived in.

62. *Ibid.*, pp. 34–36.

63. Hess was unconditionally loyal to Hitler at this time, though he deserted him later and escaped to England on May 10, 1941. See Hess's final plea at his war crimes trial in *Nazi Conspiracy*, Supp. B, pp. 133–142.

64. An example of his statements is the comment he made at the November 1, 1933, meeting of the VR: "There is only one highest authority: the one which is approved by the entire German people. This authority was given to us in the person of the Führer. There should not be made any difference anymore in the value of state Germans and Germans abroad. The folk groups [abroad] have duties to their native country and to the entire German people," (*Gesamt-volk*). Jacobsen, *Steinacher*, Doc. No. 22, p. 107.

65. *Ibid.*, Doc. No. 31, p. 164, and Doc. No. 31, p. 165.

66. For the opponents and supporters of VDA see *ibid.*, p. xiv.

67. For a figure illustrating the support given to different ethnic German groups by different German state and party authorities see *ibid.*, p. xxiii; see also respective chapters in this book.

68. The Kursell Bureau was a secret office of the NSDAP in 1936, actually a "control center for the 'defensive activities' of German minorities throughout the world," Robert L. Koehl, *RKFDV: German Resettlement and Population Policy, 1939–1945* (Cambridge, Mass.: Harvard University, 1957), pp. 36–37; see also Jacobsen, *Steinacher*, pp. 244–246.

69. Jacobsen, *Steinacher*, Doc. No. 102, p. 390.

70. Hans George von Mackensen, the German ambassador to Hungary, advised the Hungarian state secretary for minority affairs to negotiate with Lorenz and Behrends in order to settle the problems created by the activity of the Nazi ethnic German *Kameradschaftsbund*. Ránki-Pamlényi-Tikovszky-Juhász, *A Wilhelmstrasse és Magyarország* [The Wilhelm Street and Hungary] (Budapest: Kossuth Könyvkiadó, 1968), note of Mackensen, Bonn, November 24, 1937, Doc. No. 1021, p. 242.

71. Adolf Hitler, *Mein Kampf* (Boston, Houghton Mifflin, 1943), Sentry ed., p. 652.

72. Jacobsen, *Steinacher*, p. xiii, 10n, quotes Hitler's statement made to VDA representatives during an audience in December 1933, according to Dr. Robert Ernst's memoirs. In the last sentence Hitler made remarks about the Bánát Swabians living in Hungary. It is an obvious mistake. The Bánát Swabians lived in Romania and Yugoslavia until 1941. Such a mistake means either that Hitler was not familiar with the East Central European boundaries in 1933, or that Ernst's memoirs are faulty.

73. Hitler, *Mein Kampf*, p. 629.

74. *Ibid.*, pp. 647–648; Paikert, *Danube Swabians*, p. 141, 1n.

75. *R 57 neu*/1016. Report of the folk scientific work circles of VDA, Berlin, January 3, 1937, stated: "Those Germans must feel that they, too, belong to the Reich; then this feeling can be used for the benefit of the Reich."

76. For example, Hungary's *Volksdeutsche* were the responsibility of the local branch of the VDA in Karlsruhe, *R 57 neu*/1014–2. *Badische Presse*, Karlsruhe, February 3, 1934.

77. *R 57 neu*/1015-2 DAI, 26359/1933, p. 7.

78. *Ibid.*, At the 1933 VDA meeting the Czechoslovak delegation numbered eighteen, the Polish fifteen , the Hungarian and Romanian two each, and the Yugoslavian only one.

79. *R 57 neu*/1015-2, Kundschreiben No. 39, VDA.

80. The titles of these lectures were strictly academic, but the lecturers always made their presentations in the *Volksdeutsche* spirit. These trips paid returns to the Reich sometimes several years later. For example, the participants of a 1927 trip from Yugoslavia organized the "Association of Germany's Friends" in 1932, *R 57 neu*/1005-22 and 1072-49.

81. *R 57 neu*/1005-22.

82. *R 57 neu*/1015-2.

83. *R 57 neu*/1009, VDA No. 12855.

84. Jacobsen, *Steinacher*, p. 329.

85. See newspaper clippings in *R 57 neu*/1014-2.

86. *R 57 neu*/1016.

87. In Silesia during the economic crisis of 1937 the VDA recommended just that. *R 57 neu*/1016. See Chapter IV.

88. *Inland II g*, 242, R 2/11614.

89. *R 2*/14938, fol. 1.

90. *Inland II g*, 241, p. 115.

91. Paikert, *Danube Swabians*, p. 112.

92. The *Deutsche Stiftung* was organized in cooperation with the foreign ministry for the purpose of providing financial aid to the *Volksdeutsche* to lighten their economic burdens.

93. *Inland II g*, 242 and *R 2*/11614.

94. Jacobsen, *Steinacher*, Doc. No. 85, p. 328.

95. Paikert, *Danube Swabians*, p. 112

96. Example in the 1931 VDA budget: "At the disposal of the chairman RM1,321 single supports, RM410, grants, RM4,308, communication with the *Auslandsdeutsche* RM17,841." *R 57 neu*/1009-3.

97. *Inland II g*, 241. In 1936, for example, RM60,000 was sent to Romania, RM10,000 to Danzig.

98. *Inland II g*, 241, p. 33. OSSA had affiliated companies in Czechoslovakia(2), Danzig(7), Romania (2), Upper Silesia (1).

Chapter II: Sudeten German Dilemma

1. Luža, *Transfer*, pp. 3, 36. Since the Czechoslovak census of 1921 counted the Jews as an independent ethnic group to reduce the number of Germans and Hungarians, the actual number of Germans was probably 1 percent higher. For a comparison of the different minority groups and their evolution in Czechoslovakia see Alfred Bohmann, *Menschen und Grenzen*, 4 vols. (Köln: Verlag Wissenschaft und Politik, 1975), IV, 96–97.

2. Luža, *Transfer*, p. 40.

3. Elizabeth Wiskemann, *Czechs and Germans: A Study of the Struggle in the Historical Province of Bohemia and Moravia* (London: Oxford University, 1938), p. 85.

4. Luža, *Transfer*, p. 40.

5. Dr. Josef Starkbaum and Dr. H. C. Emanuel Reichenberger, *Heimat der Sudetendeutschen* (Vienna: Volkstum Verlag, 1967), pp. 273–274.

6. Tomáš Masaryk, the "Father of Czechoslovakia," was president of the Republic 1918–35. Eduard Beneš, Masaryk's closest associate, was foreign minister 1918–35, then succeeded Masaryk as president, 1935–38.

7. The Slovaks agreed to join the new Czechoslovak state on the basis of the principle of autonomy in the Pittsburgh agreement of May 1918, the Ruthenes in the Philadelphia agreement of October 1918.

8. Arnold Toynbee, *Survey of International Affairs, 1933* (London: Oxford University, 1934), p. 197. (Hereinafter referred to as Toynbee, *Survey 1933*).

9. F. W. Bruegel, "The Germans in Pre-War Czechoslovakia," in Victor S. Mamatey and Radomir Luža, eds., *A History of the Czechoslovak Republic, 1918–1942* (Princeton, N.J.: Princeton University, 1973), p. 172. For an analysis of Czechoslovakia's military-geographic and strategic conditions see A. T. Komjáthy, *The Crises of France's East Central European Diplomacy, 1933–1938* (Boulder, Colo.: East European Quarterly, distributed by Columbia University Press, 1976), p. 8.

10. Toynbee, *Survey 1933*, p. 197. However, in the field of education Switzerland was less progressive than the old Austria-Hungary; see Otto Habsburg, *Döntés Európáról* [Decision about Europe] (Munich: Amerikai Magyar Kiadó, 1955), pp. 126–128.

11. Cf. Hungary, where organization of political parties based on nationality was forbidden. See p. 44.

12. *Statistical Yearbook of Czechoslovak Republic, 1929* (Prague, 1930).

13. Bruegel, "The Germans," in Mamatey-Luža, *Czechoslovak Republic*, p. 180; see also the article of Gardslaw Cesar and Bohenrich Cerny, "Die Deutsche Irredenta und die Henleinleute in der CSR in den Jahren 1930–1938," *Czechoslovensky Caspis Historicky*, No. 1 (1962), pp. 1–17 (translation by Schubert); and *Ost Dok. 20*/hi. 23.

14. It is interesting to note that the ethnic German youngsters who began their education in the early 1920s came of age about 1935.

15. *Ost Dok. 20*/I-B3, report of a correspondent of the DAI from Prague, October 13, 1926, No. 14.

16. See the telegram sent to President Masaryk by Dr. Funks, chairman of the *Bund*, on May 23, 1934, *Ost Dok. 20*/I B-3, No. 118.

17. *Ibid.* Though Spina was an ethnic German himself, he was a member of the German Christian Socialist party, and after his resignation in 1938, "remained active in the Democratic camp." Bruegel, "The Germans," in Mamatey-Luža, *Czechoslovak Republic*, p. 181.

18. The following description is taken from *Ost Dok. 20*/I B-3, No. 5. Johanes Strauda, "Sudentendeutsche Jugendbewegung Böhmerland." (Strauda was one of the founders of the organization.)

19. *Ost Dok. 20*/I-B3, No. 7, Dr. Gustave Schmiedbach, "Die Bereitschaft."

20. *Ost Dok. 20*/I-B3, No. 6.

21. Weinberg, *Foreign Policy*, p. 108.

22. Luža, *Transfer*, p. 98, 67n. Konrad Henlein was the leader of SDP.

23. *Ost Dok. 20*/I-B3. No. 4, Karl Richard Kern, "Socialistischer Jugendverband." Kern was a member of the Executive Committee of the Deutschen *Socialdemocratischen Arbeiterpartei in der Tschechoslovakei* (DSAP).

24. For details on these economic problems the reader is referred to Antonin Basch, *The Danube Basin and the German Economic Sphere* (New York, 1943); Alois Rasin, *Financial Policy of Czechoslovakia during the First Year of its History* (Oxford, 1923); and the study of Zora P. Pryor, "Czechoslovak Economic Development in the Interwar Period," in Mamatey-Luža, *Czechoslovak Republic*, pp. 188–215.

25. Kurt Vorbach, *200,000 Sudetendeutsche Zuviel!* (Munich, 1936), p. 110; of the 8,000,000 crown loan in the Sudetenland, 89 percent was held by Germans. (Hereinafter referred to as Vorbach, *200,000*).

26. The upper limit on estates to be retained was 500 hectares. Compensation amounted to about 25 percent of postwar value. Vaclav L. Beneš, "Czechoslovak Democracy and Its Problems," in Mamatey-Luža, *Czechoslovak Republic*, p. 90, 127n.

27. For example, the Schwarzenberg family was allowed to keep nearly 50,000 hectares—and fully 40 percent of the land originally sequestered was given back to its former owners. Vorbach, *200,000*, pp. 375–376; Wiskemann, *Czechs and Germans*, pp. 147–160.

28. The number of officially registered unemployed in February 1933 was 920,000. Of that number 69 percent (634,800) were Sudeten Germans. Jan M. Michal, "Postwar Economic Development," in Mamatey-Luža, *Czechoslovak Republic*, p. 442; Luža, *Transfer*, p. 16, 68n, points out correctly that the number of unemployed in the Sudetenland included many Czech workers, but the figures indicate a disproportionate number of unemployed Germans. The proportion of total to Sudeten unemployment is estimated at 800,000 to 500,000 (62 percent Sudeten) in Department of State, *Documents on German Foreign Policy, 1918–1945* (Washington, D.C.: U.S. Government Printing Office, 1957), C. V. Eisenlohr to Neurath, Prague, April 16, 1936, Doc. No. 284. (Hereinafter referred to as *DGFP*.)

29. For example, during the period 1919–35 the German postal union members lost 7,800 jobs, which were awarded to Czechs. *Ost Dok. 20*/I, B2, No. 6. Petition of the German postal union, 1935.

30. *Ost Dok. 20*/I, A, No. 17, report of Dr. Felix Luschka at the national meeting of the Christian Socialist party in 1938.

31. Vorbach, *200,000*, pp. 136, 139.

32. In the western part of Czechoslovakia, where many German Jews lived, anti-Semitism was almost unknown and Jews rose to positions of importance within their communities, the worker movement, and in the Social Democratic Party. See Peter Meier, B.D. Weinryb, Eugene Duschinsky and Nicholas Sylvain, *The Jews in the Soviet Satellites* (Syracuse, N.Y.: Syracuse University Press, 1953), pp. 17–19. (Hereinafter referred to as *Jews in the Satellites*.)

33. Victor S. Mamatey, "The Development of Czechoslovak Democracy, 1920–1938," in Mamatey-Luža, *Czechoslovak Republic*, p. 99.

34. The Czech National Socialist party, not to be confused with the Nazi party, was led by Beneš.

35. Mamatey, "Development of Czechoslovak Democracy," pp. 178–179.

36. *Statistical Yearbook of the Czechoslovak Republic, 1929*.

37. *R 57 neu*/1009-2, No. 16216. This German majority rapidly began to lose Jewish members. With the rise of anti-Semitism, the Jews chose to side with the Czechs, hoping that the state would protect them. Because of this change in loyalty, the popular belief of ultranationalist Czechs was that the Jews were German agents, and the popular belief among the ethnic Germans was that they were Czech government agents. See Meier, *Jews in the Satellites*, pp. 58–59.

38. One of those sentenced was Paul Illing, who became secretary of the executive board of the *Sudetendeutsche Landsmannschaft* (Sudeten German Compatriots) in the German Federal Republic in 1960. *Ost Dok. Hi*/No. 6–1.

39. *DGFP*, C, I, Koch to Neurath, Prague, June 19, 1933, Doc. No. 326.

40. In September 1932 another group belonging to the Jungsturm was sentenced to jail "on charges of having attacked the safety of the state by organizing National Socialist Stormtroops," *DGFP*, C, I, Doc. No. 326, 2n.

41. This Sudeten German branch of the National Socialist group traced its history back to the German National Workers' League of Bohemia, Moravia, and Silesia in the 1890s through the pan-German Schonerer Movement in Austria-Hungary, the formation of the German Workers party in 1904, and of the German National Socialist party of Austria in 1918. After the war it split into Austrian and Sudeten German groups. *Ibid.* The latter group resembled its German counterpart in its anti-Semitism, pan-Germanism, and outer trappings. It had begun organizing in 1929. Wiskemann, *Czechs and Germans*, p. 135.

42. *DGFP*, C, II, Koch to Neurath, Prague, November 8, 1933, Doc. No. 51; June 19, 1933, Doc. No. 326 (*DGFP*, C, II, Koch to Neurath, Prague); October 5, 1933, Doc. No. 483; *Ost Dok. 20*/I, A, No. 29, p. 55.

43. *DGFP*, C, II, memorandum of Huffer, Berlin, January 12, 1934, Doc. No. 180. For a scholarly treatise on the activities of German emigrés see Lewis J. Endinger, *German Exile Politics* (Berkeley: University of California, 1956). This anti-Nazi activity undoubtedly was, to a great degree, the work of the German-Jewish members of the Social Democratic party.

44. Dr. R. Stransky, *The Educational and Cultural System of the Czechoslovak Republic* (Prague: Vladimir Zikes, 1939), p. 20. (Hereinafter referred to as Stransky, *Educational System.*)

45. Developments in schools from kindergarten to university are described in *ibid.*, pp. 53, 70–71, 89, 103–104, 111–112.

46. *Documents on International Affairs, 1938*, (London: Oxford University, 1951), II, pp. 117–120.

47. Rectors of the Czechoslovak Universities, *Czech School Facilities under the Austrian Government and German School Facilities under the Czech Government* (Prague, 1938), pp. 9–10; cited in Luža, *Transfer*, p. 41.

48. Wiskemann, *Czechs and Germans*, p. 208.

49. Calculated on the basis of Stransky, *Educational System*, p. 132.

50. Wiskemann, *Czechs and Germans*, pp. 208–212; Stransky, *Educational System*, pp. 133–137.

51. The detailed description of this university affair is in *Ost Dok. 20*/I, C1. No. 9.

52. Hitler never forgave the Sudeten German DSNAP members for their failure. Those who escaped the trial by crossing the border to Germany were "mistreated" and one of the leaders, Hans Krebs, was "shoved" into a subordinated administrative position in Berlin. *Ost Dok. 20*/I, A, No. 29, pp. 54–55.

53. *DGFP*, C, I, Koch to Neurath, Prague, March 22, 1933, Doc. No. 110.

54. *DGFP*, C, I, Doc. Nos. 132, 137, 180.

55. *DGFP*, C, I, Doc. No. 180; *Nuremberg Trials*, interrogation of Bohle, X, 13.

56. Jacobsen, *Steinacher*, Doc. No. 72.

57. *Ost Dok. 20*/I, A, No. 4, Appendix 4, p. 2.

58. The decline in the number of votes may be attributed to the turn of the Jewish intelligentsia to the Czech parties since they were "preponderantly liberal" and "linguistically and culturally assimilated" to the Czech nation. Meier, *Jews in the Satellites*, pp. 51–52.

59. *DGFP*, C, IV, Koch to Neurath, Prague, May 22, 1935; Doc. No. 99.

60. *Ost Dok. 20*/I, A, No. 4.

61. Jacobsen, *Steinacher*, p. 241; Ladislas Farago, *The Game of the Foxes* (New York: McKay, 1971), p. 15, states that Canaris told Hitler on September 8, 1935, that he "had just recruited Konrad Henlein, the Sudeten German leader, as an *Abwehr* agent." Farago's statement, is not documented, but even if it is true, it proves Henlein's orientation *away* from the Nazi party.

62. *RAA*, Judemeier to Schmidt, Prague, November 17, 1937, Doc. No. Z1 402.

63. *Ost Dok. 20*/I, A, No. 4; Jacobsen, *Steinacher*, Doc. No. 101.

64. Election results: SPD 44, Social Democrats 11, Christian Socialists 6, Agrarian 5, Sudeten German election block 9; total 75. Walter H. Mallory, ed. *Political Handbook of the World: Parliaments, Parties, and Press*, 1936 (New York: Harper, for Council of Foreign Relations, 1936), pp. 45–48.

65. *DGFP*, C, IV, Koch to Neurath, Prague, May 22, 1935, Doc. No. 99.

66. Milan Hodža was of Slovak origin and thus sensitive to minority problems.

67. This group represented a very small minority even among the leftists.

68. These two tendencies naturally received support from Austria as well as from Germany and led to bitter campaigns in the respective presses. While Austria wanted "to save the German minorities from Nazism," Germany condemned this aim as "the sabotage of Germandom." See *Deutscher Presse Verlag*, release, February 27, 1934, and *Stuttgarter Neues Tagblatt*, February 27, 1934.

69. Between 1930 and 1935 both the German and Czech areas received 576 million crowns, but the proportionately higher unemployment among the Germans meant a lower per capita benefit. F. W. Bruegel, "The Germans in Pre-War Czechoslovakia," in Mamatey-Luža, *Czechoslovak Republic*, p. 186.

70. The Reich's press had propagandized this interpretation already in 1926. A typical example is a report in the *Münchner Neue Nachrichten*, May 13, 1926, which summarized the Czech state's anti-Sudeten activities in the following three points: economic destruction through expropriation and land reform, elimination of German minorities by closing German schools, lowering the cultural level of Sudetens to secure Czech intellectual superiority.

71. Bruegel, "The Germans," in Mamatey-Luža *Czechoslovak Republic*, p. 178.

72. Seton-Watson, *Eastern Europe*, p. 282.

73. Bruegel, "The Germans," in Mamatey-Luža, *Czechoslovak Republic*, p. 178.

74. For a description of conditions and events dominating the creation of SHF see Luža, *Transfer*, p. 70.

75. The DSNAP had forwarded before its dissolution 10,000 Czech crowns for the financing of the SHF from its treasury. Henlein denied that this donation represented any obligation toward the ideology or membership of the DSNAP on his part. *Ost Dok. 20*/I, B, No. 9, affidavit of Paul Lamatsch.

76. *Ost Dok. 20*/I, A, No. 4, Appendix IV, "Konrad Henleins Beziehungen zum Reich vor 1938," interview of Dr. Fritz Bürger by Dr. Fritz Kollner (Bundesarchiv); also see Jacobsen, *Steinacher*, Doc. No. 72, p. 292.

77. For the description of this autonomist movement see Seton-Watson, *Eastern Europe*, pp. 177–180; and Komjathy, *Crises*, pp. 186–187.

78. *Ost Dok. 20*/I-B3, No. 118, May 23, 1934.

79. Mamatey, "Development of Czechoslovak Democracy," in Mamatey-Luža, *Czechoslovak Republic*, p. 156.

80. It included a secret military clause against Germany in case Hitler should try to violate the peace treaty. For further details see Kamjathy, *Crises*, pp. 100–102.

81. Poland promised that if Germany attacked France, Poland would attack Germany.

82. For a discussion of Germany's military conditions *vis-à-vis* Czechoslovakia see Komjathy, *Crises*, pp. 187–188.

83. The Czech counterintelligence service was one of the best in East Central Europe and it kept under constant surveillance every organization that might endanger national security. For example, the SHF as well as the SDP were under surveillance from the date of their foundation. Jacobsen, *Steinacher*, p. 586; and *Ost Dok. 20/*I A, No. 29.

84. *Ost Dok. 20/*I A, No. 4.

85. Luža, *Transfer*, p. 93; President Beneš did not make any distinction among pan-Germanism, Nazism, and Fascism, and called Henlein's party by all these names, thereby contributing to the presently existing confusion. See Eduard Beneš, *Munich* (Paris: Editions Stock, 1969), pp. 13, 19, 20, 23, 27, 31, *passim*.

86. *DGFP*, C, V, Eisenlohr to Neurath, Prague, May 29, 1936, Doc. No. 353. Ernst Eisenlohr requested the Reich ministry of propaganda to stop reporting on the internal affairs of the SDP until reconcilation of the leaders was complete. Dr. Walter Brand, former KB leader, and the former DSNAP members had been disputing since the 1935 election. See *ibid.*, Rente-Fink to Eisenlohr, Berlin, June 11, 1936, Doc. No. 364, regarding the settlement of this dispute, and memorandum by Attenburg, Berlin, June 15, 1936, Doc. No. 372, on a problem between Rudolf Kasper's revolutionary group and Henlein. Eisenlohr emphasized the danger of suppression of the SDP if the German connection were revealed.

87. Luža, *Transfer*, p. 93, says that Henlein met Hitler at this time, while in *Ost Dok. 20/*I, A, No. 4, Fritz Bürger says that Henlein only saw Hitler during a picture-taking session but did not have any talks with him.

88. Beneš, *Munich*, p. 20.

89. Luža, *Transfer*, p. 88, 29n.

90. *DGFP*, C, V, memo of Attenburg, Berlin, October 9, 1936, Doc. No. 578.

91. Beneš, *Munich*, Doc. No. 1, pp. 247–248.

92. *Survey 1937*, pp. 452–453.

93. *RAA*, Judmeier to Schmidt, Prague, April 27, 1937, Doc. No. Z1 187. Pol.

94. *DGFP*, D, II, Eisenlohr to Ribbentrop, Prague, February 11, 1938, Doc. No. 55.

95. *RAA*, Judmeier to Schmidt, Prague, February 13, 1937, Doc. No. Z1 77, Fol.

96. *Ibid.*, Prague, April 14, 1937, Doc. No. Z1 171, Pol.

97. *DGFP*, D, II, Conversation of Frank and Henlein with Kánya, Budapest, February 19, 1937, Doc. No. 60; *Wilhelmstrasse*, Doc. No. 111.

98. *DGFP*, D, II, Eisenlohr to Neurath, Prague, December 10, 1937, Doc. No. 27.

99. *Survey 1937*, I, 454. The policeman apparently did strike Frank, though unaware that he was a deputy and thus protected by parliamentary immunity, but then Frank lost control and fought the police. *DGFP*, D, II, p. 27.

100. *DGFP*, D, II, Forster to Neurath, Paris, November 16, 1937, Doc. No. 21.

101. Luža, *Transfer*, p. 103.

102. *DGFP*, D, II, Eisenlohr to Neurath, Prague, October 22, 1937, Doc. No. 5.

103. Luža, *Transfer*, p. 106; *Nuremberg Trials*, XXV, "Hossbach Memorandum," November 10, 1937, Doc. No. 386-PS. (Colonel Friedrich Hossbach, Hitler's adjutant, made notes of the conference in the Reich Chancellery on November 5, 1937.)

104. *RAA*, Judmeier to Schmidt, Prague, November 4, 1937, Doc. No. Z1, 383, Fol.

105. *Ibid.*, Judmeier to Schmidt, Prague, November 22, 1937, Doc. No. Z1.413, Pol.

106. *RAA*, Judmeier to Schmidt, Prague, November 25, 1937, Doc. No. Z1.415, Pol.

107. *DGFP*, D, II, Henlein to Neurath, Prague, November 19, 1937, Doc. No. 23.

108 Luža, *Transfer*, p. 106.

109. *DGFP*, D, II, Henlein to Neurath, Prague, November 19, 1937, Doc. No. 23. Henlein's report appears to have been directly influenced by the Czechoslovak government's surprisingly conciliatory reply to Hitler's demand two weeks earlier for the right to organize Reich Germans living in Czechoslovakia into Nazi formations. Since the power struggle within the SDP between Frank and Henlein was still going on, it seemed expedient to Henlein to secure Hitler's backing by disavowing his previous moderate policy. Thus we may interpret this report as an attempt by Henlein to jump on the bandwagon of the Nazi group within the SDP.

110. Out of this ten million, 3.75 million lived in Czechoslovakia. This number included 350 thousand Jewish Germans. Meier, *Jews in the Satellites*, pp. 53–54.

111. *Documents on International Affairs, 1938*, II, pp. 12–13.

112. *Ibid.*, pp. 117–120.

113. *Survey 1938*, II, p. 62.

114. *DGFP*, D, II, Friedrich Burger to Mackensen, Prague, March 18, 1938, Doc. No. 89.

115. *DGFP*, D, II, Eisenlohr to Ribbentrop, Prague, March 24, 1938, Doc. No. 103.

116. *Ibid.* Dr. Czech was of the Jewish faith.

117. The National Defense Law allowed the government to nationalize land in the border area. It was more often used against the Germans than the Czechs.

118. *DGFP*, D, II, Eisenlohr to Ribbentrop, Prague, March 24, 1938, Doc. No. 103, and p. 235.

119. J. W. Bruegel, *Czechoslovakia before Munich: The German Minority Problem and British Appeasement Policy* (Cambridge: University Press, 1973), p. 173.

120. *DGFP*, D, II, unsigned report about the meeting of Henlein with Frank, undated, Doc. No. 107.

121. *DGFP*, D, II, Ribbentrop to Eisenlohr, Berlin, March 29, 1938, Doc. No. 109. Present from the SDP were also Kungel and Kreisel; from VoMi, Lorenz and Haushofer; from the foreign ministry, Ribbentrop, von Mackensen, Weizsäcker, Eisenlohr, Stieve, Twardowski, Kordt, and Attenburg.

122. *DGFP*, D, II, Eisenlohr to Ribbentrop, Prague, March 31, 1938, Doc. No. 112.

123. *Survey 1938*, II, p. 95; *DGFP*, D, II, unsigned memorandum of Henlein's Karlsbad demands, undated, Doc. No. 135.

124. Gerhard L. Weinberg, "The May Crisis, 1938," *The Journal of Modern History*, XXIX (September 1957): 215, 217.

125. *Ibid.*, p. 219; *Survey 1938*, II, p. 123.

126. *Survey 1938*, II, pp. 125–126.

127. For details of British and French efforts see *ibid.*, pp. 128–135, 138.

128. *Ibid.*, pp. 141, 143.

129. *DGFP*, D, II, Hitler's directives for "Operation Green," Berlin, May 30, 1938, Doc. No. 221.

130. *DGFP*, D, II, minutes of Weizsacker, Prague, June 18, 1938, Doc. No. 257.

131. *Survey 1938*, II, pp. 156–158, 184–187.

132. *Ibid.*, pp. 206–208.

133. Her Majesty's Stationery Office, *Documents on British Foreign Policy* (Oxford: Her Majesty's Stationery Office, 1958), 3rd ser., I, Halifax to Newton, Prague, July 18, 1938, Doc. No. 508. (Hereinafter referred to as *DBFP*.)

134. *Survey 1938*, II, pp. 211–212.

135. *DGFP*, D, II, Burger to Altenburg, Prague, August 17, 1938, Doc. No. 366.

136. *Survey 1938*, II, p. 215.

137. Bruegel, *Czechoslovakia before Munich*, pp. 231, 244.

138. *DGFP*, D, II, Doc. Nos. 407, 417; Bruegel, *Czechoslovakia before Munich*, p. 239.

139. *DGFP*, D, II, Hencke to Ribbentrop, Prague, August 30, 1938, Doc. No. 599.

140. *Survey 1938*, II, pp. 227–230; *DBFP*, 3rd ser., 1, Strang to Henderson, Berlin, July 21, 1938, Doc. No. 530.

141. *DBFP*, 3rd ser., II, Newton to Halifax, Prague, September 2, 1938, Doc. No. 746.

142. *Survey 1938*, II, 237–238.

143. *DGFP*, D, II, Hencke to Ribbentrop, Prague, September 7, 1938, Doc. No. 438.

144. *Survey 1938*, II, 253. Bruegel, *Czechoslovakia before Munich*, pp. 250–251.

145. *Survey 1938*, II, 256.

146. Julius Mader, *Hitler's Spionage General Sagen Aus* (Berlin: Verlag der Nation, 1971), pp. 135, 154. The organization of the *Sudetendeutsche Freikorps* on German territory was necessitated by the unexpected apathy of the ethnic Germans. Only the most radical elements in the ethnic group, Nazi and teenage boys, were willing to undertake sabotage acts against the Czechs, and they felt themselves to be in such a minority that they preferred to escape to Germany. The German army command was divided in its opinion of the usefulness of these escapees. They were considered by some as good material for commando duty because of their knowledge of the terrain. Others wanted no part of this irregular group. The total number of men in the SDU Freikorps was 40,000; the percentage of actual Sudeten Germans was only 0.001 percent. While the Freikorps tried to mobilize ethnic German as well as world opinion on the side of Germany, the SDP had issued an ultimatum.

147. *DGFP*, D, II, Doc. Nos. 466, 467, 472, 474, 490, 491.

148. *DGFP*, D, II, Doc. Nos. 502, 513, 515, 520.

149. With the Munich crisis began the last phase of the tragedy of Czechoslovakia. This phase was dominated by the Great Powers and the Sudeten Germans' role in it was unimportant, thus negligible with regard to this study.

Chapter III: The Swabians of Hungary

1. Burgenland, formerly Hungarian territory, was awarded to Austria under the Trianon Treaty, with the exception of the city of Sopron, where a plebiscite was held and the population decided to remain within Hungary.

2. 1920 census.

3. In the *Ausgleich* the Habsburgs had recognized Hungary as an independent state to be ruled according to its own constitution. Accordingly, the monarchy was transformed into a "dual monarchy" and its official name changed to Austria-Hungary.

4. Paikert, *Danube Swabians*, p. 42.

5. Hungary was declared a kingdom by the first parliament, which was elected after the dictatorship of the proletariat. Because of the restrictions of the victorious Entente, the throne remained vacant and a regent was elected in the person of Admiral Nicholas Horthy on March 1, 1921.

6. For details see Macartney, *Hungary and Her Successors*, p. 445, *passim*. A peculiarity of the Hungarian situation was that the Jews were not registered as a separate minority group. They had been emancipated in the nineteenth century, and they subsequently assimilated to the Magyar nationality. They came to regard themselves, and to be regarded by the rest of the population, as a religious and not a national or racial group. For this reason, there were no prominent Jewish members in the ethnic German group in Hungary. Meier, *Jews in the Satellites*, pp. 373–384.

7. Paikert, *Danube Swabians*, p. 48, regards these Orders as the fulfillment of the obligations prescribed by the Trianon Treaty, while C. A. Macartney, *October Fifteenth* 2 vols. (Edinburgh: University Press, 1961), I, 69, interprets them as an attempt to reestablish Hungarian control over the different minorities.

8. Non-Magyar nationalities were only 7.9 percent. L'Office Central Royal Hongrois de Statistique, *Annuaire Statistique Hongrois, 1932* (Budapest: Athenaeum, 1933), p. 12.

9. *R 57 neu*/1014-1; *Ost Dok. 16 Rum.*/17, p. 77; *Ost Dok. 17/22*, fol. 1, p. 15; *Ost Dok. 16 Ung.*/27; Anton Valentin, *Die Banater Schwaben* (Munich: Südestdeutsche Kulturbund, 1959), p. 70; Hans Herrschaft, *Das Banat* (Berlin: Verlag Grenze und Ausland, 1942), pp. 150–167; Bohmann, *Menschen und Grenzen*, II, 131.

10. Dr. Dezsö Sulyok, *A Magyar Tragédia* [Hungarian Tragedy] (Newark, N.J.: author's ed., 1954), pp. 29–47; Ödön Málnási, *A Magyar Nemzet Öszinte Története* [Sincere History of the Hungarian Nation] (Munich: Mikes Kelemen Kör, 1959), pp. 14–148.

11. Bohmann, *Menschen und Grenzen*, II, 52.

12. For a review of the cultural contributions and names of ethnic Germans in Hungary see Eugen Thurner, *Handbuch der Kulturgeschichte* (Konstanz, 1963); *Lieferung* 17/18 and 25/26; Ferencz Helle, *A Magyar német müvelödési kapcsolatok története* [History of the Hungarian-German Cultural Relations] (Budapest, 1942); Béla Pukánszky, *Német polgárság magyar földön* [German Petty Bourgeoisie in Hungary] (Budapest, 1940).

13. Macartney, *Hungary and Her Successors*, pp. 451–452.

14. The following data are taken from Alajos Kovács, *A németek helyzete Csonka-Magyarországon a statisztika megvilágitásában* [The Situation of Germans in Mutilated Hungary in the Light of Statistics] (Budapest, 1936), pp. 25–28, 49–56.

15. Paikert, *Danube Swabians*, p. 34.

16. *Annuaire Statistique Hongrois, 1932*, p. 12. The statistics in the following paragraphs were taken, unless otherwise indicated, from this reference book published annually by the government.

17. This number was naturally challenged by minority group leaders and by historians who corrected it according to their different sources and also interpreted it differently. See Macartney, *October Fifteenth*, I, 70; Paikert, *Danube Swabians*, p. 41; Seton-Watson, *Eastern Europe*, p. 283.

18. Based on the average for the years 1928–1930.

19. Calculations are based on the 1926, 1928 and 1930 statistics.

20. Treaty of Trianon, Articles 54–60.

21. Paikert, *Danube Swabians*, p. 56.

22. No. 110478a/VKM-1923.

23. 1:52 in the A type, 1:49 in the C type.

24. Ethnic Germans were 6.3 percent of the whole population; ethnic German students were 6.2 percent of the whole elementary student group.

25. "Bourgeois" schools (*polgári iskola*) roughly correspond to the four upper grades of the present-day elementary schools.

26. Macartney, *October Fifteenth*, I, 70.

27. For the full text of his speech see *Képviselöházi napló* [Parliamentary Reports] (Budapest, 1933) XV, 210–215.

28. Between 1930 and 1932 the number of Type A schools declined from 47 to 46 and Type C schools from 387 to 382, while the number of Hungarian schools increased from 6,217 to 6,310.

29. *Parliamentary Reports*, pp. 210–215.

30. "Bleyer was threatened, his wife ill-treated," by university students. Jacobsen, *Steinacher*, p. 80.

31. *Wilhelmstrasse*, report of Professor Bleyer to the German embassy in Hungary, Budapest, August 11, 1933, Doc. No. 13.

32. *DGFP*, C, I, Roediger (councillor of the cultural department of the German foreign ministry) to the legation in Hungary, Berlin, August 11, 1933, Doc. No. 400.

33. *Wilhelmstrasse*, Professor Bleyer's report to the German legation, Budapest, August 11, 1933, Doc. No. 13.

34. *Ibid.*

35. *Völkischer Beobachter* was the official newspaper of the German Nazi party. For a very informative short account of the history of the press in Germany see Oron F. Hale, *The Captive Press in the Third Reich* (Princeton, N.J.: University Press, 1964).

36. *Wilhelmstrasse*, Roediger to Schoen, Berlin, August 1, 1933, Doc. No. 12.

37. Bullock, *Hitler*, p. 277, 281.

38. Hitler to Richard Breitung, editor of the *Leipziger Neuste Nachrichten*, in Harold C. Deutsch, *Hitler and His Generals* (Minneapolis: University of Minnesota, 1974), pp. 2–5.

39. *Wilhelmstrasse*, Hans Schoen, German ambassador to Hungary, to the Foreign Ministry, Budapest, June 21, 1933, Doc. No. 8.

40. Deutsch, *Hitler and His Generals*, p. 5.

41. *Wilhelmstrasse*, Bülow's note about the visit of Masirevich to Hitler, Berlin, September 20, 1933, Doc. No. 15.

42. *DGFP*, C, II, Mackensen to the Foreign Ministry, Budapest, December 14, 1933, Doc. No. 123.

43. *DGFP*, C, II, Memorandum by Neurath, Berlin, January 18, 1934, Doc. No. 192.

44. *Wilhelmstrasse*, Mackensen to Neurath, Budapest, February 6, 1934, Doc. No. 18.

45. It cannot be discovered who initiated the Gratz-Mackensen meeting. Did Mackensen ask for information or did Gratz volunteer it? In any case, Gratz's action touches very closely the limit of loyalty. After all, any information given to Mackensen served German diplomacy and not the Hungarian government. *Ibid.*, Doc. No. 18-1.

46. The irony of this negative reply is that it was given by a government committee of Gömbös, Kersztes-Fischer, Hóman (of German ancestry), Kánya, Darányi, and Pataky (of Hungarian ancestry), and the three with partial German blood represented the uncompromising Hungarian standpoint.

47. *DGFP*, C, II, Gömbös to Hitler, Budapest, February 14, 1934, Doc. No. 652.

48. Walter Schneefuss, *Deutschtum in Süd-Ost-Europa* (Leipzig: Wilhelm Goldmann Verlag, 1939), pp. 75–76.

49. If we accept Paikert's statement, i.e., ethnic German intellectuals numbered only 1,761 persons (*Danube Swabians*, p. 34), they were only 0.3 percent of the ethnic German population.

50. Macartney, *October Fifteenth*, I, 171.

51. Schneefuss, *Deutschtum*, p. 77.

52. Macartney, *October Fifteenth*, I, 171.

53. Schneefuss, *Deutschtum*, p. 77.

54. *DGFP*, C, II, Gömbös to Hitler, Budapest, February 14, 1934, Doc. No. 252.

55. The first draft of Hitler's reply was prepared on February 28, 1934, by Reichminister Hans Heinrich Lammers, but Hitler did not sign it. The letter was rescheduled to be sent in May, and then postponed indefinitely. *Wilhelmstrasse*, Doc. No. 22, 2n.

56. It was certainly not a moral policy to use the ethnic Germans and their grievances as a weapon against Hitler, but Gömbös knew that Hitler was unmoved by moral arguments.

57. *Wilhelmstrasse*, Mackensen to Stieve, Budapest, November 30, 1934, Doc. No. 29.

58. *Wilhelmstrasse*, Harlo Schnurre, councillor of the German embassy, to Neurath, Budapest, February 12, 1935, Doc. No. 31.

59. Basch's case of 1934 was continued at the same time in a higher appellate court.

60. Tibor Eckhardt and Endre Bajcsy-Zsilinszky from the Smallholder party. See the daily correspondence of Bajcsy-Zsilinszky and Gratz published in the daily *Szabadság* [Liberty], Budapest, February 10, 1935.

61. *Wilhelmstrasse*, Doc. No. 31.

62. *Ibid.* Schnurre's conversation with Kussbach, Budapest, March 6, 1935, Doc. No. 32.

63. Since the UDV was a cultural association and not a political party, they could not run as candidates of the UDV or of ethnic German groups.

64. *Wilhelmstrasse*, Mackensen to Neurath, Budapest, April 6, 1935.

65. For a description of Gömbös's East Central European policy see Komjathy, *Crises*, pp. 122–124.

66. *R 57 neu*/No. 1016, members of the advisory board of the *Bund der Auslandsdeutschen*, Group II, in 1930.

67. Jacobsen, *Steinacher*, Doc. No. 13, p. 80.

68. *Dresdener Anzeiger, December 3, 1932, in R 57 neu*/1013–2.

69. *R 57 neu*/No. 1016, p. 4, German press reports from Hamburg, VDA, without number, March 17, 1933.

70. Jacobsen, *Steinacher*, pp. 7, 6n, and 80.

71. *DGFP*, C, IV, Mackensen to Neurath, Budapest, November 21, 1935, Doc. No. 424.

72. *Ibid.*

73. Germany increased its share of Hungary's export-import trade by 10 percent from 1933 to 1934. For the importance of German trade from Hungary's point of view see Komjathy, *Crises*, pp. 111, 119–120.

74. The cooperative or "magyarized" Swabians were called mockingly "magyarone" by the radical Germans. Jacobsen, *Steinacher*, Doc. No. 103, p. 392.

75. These actions of the VDA and Steinacher cast doubt on his claims that he always served the interest of the Reich and of the ethnic Germans and that he never promoted Nazism among the ethnic Germans. The fact is that Basch's group represented in 1935 only a small minority of ethnic Germans, his group was definitely Nazi oriented, and the interest of the Reich was at that time to avoid any misunderstanding with the Hungarian government. Steinacher justified his actions by picturing Basch as the "true representative" of the Swabians. Jacobsen, *Steinacher*, pp. 392–393.

76. *Budapesti Hirlap*, Budapest, June 15, 1935.

77. Egyed Faulstich was a medical doctor, one of Basch's colleagues in the leadership of the *Volksdeutsche Kameradschaft*. Richard Huss, professor at the University of Debrecen, was the honorary president of the UDV and also a member of the Basch-led radical group.

78. Steinacher supported the Basch group.

79. *Wilhelmstrasse*, Mackensen to Neurath, Budapest, June 26, 1935.

80. The *Deutsche-Ungarische Heimblätter* was financed entirely by the German embassy. Legally it was the personal property of Kussbach. After the June split Kussbach prohibited the publication of the last issue of the paper, arguing that Basch's editorship alienated exactly those Hungarian elements whose support the UDV needed most. He refused to publish that issue of the paper, even when the German embassy ordered him to do so. *Wilhelmstrasse*, Doc. No. 35.

81. Because legally it was his publication.

82. *DGFP*, C, IV, unsigned memorandum, Berlin, September 27, 1935.

83. *Ibid.*

84. *DGFP*, C, IV, memorandum by Neurath, Berlin, September 30, 1935, Doc. No. 314.

85. *DGFP*, C, IV, Mackensen to Neurath, Budapest, October 7, 1935, Doc. Nos. 337, 307, enclosure.

86. *DGFP*, C, IV, Mackensen to Neurath, Budapest, November 21, 1935, Doc. No. 424.

87. *Ibid.*

88. After exchanging the German marks in the black market for Hungarian Pengö.

89. Calculated on the basis of Board of Governors of the Federal Reserve System, *Banking and Monetary Statistics* (Washington, D.C., 1943), pp. 671–672.

90. *Budapesti Hirlap*, Budapest, May 7, 1935, p. 9.

91. *DGFP*, C, IV, Doc. No. 424.

92. *DGFP*, C, IV, Mackensen to Neurath, Budapest, November 21, 1935, Doc. No. 424.

93. Admiral Nicholas Horthy was regent of Hungary; Count István Bethlen was prime minister, 1921–1931.

94. Macartney,*October Fifteenth*, I, p. 173.

95. Those who wanted to restore the Habsburgs to the Hungarian throne. Their leaders came mostly from the Catholic clergy.

96. *DGFP*, C, IV, Stieve to Mackensen, Berlin, January 30, 1936.

97. Macartney, *October Fifteenth*, I, p. 172.

98. *DGFP*, C, IV, Stieve to Mackensen, Berlin, January 30, 1936, Doc. No. 527.

99. He died in Munich in the hospital after a long period of illness with kidney disease.

100. Macartney, *October Fifteenth*, I, 179.

101. For details see *Wilhelmstrasse*, Doc. No. 39, 2n.

102. Macartney, *October Fifteenth*, p. 178.

103. See Chapter VII for details.

104. The UDV was only a shadow of its former self by 1937.

105. *Wilhelmstrasse*, Mackensen to Neurath, Budapest, November 29, 1936, Doc. Nos. 73, 73-1, 73-2. The following narrative is based on these documents.

106. These points were accepted by the foreign ministry and served as a basis for negotiation with Kozma.

107. Order in Council No. 11,000/1935 ME introduced a standard school type for minorities, thus eliminating the A, B, C type schools. In the new schools, with the exception of subjects dealing with "national knowledge" (*nemzeti ismeret*), all subjects were taught in the mother tongue of the students. In grades 4–6 the same subjects were repeated, but the subjects were taught in the Magyar language (and vice versa).

108. *Wilhelmstrasse*, Doc. Nos. 73, 73-1, 73-2.

109. The transferred members were teachers in the state school system and so the government had the right to transfer them from one school to another. It is undeniable that their transfer tended to weaken the *Kameradschaft*.

110. One of the authors (Komjathy) was acting as interpreter for a visiting *Hitlerjugend* group in 1940 and got a copy of this map through the indiscretion of a Hitler youth. It was submitted at once to the battalion commander of the Ludovica Military Academy, where the author served as a cadet.

111. Quoted in Macartney, *October Fifteenth*, I, 172.

112. *Wilhelmstrasse*, memorandum of the foreign ministry, Berlin, December 14, 1936, Doc. No. 76-2.

113. During the summer of 1936 several Reich German students were arrested by the Hungarian authorities and expelled from Hungary for spreading Nazi propaganda in Swabian villages. *Wilhelmstrasse*, Werkmeister, Councillor of the German embassy, to Neurath, Budapest, March 10, 1937, Doc. No. 84.

114. *Wilhelmstrasse*, Mackensen to Stieve, Budapest, November 30, 1934, Doc. No. 29.

115. See Chapter VII.

116. Mathias Annabring, *Das Ungarländische Deutschtum* (Stuttgart: Südoststimmen, 1952), II, 11.

117. Lóránt Tilkovszky, "A Volksbund szerepe Magyarország második világháborús történetében" [The Role of the Volksbund in the History of Hungary during World War II] in *Történelmi Szemle* [Historical Review], XI, No. 3 (1968), 296.

118. *Ibid.*, Macartney, *October Fifteenth*, I, 217.

119. Macartney, *October Fifteenth*, I, 217.

Chapter IV: Ethnic Germans of Poland

1. For a detailed description and analysis of the peace negotiations concerning Poland see Piotr S. Wandycz, *France and Her Eastern Allies, 1919–1925* (Minneapolis: University of Minnesota, 1962), pp. 29–48.

2. Census of September 30, 1921. *Commission Statistique de la République Polonaise,* 1925–26, p. 26.

3. William John Rose, *The Drama of Upper Silesia* (Brattleboro, Vt.: Stephen Daye Press, 1935), p. 204.

4. Helmuth Fechner, *Deutschland und Polen, 1772–1945* (Wurzburg: Holzner Verlag, 1964), p. 156.

5. *Ibid.*, pp. 111, 159.

6. Ludwig Denne, *Das Danzig Problem in der Deutschen Aussenpolitik, 1934–1939* (Bonn: Ludwig Rohrscheid Verlag, 1959), p. 33.

7. The following description is based on League of Nations, *Ten Years of World Cooperation* (Geneva: Secretariat of the League of Nations, 1930), pp. 382–387.

8. OSSA had the following affiliated companies in Danzig: *Landwirtschaftliche Band Creditverband Weichselgau, Weichselgau Wirtschaftliche Beratungsstelle, Kreditgenossenschaft Agraria, Agraria Betriebwissenschaftlich Abteilung, Rentenablosungsfond, Land G.m.b.H. Inland IIg,* No. 241, p. 33.

9. Denne, *Danzig-Problem*, pp. 39, 62.

10. *Ibid.*, p. 44, *RAA*, Hoffinger to Berger Waldenegg, Warsaw, November 21, 1934, Doc. No. 146/Pd./1934.

11. For a description of this power struggle by Rauschning himself see Hermann Rauschning, *The Conservative Revolution* (New York: Putnam, 1941), pp. 12–33.

12. Denne, *Danzig Problem*, p. 55.

13. For further details of Pilsudski's diplomacy concerning Germany see Komjathy, *Crises*, pp. 32–35.

14. The smallholder German peasant class characteristic of ethnic German settlements in East Central Europe was insignificant in Prussia and Silesia. On the other hand, in Posen and Pomerelia medium-size farms were in the majority.

15. The peace treaty marked out the borders between Germany and Poland, disregarding the ownership of land. Thus there were landlords whose estates were partly in Germany and partly in Poland. Also, industries belonging to the same owner were separated by the new frontiers. Special agreements tended to ease the problems created for these "double proprietors."

16. Rose, *Drama of Upper Silesia*, p. 207.

17. All those Germans who had migrated before 1908 to the territories now belonging to Poland, as well as those who had not lived in these territories for at least fifteen years uninterruptedly, were refused Polish citizenship. Fechner, *Deutschland und Polen*, p. 159.

18. Denne, *Danzig-Problem*, p. 34.

19. Reports of the VDA complained even in 1937 about the apathy of Silesian workers concerning nationality questions. *R 57 neu*/1016.

20. Rose, *Drama of Upper Silesia*, p. 238.

21. According to the minority treaty, a German school was to operate in every community where there were at least forty ethnic German students. Fechner, *Deutschland und Polen*, p. 160.

22. Rose, *Drama of Upper Silesia*, pp. 268–270.

23. The Mixed Commission was organized originally to solve technical and economic disputes, but it soon became a forum for all kinds of minority problems.

24. Rose, *Drama of Upper Silesia,* pp. 268–270.

25. Calculated on the basis of Rose, *Drama of Upper Silesia*, p. 285.

26. Wandycz, *Eastern Allies*, pp. 352–353; Rose, *Drama of Upper Silesia*, p. 238; Denne, *Danzig-Problem*, p. 37. Denne omits the original German refusal to renew the coal convention and blames the Polish government alone for the economic war.

27. Rose, *Drama of Upper Silesia*, p. 238.

28. *Ibid.*, p. 301.

29. *Ibid.*, p. 321.

30. The reorganization of the German army was projected to start in 1935. Department of State, *Foreign Relations of the United States, 1934*, 5 vols. (Washington, D.C.: U.S. Government Printing Office, 1935), I, German ambassador to Secretary of State, Washington, April 21, 1934, pp. 56–57.

31. The Westerplatte incident is described in Jósef Lipski, *Diplomat in Berlin, 1933–1939*, edited by Waclav Jedrzejewicz (New York: Columbia University, 1968), pp. 46–59. (Hereinafter referred to as *Lipski Papers*.) See also Roos, *Poland und Europa*, pp. 61–71; Komjáthy, *Crises*, pp. 42–43.

32. *RAA*, evaluation of Hoffinger, Austrian ambassador to Poland, on the second anniversary of the pact, Warsaw, January 31, 1936, Doc. No. 15 Pol./1936.

33. Polish youth gangs destroyed fifty-seven *Volksbund* clubhouses. The police closed down fourteen *Volksbundheime* and "denied the freedom of assembly to the *Volksbund*," *R 57 neu*/1094-4, p. 15. Atrocities against individuals are listed in *R 57 neu*/1012-2.

34. *R 57 neu*/1094-4, p. 15.

35. *R 57 neu*/1014-1; *R 57 neu*/1014-2; Jacobsen, *Steinacher*, p. 135.

36. See, for example, reports in *Heidelberger Tageblatt*, February 6, 1933, and *Münchner Nachricht*, February 10, 1933.

37. 1933 was also the year when the old leadership of the VDA was eliminated. Steinacher, the new leader, was received by Hitler in December 1933, but was not informed about the upcoming Nonaggression Pact. Jacobsen, *Steinacher*, Doc. No. 24.

38. *R 2*/14938, fol. I, finance ministry to AA, without date (probably late 1933 or early 1934).

39. *RAA*, Hoffinger to Dollfuss, Warsaw, January 26, 1934, Doc. No. 10 Pol/1934.

40. For a review of French domestic political problems see Edouard Bonnefous, *Histoire Politique de la Troisième République*, 6 vols. (Paris: Presses Universitaires de France, 1962). For a detailed discussion of these problems see Komjathy, *Crises*, pp. 52–64, 98–103, 264.

41. Waclaw Jedrzejewicz, "The Polish Plan for a 'Preventive War' against Germany in 1933," *The Polish Review*, XI, No. I (Winter 1966), 62–91.

42. For the text of the German-Polish declaration see *Nazi Conspiracy*, VIII, 368–369.

43. See p. 79.

44. Meier, *Jews in the Satellites*, p. 209.

45. *R 57 neu*/1094-4, *Volksbund* report about Silesia, December 18, 1933, p. 14.

46. Theodor Bierschenk, *Die deutsche Volksgruppe in Polen, 1934–1939* (Würzburg: Holzner Verlag, 1954), p. 30.

47. *Ibid.*, p. 31, 34.

48. *Ibid.*, p. 40.

49. Jacobsen, *Steinacher*, p. 531.

50. *Ibid.*, p. 532.

51. For an analysis of Poland's foreign policy alternatives, see Komjathy, *Crises*, pp. 43–47.

52. Chief Bureau of Statistics of the Republic of Poland, *Concise Statistical Year-Book of Poland*, 1937 (Warsaw: Chief Bureau of Statistics, 1937). The number of ethnic Germans in Poland varies according to the source. The greatest numbers are mentioned in *R 57 neu*/1009-2, No. 12855: 2,200,000; the smallest in the *Statistical Year-Book*, 1937: 740,000. Since it is impossible to reconcile these figures, for the purpose of our calculations we have used the Polish numbers wherever possible.

53. Rauschning, *Conservative Revolution*, pp. 13–33; Komjathy, *Crises*, pp. 34–35.

54. German leaders called this friendly attitude toward the Jews "lethargy." Bierschenk, *Deutsche Volksgruppe*, p. 41.

55. Jacobsen, *Steinacher*, p. 531; Bierschenk, *Deutsche Volksgruppe*, p. 42.

56. *R 57 neu*/1094-4, p. 17.

57. *Inland II g*, 241, p. 33. See note 8 of this chapter.

58. *Lipski Papers*, p. 137.

59. *RAA*, Hoffinger to Dollfuss, Warsaw, June 16, 1934, Doc. No. 67, Pol./1934.

60. *Lipski Papers*, pp. 141–142.

61. *RAA*, Hoffinger to Dollfuss, Warsaw, June 29, 1934, Doc. No. 72, Pol./1934.

62. *RAA*, Hoffinger to Berger-Waldenegg, Warsaw, September 14, 1934, Doc. No. 118, Pol./1934.

63. Komjathy, *Crises*, pp. 104–105.

64. German Foreign Office, *Documents on the Events Preceding the Outbreak of the War* (Berlin, 1939), Consul General von Kuchler to AA, Thorn, May 18, 1936, Doc. No. 66. (Hereinafter referred to as *German White Book*.)

65. *Lipski Papers*, pp. 266–270.

66. *German White Book*, conversation of Neurath with Lipski, Berlin, November 13, 1936, Doc. No. 67.

67. The crisis was triggered by the visit of a German battleship to Danzig. For details see *Lipski Papers*, pp. 257–278.

68. Burckhardt was a friend of Weizsäcker and was nominated by him for the position. Ernst von Weizsäcker, *Memoirs* (London: Gollancz, 1951), pp. 146–147, 188. Hitler "recommended" Forster's cooperation with the AA in order not to worsen Polish-German relations. Carl J. Burckhardt, *Meine Danziger Mission, 1937–1939* (Munich: Verlag Georg D. W. Callweg, 1960), p. 67.

69. His appointment was announced by the secretary general of the League of Nations, Joseph Avenol, on February 17, 1937. Burckhardt, *Mission*, p. 69.

70. Denne, *Danzig-Problem*, p. 129.

71. *Lipski Papers*, Doc. Nos. 66–77. Hitler suggested, and Lipski accepted, a compromise statement according to which the two states agreed that the Polish-German "relations should not be disturbed by the Danzig question." *DGFP*, D, V, memorandum by Neurath, Berlin, October 23, 1937, Doc. No. 16.

72. Documents describing the Beck-Hitler and Beck-Ribbentrop conversations are in *DGFP*, D, V, Doc. Nos. 119, 120; *Polish White Book*, Doc. Nos. 48–52; *Lipski Papers*, Doc. No. 132.

73. *DGFP*, III, IV, G, Shepherd to Halifax, Danzig, January 28, 1939, Doc. No. 47.

74. Statistics used in this paragraph are found in Hans-Adolf Jacobsen, *Nationalsozialistische Aussenpolitik, 1933–1938* (Frankfurt: Alfred Metzner Verlag, 1968), pp. 590–591. (Hereinafter referred to as Jacobsen, *Aussenpolitik*.)

75. *Der Aufbruch*, April 5, 1936. Quoted in Richard Breyer, *Das Deutsche Reich und Polen, 1932–1937: Aussenpolitik und Volksgruppenfragen* (Würzburg: Holzner Verlag, 1955), pp. 242–243. (Hereinafter referred to as Breyer, *Deutsche Reich und Polen*.)

76. Jacobsen, *Steinacher*, pp. 537–538.

77. *RAA*, Hoffinger to Berger-Waldenegg, Warsaw, January 11, 1935, Doc. No. 2, Pol./1935.

78. Jacobsen, *Aussenpolitik*, p. 591.

79. Abt. VI A, Deutschtum 2, Bd. 15, VDA. Treasurer's report to Reichstelle für Devisenbewirtschaftung Berlin, June 29, 1936, in Jacobsen, *Aussenpolitik*, pp. 671–672.

80. Jacobsen, *Aussenpolitik*, p. 592.

81. *Lipski Papers*, Lipski to Beck, Berlin, May 5, 1935, Doc. No. 42.

82. *Inland II g*, 220, Deutschtum, Bd. 1, Twardowski to Kursell, Berlin, May 29, 1936, in Jacobsen, *Aussenpolitik*, pp. 593–595.

83. Breyer, *Deutsche Reich und Polen*, p. 245.

84. Jacobsen, *Aussenpolitik*, pp. 593–595. The JDP papers were *Der Aufbruch* in Kattowitz, *Deutsche Nachrichten* in Posen, and *Völkische Anzeiger* in Lodz.

85. *Inland II g*, 221, Deutschtum, Bd. 2, in Jacobsen, *Aussenpolitik*, p. 595.

86. *R 57 neu*/1092 Pol. 23.

87. Bierschenk, *Deutsche Volksgruppe*, p. 234.

88. *Ibid.*, pp. 234–237; *RAA*, Hoffinger to Berger-Waldenegg, Warsaw, April 19, 1935, Doc. No. 41, Pol./1935; Breyer, *Deutsche Reich und Polen*, p. 257.

89. Bierschenk, *Deutsche Volksgruppe*, pp. 242–244, 255–256.

90. Breyer, *Deutsche Reich und Polen*, pp. 39–45. Almost all the German Protestants lived in the former German territory; therefore our study concentrates on the survey of religious conditions in this territory.

91. Rose, *Drama of Upper Silesia*, pp. 306–306.

92. *Ibid.*, p. 307.

93. *Ibid.*, p. 312.

94. *Ibid.*, p. 313.

95. After the new voting regulations of July 8, 1935, redistricting made it difficult for the German group to elect its own candidates. However, in order to have German minority representatives in the parliament, the Polish government drafted Hassbach and Wiesner.

96. Jacobsen, *Steinacher*, pp. 527, 529–530.

97. Anthony Polonsky, *Politics in Independent Poland, 1921–1939* (Oxford: Clarendon, 1972), p. 464.

98. Bierschenk, *Deutsche Volksgruppe*, p. 233.

99. W. E. Moore, *Economic Demography of Eastern and Southern Europe* (Geneva, 1945), p. 63.

100. *RAA*, Hoffinger to Berger-Waldenegg, Warsaw, February 21, 1936, Doc. No. 30/Pol/1936. For a comparison with 1935 figures see *German White Book*, Lütgens, German consul general at Posten, to AA, Posen, February 18, 1935, Doc. No. 55.

101. *RAA*, Doc. No. 30/Pol./1936.

102. *RAA*, Hoffinger to Berger-Waldenegg, Warsaw, January 31, 1936, Doc. No. 15./Pol. 1936, fol. 878.

103. Hans Kohnert, "Agrarreformstatistik aus Polen," *Nation and Staat*, XII (1939), 618–619. (Hereinafter cited as Kohnert, "Agrarreformstatistik.")

104. Breyer, *Deutsche Reich und Polen*, p. 54.

105. Excluding nursery schools (49 with 1,600 pupils) and private primary schools (234 with 15,100 pupils). Calculated on the basis of Polish Ministry of Information, *Concise Statistical Year-Book of Poland*, September 1939–June 1941 (Glasgow: University Press, 1941), pp. 138–139. (Hereinafter cited as *Statistical Year-Book*, 1941.)

106. The following information about Upper Silesia is from Rose, *Drama of Upper Silesia*, pp. 288–292.

107. *R 57 neu*/1093-21, report on the German schools in Poland, August 29, 1935.

108. *R 57 neu*/1094-4, report of Volksbund in Polish Silesia, December 18, 1933.

109. *R 57 neu*/1097-1, *Neue Lodzer Zeitung*, October 31, 1937.

110. *Ibid.*, *Täglische Rundschau*, August 2, 1932.

111. Bierschenk, *Deutsche Volksgruppe*, p. 157.

112. *Ibid.*, pp. 277–279.

113. *RAA*, Hoffinger to Schuschnigg, Warsaw, June 12, 1936, Doc. No. 70 Pol./1936.

114. *Ibid.*

115. The following data are from *Statistical Year-Book*, 1941, p. 115; Bierschenk, *Deutsche Volksgruppe*, pp. 266–267.

116. *DGFP*, D, V, Bismarck, deputy director of the political department, memorandum, Berlin, November 25, 1937, Doc. No. 23.

117. *R 57 neu*/1016; report of the Scientific Work Circle of VDA, Berlin, January 3, 1937, pp. 10–11.

118. The following political-military evaluation does not contradict the Hossbach Memorandum, which was based on the possibility of a French involvement. The present discussion involves only the military necessity of neutralizing Poland. For the Hossbach memorandum, see *DGFP*, D, I, Doc. No. 19.

119. *Lipski Papers*, Lipski to Beck, Berlin, June 19, 1937, Doc. No. 65.

120. For a description of cultural activities of the Polish government among the Poles in Germany see *R 57 neu*/1016. For a description of Poland's commercial and financial activities in Germany see *Inland II g*, 241, p. 31.

121. *Lipski Papers*, Lipski to Beck, Berlin, November 5, 1937, Doc. No. 73. *Inland II g*, 248, pp. 1–6, No. e. o. Kult. A. 1148 TS. Verh. geh. Ang. 2.

122. *DGFP*, D, I, Hossbach memorandum, Berlin, November 5, 1937, Doc. No. 19.

123. Anna M. Cienciala, *Poland and the Western Powers, 1938–1939* (London: Routledge & Kegan Paul, 1968), p. 39.

124. *Lipski Papers*, p. 359.

125. *Ibid.*, pp. 313–317.

126. *German White Book*, Walther, German Consul-General in Posen, to AA, Posen, February 22, 1938, Doc. No. 157.

127. Kohnert, "Agrarreformstatistik," p. 618. Figures for the rest of the paragraph are from this source.

128. *DGFP*, D, V, Ribbentrop to Moltke, Berlin, June 29, 1938, Doc. No. 44. Cf. *German White Book*, Doc. Nos. 125, 128, 171.

129. *DGFP*, D, V, Schliep, head of Political Division V, memorandum, Berlin, July 8, 1938, Doc. No. 47.

130. In Upper Silesia about 8,000 tenants families' lives were affected by this policy. Rose, *Drama of Upper Silesia*, p. 250. See also *German White Book*, Doc. No. 93.

131. *R 57 neu*/1094-4. *German White Book*, Nöldeke, German consult general at Kattowitz, to AA, Kattowitz, November 8, 1938, Doc. No. 131; Nöldeke to AA, Kattowitz, November 24, 1938, Doc. No. 134. See also Doc. Nos. 105, 107, 108, 136, 141.

132. *German White Book*, Woermann to German chargé d'affaires in Warsaw, Berlin, November 26, 1938, Doc. No. 121.

133. *German White Book*, Fries, official in cultural department of AA, memorandum, Berlin, January 25, 1938, Doc. No. 111.

134. *Ibid.*, Twardowski to Moltke, Berlin, May 27, 1938, Doc. No. 114.

135. *Ibid.*, Walther to Ribbentrop, Posen, October 10, 1938, Doc. No. 129.

136. *Ibid.*, Doc. No. 114; *ibid.*; Nöldeke to Ribbentrop, Kattowitz, January 26, 1939, Doc. No. 143; *DGFP*, D, V, Schliep memorandum, Berlin, July 8, 1938, Doc. No. 47.

137. *German White Book*, Küchler, German consult general at Thorn, to Ribbentrop, Thorn, November 23, 1938, Doc. No. 133; and December 30, 1938, Doc. No. 139.

138. *Ibid.*, Küchler to Ribbentrop, Thorn, December 29, 1938, Doc. No. 138.

139. *R 57 neu*/1097-1, *Deutsche Schulzeitung in Polen*, November 15, 1938.

140. The following complaints and the Polish response are listed in *German White Book*, Woermann to Wühlisch, German chargé d'affaires in Warsaw, Berlin, November 26, 1938, Doc. No. 121; Moltke to Ribbentrop, Warsaw, Ddecember 20, 1938, Doc. No. 123. The German rebuttal is in *ibid.*, Woermann to Moltke, Berlin, February 1, 1939, Doc. No. 125.

141. *German White Book*, Moltke to Ribbentrop, Warsaw, December 11, 1937, Doc. No. 109.

142. *Ibid.*, Walther to Ribbentrop, Posen, October 10, 1938, Doc. No. 129.

143. *DGFP*, D, V, Schliep memorandum, Berlin, March 3, 1939, Doc. No. 134.

144. *German White Book*, Küchler to Ribbentrop, Thorn, June 23, 1939, Doc. No. 387.

145. *Ibid.*, Moltke to Ribbentrop, Warsaw, July 5, 1939, Doc. No. 394.

146. *Ibid.*, Matuschka to Ribbentrop, Posen, August 15, 1939, Doc. No. 411.

147. *Ibid.*, Küchler to Ribbentrop, Thorn, December 29, 1938, Doc. No. 138.

148. *Ibid.*, January 19, 1939, Doc. No. 142.

149. *Ibid.*, Damerau, German consul at Teschen, to Ribbentrop, Teschen, June 2, 1939, Doc. No. 377. The majority shareholders in this home were Reich Germans—256 shares compared with 179 held by minority Germans.

150. *Ibid.*, Walther to Ribbentrop, Posen, June 16, 1939, Doc. No. 383.

151. *Ibid.*, Ehrenhauss, German consul at Teschen, to Ribbentrop, Teschen, July 13, 1939, Doc. No. 399.

152. *Ibid.*, Walther to Ribbentrop, Posen, August 12, 1939, Doc. No. 409.

153. *Ibid.*, Damerau to Ribbentrop, Teschen, August 18, 1939, Doc. No. 414.

154. Poland acquired the territory by presenting the Czech government with an ultimatum; the Hungarians received their territories by the decision made in Vienna in 1938. Germany, of course, annexed the Sudetenland after the Munich agreement. For the details of these procedures see John W. Wheeler-Bennett, *Munich: Prologue to Tragedy*, London: Macmillan, 1966; Royal Institute of International Affairs, *Survey of International Affairs, 1938*, 2 vols., London, New York: Oxford University, 1951, Vol. II; Keith Eubank, *Munich* (Norman, Okla.: University of Oklahoma, 1963); Francis L. Loewenheim, ed., *Peace or Appeasement* (Boston: Houghton Mifflin, 1965), Eduard Beneš, *Munich* (Paris: Editions Stock, 1969); Anna M. Cienciala, *Poland and the Western Powers* (London: Routledge & Kegan Paul, 1968); Jósef Lipski, *Diplomat in Berlin, 1933–1939*, edited by Waclav Jedrzejewicz (New York: Columbia University, 1968); Anthony Polonsky, *Politics in Independent Poland, 1921–1939* (Oxford: Clarendon, 1972); Roman Debicki, *Foreign Policy of Poland, 1919–1939* (New York: Praeger, 1962).

155. Ministère des Affaires Étrangères, *Le Livre Jaune Francais* (Paris: Imprimerie Nationale, 1939), Doc. Nos. 28, 29. (Hereinafter referred to as *French Yellow Book*.)

156. *Foreign Relations of the United States, 1938–1945*, 1938, I, 85; Cienciala, *Poland and the Western Powers*, p. 169.

157. The argument started with the signing of the Franco-Soviet Mutual Assistance Treaty on May 2, 1935. It was directed against Germany, but French diplomacy failed to secure Poland's consent beforehand, as well as afterward. Thus the treaty remained a worthless piece of paper. For details see Komjathy, *Crises*, pp. 61–62.

158. *DGFP*, D, V, conversation of Ribbentrop with Lipski, Berchtesgaden, October 24, 1938, Doc. No. 81; *Lipski Papers*, Doc. No. 124; Ministerstwo Spraw Zagraniczynch, *Official*

Documents Concerning Polish-German and Polish-Soviet Relations, 1933–1939 (London, 1940), Lipski to Beck, Berlin, October 25, 1938, Doc. No. 44. (Hereinafter referred to as *Polish White Book.*)

159. The Anti-Comintern Pact was signed between Germany and Japan in Berlin on November 25, 1936. It placed the anti-Soviet policy of the signatories on an ideological basis.

160. 320,000 Germans out of a total population of 400,000. German statistics in *R 57 neu*/1009-2, No. 12855.

161. Polonsky, *Independent Poland, p. 447.*

162. *Concise Statistical Yearbook of Poland 1937.*

163. The modernization of Polish war industry began only in 1936 and lagged behind the projected production because of budget problems. Polonsky, *Independent Poland*, pp. 488–499. Thus Poland remained dependent on French arms shipment, which became more and more uncertain because France distrusted Poland on account of Polish participation in the destruction of Czechoslovakia. Even the force of the Franco-Polish Mutual Assistance Treaty was questioned. General Maurice Gamelin, *Servir*, 2 vols. (Paris: Plon, 1946), II, 380; Ciencila, *Poland and the Western Powers*, pp. 170–171.

164. *Lipski Papers*, pp. 313–317.

165. *DGFP*, D, V, memorandum by Ribbentrop, Berlin, December 2, 1938, Doc. No. 106.

166. *Polish White Book*, Beck's instructions to Lipski, Warsaw, October 31, 1938, Doc. No. 45. Also see *Lipski Papers*, p. 458 and 15n.

167. In October 1938–January 1939. *DGFP*, D, V, Doc. Nos. 72, 82, 121.

168. *DGFP*, D, V, memorandum by Aschmann, director of the information and press department, Berlin, December 5, 1938, Doc. No. 110.

169. Burckhardt, *Mission*, p. 266.

170. See, for example, *German White Book*, Matuschka to Ribbentrop, Posen, February 28, 1939, Doc. No. 150. Also see Doc. Nos. 129, 140, 146, 152, 155.

171. Burckhardt, *Mission*, p. 266.

172. *Ost Dok. 2*/312, "A Little Contribution to the Theme: So Was the East-German Fatherland Gambled Away" by Hermann von Bülow, p. 26.

173. *Ost Dok. 7*/40, p. 157; Breyer, *Deutsche Reich und Polen*, p. 262. For the Polish interpretation see Polish Ministry of Information, *The German Fifth Column in Poland* (London: Hutchinson, 1940), Deposition No. 410.

174. For example, Hermann Rauschning, president of the Danzig senate, resigned on November 23, 1934. Denne, *Danzig-Problem*, p. 53.

175. Burckhardt, *Mission*, p. 266.

176. *Inland II g*, 242, pp. 38–39.

177. *Lipski Papers*, Lipski to Beck, Berlin, April 29, 1939, Doc. No. 142. *Polish White Book*, Beck's speech to the Diet, May 5, 1939, Doc. No. 77.

178. Sir Neville Henderson, *Failure of a Mission* (New York: Putnam, 1940), p. 243.

179. First contact was made by Ambassador Litvinov on April 17, visiting Weizsäcker in the foreign ministry. *DGFP*, D, VI, minutes of the conversation, Berlin, April 17, 1939, Doc. No. 211.

180. *DGFP*, D, VI, Moltke to Ribbentrop, Berlin, May 10, 1939, Doc. No. 355.

181. *DGFP*, D, VI, memorandum by Clodius (official of the foreign minister's secretariat), Berlin, May 15, 1939, Enclosures 1 and 2, Doc. No. 387. The numbers mentioned in *DGFP* and other German sources differ greatly from the Polish statistics, but since they provided the basis for the German calculations, we have accepted them in this case. Cf. note 52 in this chapter.

182. *Inland II D*, 3/3 Deutsche Stiftung to VDA, July 13, 1938; *Inland II g*, 242, AA to Army Intelligence Department, October 27, 1938.

183. Paul Leverkuehn, *German Military Intelligence* (London: Weidenfeld & Nicolson, 1954), p. 82.

184. *Ost Dok.* 7/40, p. 157.

185. The following data are taken from *Inland II g*, No. 242, Appendix, pp. 101–102.

186. *Ibid.*

187. Peter Aurich, *Der Deutsch-Polnische September 1939: Eine Volksgruppe zwischen den Fronten* (Munich, 1969), p. 111.

188. De Jong, *Fifth Column*, p. 48.

189. Cf. *Marsch der Deutschen in Polen: Deutsche Volksgenossen im ehemaligen Polen, Berichten über Erlebnisse in den Septembertagen 1939* (Berlin, 1940), p. 14, with Aurich; *Deutsch-Polische September*, p. 6. These numbers, of course, are denied by Polish authorities, who charge that the losses are highly exaggerated. A West German study of December 31, 1961, put the number of prewar losses of ethnic Germans at 3,841. *Ost Dok.* 7/40, Poland, p. 17.

190. The evacuation began with the women and children during early summer and ended with the evacuation order for all *Reichsdeutsche* on August 25, 1939. De Jong, *Fifth Column*, p. 148; *DGFP*, D, VII, Doc. No. 286.

191. De Jong, *Fifth Column*, p. 38.

192. This group consisted of Sudeten German volunteers and numbered seventy men under the leadership of a Dr. Herzner. Aurich, *Deutsch-Polnische September*, p. 111, and Mader, *Spionage Generale*, pp. 13–14.

193. Mader, *Spionage Generale*, p. 319.

194. For the text of the document, see *ibid.* pp. 116–121.

195. The collection of *Volksdeutsche* experiences concerning Polish terror is in *Ost Dok.* 7/8 and *Ost Dok.* 7/40; de Jong, *Fifth Column*, p. 156.

196. *Ost Dok.* 7/4, p. 712, and de Jong, *Fifth Column*, p. 50. The number of murdered *Volksdeutsche* amounted, according to German sources, to 13,000. Since this number was published by German Nazi authorities, it should be treated with skepticism. See also note 189 above.

197. *DGFP*, D, VII, Veesenmeyer, special representative in Danzig, to Weizsäcker, Danzig, August 22, 1939, Doc. No. 172, and Weizsäcker's reply on the same day, Doc. No. 182.

198. *Ibid.*, Doc. Nos. 202, 235.

199. Cf. the Soviet partisan activities in which the Soviet Army provided only the leadership for the partisans, who were recruited from the local population by different methods to serve in the partisan units.

200. Lipski expressed this hope to Dahlerus, *Nuremberg Trials*, Dahlerus testimony, XIX, 368.

201. *Ibid.* Also see IX, 470.

202. *Ost Dok.* 2/312, Hermann von Bülow, "A little contribution to the theme: So was East-German Fatherland gambled away," p. 26. This and the following description are based on that report.

203. Aurich, *Deutsch-Polnische September*, p. 16.

204. *French Yellow Book*, Noël to Bonnet, Warsaw, May 3, 1939, Doc. No. 117.

205. *Ibid.*, Noël to Bonnet, Warsaw, April 1, 1939, Doc. No. 90.

206. *Ibid.* Noël reports that during the showing of newsreels in movie theaters, pictures of Germans in military uniforms provoked the "liveliest reactions."

207. *German White Book*, Doc. Nos. 349, 350, 352, 353, 354, 355, 357, 358, 359.

208. The following data are from *French Yellow Book*, Tournelle, French consul in Danzig, to Bonnet, Danzig, April 5, 1939, Doc. No. 91.

209. *Ibid.*, The coup was actually planned by Gauleiter Forster but its execution was prevented by the intervention of Senate President Greiser.

210. *Ibid.*, Tournelle to Bonnet, Danzig, April 5, 1939, Doc. No. 91. *Polish White Book*, Lipski to Beck, Berlin, April 6, 1939, Doc. No. 70. *French Yellow Book*, De Vaux Saint Cyr, French chargé d'affaires in Berlin, to Bonnet, Berlin, April 8, 1939, Doc. No. 95.

211. Some of these measures were: evacuation of rolling stock, barges, and wholesale merchandise; termination of credits; special export permits; currency devaluation. *French Yellow Book*, Tournelle to Bonnet, Danzig, April 5, 1939, Doc. No. 91.

212. *German White Book*, Graf, German consul general at Thorn, to Ribbentrop, Thorn, March 30, 1939, Doc. No. 354.

213. *Ibid.*, Noël to Bonnet, Warsaw, May 2, 1939, Doc. No. 17.

214. The relevant portion of the Polish constitution is Article 109.

215. *French Yellow Book*, Doc. No. 117.

216. *Ibid. Volksgruppenrecht* meant, according to the German terminology, that ethnic Germans everywhere had to give their first allegiance to the Führer, that is, they were not members of a minority but of the Reich.

217. For a description of this incident see *German White Book*, von Berchem, German consul at Lodz, to Ribbentrop, Lodz, May 15, 1939, Doc. No. 370. *ibid.*, May 18, 1939, Doc. No. 371.

218. *German White Book*, Petition of the Representatives of the German Minority to the President of the Polish Republic, May 12, 1939, Doc. No. 369.

219. Much of the "proof" of subversion is based on the Polish Ministry of Information's *German Fifth Column in Poland*. It consists largely of hearsay evidence, as the following examples demonstrate. In Deposition No. 412 Captain A.E. reported what Lieutenant B.Z., "now dead," had told him about a shortwave station that "was said to have been installed" by German agents. In Deposition No. 339 Captain Ch. "learned from an eyewitness" his evidence. Deposition No. 118 by Major R. told of an agent who "was killed at once; all he had on him was German money; he had no document." In Appendix II, the French consul, M. R. Chaulet, notes that "there was talk of" arrests for which "occasionally it was possible to obtain official confirmation." In a typical episode he said, "it was learnt" that a Protestant pastor and others had fought Polish troops. "The truth of this story was confirmed by what followed," that is, the pastor was arrested, "given a warm time by the colonel," and probably shot. On the other hand, Mader, East German historian, in *Spionage Generale*, pp. 318–319, cites only two instances in which ethnic Germans in Poland aided German sabotage teams.

Chapter V: Saxons and Swabians of Romania

1. The first king of Romania was Charles of Hohenzollern (1881–1914) who was invited to the throne of the Romanian principality in 1866.

2. Jean Morini-Comby, *Les Échanges Commerciaux Entre la France et les États Successeurs de l'Empire Austro-Hongrois* (Paris: Centre d'Études de Politique Étrangère, 1936), p. 46.

3. For the text of the Karlsburg Declaration see Theodore Schieder, ed., *Documents on the Expulsion of the Germans from Eastern-Central Europe*, 4 vols. (Bonn: Federal Ministry for Expellees, Refugees, and War Victims, 1961), III, 125.

4. For details see p. 108–109.

5. Dr. Theodore Grentrup, *Das Deutschtum an der Mittleren Donau in Rumanien und Jugoslawien* (Munster: Aschendorfsche Verlag, 1930), p. 14.

6. Anton Valentin, *Die Banater Schwaben* (Munich: Südostdeutsche Kulturwerk, 1959), p. 194.

7. Grentrup, *Deutschtum*, p. 5.

8. See pp. 108–109.

9. Meier, *The Jews in the Satellites*, p. 496.

10. *Ibid.*, pp. 499, 501.

11. *Brevariul statistic al Romanei* (Bucharest, 1939), pp. 53–60.

12. Alfred Bohmann, *Menschen und Grenzen*, 4 vols. (Koln: Verlag Wissenschaft und Politik, 1969), II, 112.

13. For the details of the history of Transylvania Saxons consult Friedrich Teutsch *Die Siebenburger Sachsen in Vergangenheit und Gegenwart* (Hermannstadt: W. Krafft Verlag, 1924), and Friedrich Muller-Langenthal, *Die Geschichte der Deutschen in Rumänien* (Hermannstadt: Verlag Krafft und Drotleff, 1938).

14. C. A. Macartney, *Hungary: A Short History* (Chicago: Aldine, 1962), p. 23.

15. Bálint Hóman and Gyula Szekfü, *Magyar Történet* [Hungarian History], 5 vols. (Budapest: Királyi Magyar Egyetemi Nyomda, 1936), V, 122.

16. According to the 1910 census there were 229,028 Lutherans out of 235,085 Saxons.

17. Lecture of Béla K. Király, "Renaissance and Reformation in Hungary," presented in Session 43 of the meeting of the American Historical Association in San Francisco, 1973.

18. Jászi, *Dissolution of the Habsburg Monarchy*, p. 332.

19. Hans Herrschaft, *Das Banat* (Berlin: Verlag Grenze und Ausland, 1942), p. 69.

20. This help was very considerable. The peasants were fitted out with four horses, one cow, agricultural tools, daily pay during the travel, free land, and three years' tax exemption. *Ibid.*, p. 81.

21. The full text of this petition is in Valentin, *Banater Schwaben*, pp. 142–146.

22. For the history of the German settlements in Bukovina see Franz Lang, ed., *Buchenland: Hundertfünfzig Jahre Deutschtum in der Bukowina* (Munich: Verlag des Südostdeutschen Kulturwerks, 1961).

23. *Ibid.*, p. 78.

24. Bohmann, *Menschen und Grenzen*, II, 112.

25. For the full text of the German demands see Lang, *Buchenland*, pp. 118–119.

26. Stephen Fischer-Galati, ed. *Romania* (New York: Praeger, 1957), p. 9.

27. On the other hand, the acquisition of Bessarabia created a continuous problem for Romanian-Soviet relations. For further details see R. W. Seton-Watson, *A History of the Romanians from Roman Times to the Completion of Unity* (Cambridge: University Press, 1934), Chapters 15–17; L. Y. Stavrianos, *The Balkans Since 1453* (New York: Holt, Rinehart & Winston, 1966), pp. 565–566; Komjathy, *Crises*, pp. 20–21.

28. Bohmann, *Menschen und Grenzen*, II, 108.

29. Although the German ethnic groups in Bessarabia became politically active only after 1930, the Saxon leader Fritz Fabritius began to keep closer contact with them and spread Nazi ideas among them.

30. The revisionists constantly demanded the revision of the Trianon Treaty, according to whose resolution Hungary lost Transylvania and part of the Bánát to Romania.

31. Seton-Watson, *Eastern Europe*, p. 279.

32. *Ibid.*, p. 320.

33. Grentrup, *Deutschtum*, pp. 313–317.

34. *Ost Dok. 16 Rum./90*, communication of Gerhard Fabritius, son of Fritz Fabritius, to the Bundesarchiv, p. 1.

35. Herrschaft, *Banat*, p. 199.

36. Bund was the popular name of the *Verband der Deutschen in Grossrumänien*.

37. Herrschaft, *Banat*, p. 198.

38. Valentin, *Banater Schwaben*, pp. 82–83.

39. Herrschaft, *Banat*, p. 199.

40. *Ost Dok. 16 Rum.*/90, p. 1.

41. Bohmann, *Menschen und Grenzen*, II, 149.

42. Calculated on the basis of *ibid.*, pp. 149–151.

43. Seton-Watson, *Eastern Europe*, p. 273.

44. Grentrup, *Deutschtum*, p. 51; Teutsch, *Siebenbürger Sachsen*, p. 304.

45. The expression "ruling church," according to the explanation of the Romanian patriarch, was not an indication of their desire to rule but a "simple reinstatement of the existing situation." Grentrup, *Deutschtum*, p. 106.

46. *Ibid.*

47. Patronage right: the landlord took care of the parish's material needs, providing land, giving donations for building maintenance, etc. For these services he had the right to be consulted when the bishop appointed the village priest and he had a seat in the church next to the altar, inside the communion rail.

48. Seton-Watson, *Eastern Europe*, p. 77.

49. The American Committee on the Rights of Religious Minorities, *Roumania Ten Years After* (Boston: Beacon, 1929), pp. 90–107. This report is slightly pro-minority. A strong defense of the Romanian government's and authorities' policy is in Charles Upson Clark, *United Roumania* (New York: Dodd, Mead, 1932), pp. 344–357.

50. The following information is quoted from the *Stimmen der Minderheiten*, December 1926, p. 342, and April 1927, p. 145.

51. Stavrianos, *Balkans*, p. 693. Juliu Maniu was the leader of the National Peasant party and prime minister on and off from 1928 to 1944.

52. Grentrup, *Deutschtum*, pp. 205–206.

53. It is interesting to note that while in Hungary this right of parents was considered by the ethnic German leaders as an instrument to "destroy Germandom," in Romania it was considered as a "beautiful dream" denied in practice by the authorities. *Ibid.*, pp. 226–227.

54. Calculated on the basis of *ibid.*, p. 244, and Teutsch, *Siebenbürger Sachsen*, p. 349.

55. Paikert, *Danube Swabians*, p. 251.

56. Jacobsen, *Steinacher*, p. 18.

57. The Iron Guard of Corneliu Codreanu was persecuted violently during the fall of 1933 by the Liberal government of Ion Duca. Prince Michel Sturdza, *The Suicide of Europe* (Boston: Western Islands, 1968), p. 55.

58. *Ost Dok. 16 Rum.*/90, p. 4; Herrschaft, *Banat*, p. 199.

59. Jacobsen, *Steinacher*, p. 559.

60. Herrschaft, *Banat*, p. 200.

61. Paikert, *Danube Swabians*, p. 252.

62. Schieder, *Documents*, III, pp. 35, 37.

63. *Ost Dok. 16 Rum.*/90, p. 4.

64. Herrschaft, *Banat*, p. 201.

65. *Ost Dok. 16 Rum.*/90, pp. 4, 12.

66. *Ibid.*, p. 1.

67. *Ost Dok. 16 Rum.*/90, pp. 4–8.

68. *Ibid.*

69. *Ost Dok. 16 Rum.*/17, conversation of Dr. Edouard Keintzel with Johann Wüscht, Koblenz, February 11, 1960, p. 13.

70. *Inland II A/B*, Nazi Ortsgruppen im Auslande, I, 226–231, April 30, 1934.

71. *Ost Dok. 16 Rum.*/90, p. 5.

72. *Ibid.*, p. 14.

73. *Ost Dok. 16. Rum.*/90, p. 9.

74. Stephen Fischer-Galati, "Fascism in Romania," in *Native Fascism in the Successor States, 1918–1945*, edited by Peter F. Sugar (Santa Barbara, Cal.: ABC-Clio, 1971), p. 113.

75. Valentin, *Banater Schwaben*, p. 84.

76. *DGFP*, C, V, unsigned memorandum, Bucharest, July 7, 1936, Doc. No. 440.

77. The literature on the Iron Guard is very extensive. The reader may consult the following works: Andreas Hillgruber, *Hitler, König Carol und Marschall Antonescu: Die Deutsch-Rumanische Beziehungen 1938–1944* (Wiesbaden: Franz Steiner Verlag, 1954); Nicholas Nagy-Talavera, *The Green Shirts and Others* (Stanford: Hoover Institution, 1970); H. L. Roberts, *Rumania: Political Problems of an Agrarian State* (New Haven, Conn.: Yale University Press, 1951); Prince Michel Sturdza, *The Suicide of Europe* (Boston: Western Islands, 1968); Peter Sugar, ed., *Native Fascism in the Successor States, 1918–1945* (Santa Barbara, Cal.: ABC-Clio, 1971).

78. The Iron Guard was the militant wing of the Legionary movement. Fischer-Galati, "Fascism in Rumania" in Sugar, *Native Fascism*, pp. 116–117.

79. Sturdza, *Suicide of Europe*, p. xvii.

80. Fischer-Galati, "Fascism in Rumania" in Sugar, *Native Fascism*, p. 116.

81. *Nazi Conspiracy and Aggression*, III, Annex II, 36.

82. *Ibid.*, pp. 37, 39.

83. *DGFP*, D, XI, Fabricius to Ribbentrop, Bucharest, November 1, 1940, Doc. No. 269.

84. *DGFP*, D, XII, von Killinger to Ribbentrop, Bucharest, February 26, 1941, Doc. No. 94.

85. *DGFP*, D, XII, Antonescu to Killinger, Bucharest, March 1, 1941, Doc. No. 118.

86. *DGFP*, D, XII, Weizsäcker to Himmler, Berlin, March 15, 1941, Doc. No. 169. See also Sturdza, *Suicide of Europe*, p. 40, and Walter Hagen, *Die Geheime Front* (Zurich, 1950), pp. 292–293, which explains the internment as reprisal for an escape attempt by Sima.

87. Hillgruber, *Hitler*, pp. 10–11.

88. Joseph Rothschild, *East Central Europe between the Two World Wars* (Seattle & London: University of Washington, 1974), p. 310.

89. *DGFP*, D, V, Fabricius to Ribbentrop, Bucharest, May 22, 1938, Doc. No. 205.

90. *Ibid.*, 1 n.

91. *DGFP*, D, V, Fabricius to Ribbentrop, Bucharest, September 30, 1938, Doc. No. 228.

92. *DGFP*, D, V, conversation between Göring and Carol, Leipzig, November 26, 1938, Doc. No. 257, enclosure.

93. Hillgruber, *Hitler*, p. 110.

94. *Ost Dok. 16 Rum.*/87 fol. 1, interview with Dr. W. Bruckner, former *Volksgruppenführer* in Romania, Koblenz, October 11, 1969, p. 14.

95. *DGFP*, D, V, memorandum by Twardowski, Berlin, November 23, 1938, Doc. No. 253.

96. *Inland II D 15 14/12*, Fabricius to Ribbentrop, Bucharest, December 14, 1938.

97. Hillgruber, *Hitler*, p. 110.

98. *Ost Dok. 16 Rum.*/90, p. 13.

99. *DGFP*, D, VI, report of Dr. Brückner, *Gauleiter* of the German community in Transylvania, Berlin, May 3, 1939, Doc. No. 319; *Ost Dok. 16 Rum.*/9 fol. 1.

100. *Ibid.*

101. *Inland II D,* Fabricius to Neurath, Bucharest, December 14, 1937, and 1938, Doc. Nos. 20/10.1 and 14/12.

102. *R 2/25083* fol. 1, memorandum of Dr. Lammers, Berlin, October 9, 1939. The ethnic Germans learned about this decision from the October 6, 1939, Reichstag speech of Hitler and it caused considerable unrest among them.

103. *DGFP,* D, X, Fabricius to Ribbentrop, Bucharest, June 28, 1940, Doc. No. 50.

104. *R 59* VoMi, Vol. 59, complaints of ethnic Germans, November 1940. For further ethnic German views see Schieder, *Documents,* III, Documentation, 187, passim.

105. *DGFP,* D, VI, conversation of Hitler with Gafencu, Berlin, April 19, 1939, Doc. No. 234; Vol. VII, Fabricius to Ribbentrop, Bucharest, September 2, 1939, Doc. No. 547.

106. Herrschaft, *Banat,* pp. 202–203.

107. *DGFP,* D, X, German-Romanian protocol, Vienna, August 30, 1940, Doc. No. 413.

108. For the text of Decree-Law No. 830/1940 see Schieder, *Documents,* III, 130–131.

109. *Inland II D* 62–15 3/91, VoMi to Ribbentrop, Berlin, September 3, 1941, complains that the arianization policy (which was intended to give Romanians more control over their own economy) was becoming more a pure romanization policy. Confiscated Jewish property could only be taken over by pure Romanians. VoMi asked the German embassy in Bucharest to back VD demands for equality on the basis of the Vienna protocol. *Inland II D* 62-15 20/1.1, Dr. Kurt Streitfeld to *Verbindungsstelle Bukarest,* December 10, 1941, also reports on anti-German laws.

110. *Ost Dok. 16 Rum./8* fol. 1.

111. Schieder, *Documents,* III, 38.

112. *Ost Dok. 16 Rum./90,* p. 17.

113. *Ost Dok. 16 Rum./9* fol. 1, statement of Wolfram A. Brückner; *DGFP,* D, VI, note of Twardowski, Berlin, May 3, 1939, Doc. No. 319; *Ost Dok. 16 Rum./72* fol. 1, letter of Franz Besinger, October 20, 1960, p. 2. Besinger's attempt to prevent Schmidt's dissolution of the "deutsche Nachbarschaft" brought him a warning from VoMi that there was still room for him in a concentration camp.

114. *Ost Dok. 16 Rum./87* fol. 1, interview with Dr. Wolfram Brückner, October 11, 1969, p. 20; *Ost Dok. 16 Rum./5* fol. 1, interview with Friedrich Cloos, November 27–29, 1963, pp. 24–25; *Ost Dok. 16 Rum./6* fol. 1, interview with Hans Ewald Frauenhoffer, January 22, 1961, p. 25.

115. *R 57 neu/1103-1, Press. Korrespondenz,* October 1940; *DGFP,* D, XI, unsigned letter of Fabricius to Luther, director of the department for German internal affairs, Bucharest, December 3, 1940, Doc. No. 445.

116. Paikert, *Danube Swabians,* p. 253.

117. For samples of such letters see *Inland D* VIII 213 g.

118. For the text of the school law see Schieder, *Documents,* III, Annex 5, 132–135.

119. *Ibid.,* p. 125.

120. *Ibid.,* Annex 5, p. 135.

121. *Ost Dok. 16 Rum./15b.* Schmidt forced the youth organization to accept the "new principles." With that step the organization lost all its cultural and spiritual goals and became a rude "pre-training camp for the SS."

122. Schieder, *Documents,* III, 56.

123. *R 57 neu/1103-1, Siebenbürgisch-Deutsches Tageblat,* October 3, 1940.

124. NO-1782, Killinger to Ribbentrop, February 26, 1941, quoted in Schieder, *Documents,* III, 56.

125. Schieder, *Documents,* III, 57.

126. For the full text of the SS agreement, see *ibid.,* Annex 8, pp. 148–151.

127. The sources concerning the number of *Volksdeutsche* recruited for the SS in Romania are highly contradictory. The lower figure given by Schieder, *Documents*, III, 60–61, is based on the official final report of SS General Berger. The higher figure quoted by Joseph B. Schechtman, *Postwar Population Transfers in Europe, 1945–1955* (Philadelphia: University of Pennsylvania, 1962), p. 269, is not documented. *Inland II D* 3/2, VoMi report of October 18, 1944, also gives the figure of 60,000.

128. Schieder, *Documents*, III, 60.

129. *Ibid.*, pp. 60, 61, 87n.

130. *Ibid.*, p. 61.

Chapter VI: Ethnic Germans of Yugoslavia

1. Bohmann, *Menschen und Grenzen*, II, 229.

2. Seton-Watson, *Eastern Europe*, pp. 217–230.

3. Bohmann, *Menschen und Grenzen*, II, 237. On the other hand, Ljubisa Stojkovíc and Milos Martić, *National Minorities in Yugoslavia* (Beograd: Publishing and Editing Enterprise "Jugoslavija," 1952), p. 6, states that the minority treaty was incorporated in the Yugoslavian constitution.

4. Treaty of Trianon with Hungary, St. Germain with Austria, Neuilly with Bulgaria.

5. Komjathy, *Crises*, pp. 83–85.

6. *DGFP*, D, IV, memorandum of Clodius, Berlin, January 7, 1938, Doc. No. 159.

7. Yugoslavian census of 1921.

8. Vojvodina is called in Hungarian Bácska, in German Batschka.

9. *R 57 neu*/1070-71.

10. At the time of dissolution the membership was 55,000. *Ibid.*

11. Grentrup, *Deutschtum*, p. 54.

12. Bohmann, *Menschen und Grenzen*, II, 229.

13. Grentrup, *Deutschtum*, p. 55.

14. Calculated on the basis of *ibid.*

15. *Ibid.*, p. 20.

16. Unless otherwise noted, the following description of German education in Yugoslavia is based on Bohmann, *Menschen und Grenzen*, II, 237–240.

17. *RAA 87*/Pol., Hoennig to Dollfuss, Belgrade, July 6, 1933.

18. *Ibid.*

19. Bohmann, *Menschen und Grenzen*, II, 238–239.

20. *Ibid.*, p. 246.

21. *Ibid.*, p. 243.

22. Johann Wüscht, *Ursachen und Hintergründe des Schicksals der Deutschen in Jugoslawien* (Kehl: author's ed., 1966), p. 11.

23. Grentrup, *Deutschtum*, p. 151.

24. Theodor Schieder, ed., *Dokumentation der Vertreibung der Deutschen aus Ost-Mitteleuropa*, 5 vols. (Bonn: Bundesministerium für Vertriebene, Flüchtlinge und Kriegsgeschädigte, 1956–61), V, 31E, 13n.

25. Grentrup, *Deutschtum*, p. 151.

26. Schieder, *Vertreibung*, V, 29E, 31E, 13n.

27. Jacobsen, *Steinacher*, p. 564.

28. Calculated on the basis of Schieder, *Vertreibung*, V, 15E.

29. *Annuaire statistique Yugoslavia*, 1936, pp. 88–89.

30. Schieder, *Vertreibung*, V, 15 E.

31. *Ibid*. This was also true in the area of Gottschee, *ibid*., p. 18 E, although elsewhere in Slovenia there were larger German holdings, which were the hardest hit by reform. *Ibid*. p. 31 E, 13 n.

32. Wüscht, *Ursachen*, p. 19.

33. Jacobsen, *Steinacher*, p. 564. See also Wüscht, *Beitrag*, p. 56.

34. Schieder, *Vertreibung*, V, 18 E.

35. Calculated on the basis of Johann Wüscht, *Slowenen und Deutsche* (Kehl: author's ed., 1975), p. 15.

36. Schieder, *Vertreibung*, V, 16 E and 4 n.

37. Calculated on the basis of Bohmann, *Menschen und Grenzen*, II, 234.

38. Moore, *Economic Demography*, p. 125.

39. Wüscht, *Ursachen*, p. 13.

40. *Inland II D* 6/2, 62–41, VoMi report, August 29, 1941, p. 3.

41. Schieder, *Vertreibung*, V, 16 E, 6 n.

42. *Ibid*., p. 16 E.

43. *Inland II D* 6/2, 62–41, p. 3.

44. Valentin, *Banater Schwaben*, p. 93.

45. Schieder, *Vertreibung*, V, 16 E.

46. Valentin, *Banater Schwaben*, p. 93.

47. *R 57 neu*/1009-2 No. 12855.

48. *R 57 neu*/1070-71.

49. *R 57 neu*/1070, I-66.

50. *R 57 neu*/1070-71.

51. *Ibid*.

52. *R 57 neu*/1070.

53. *Pressebericht*, March 1934, November 21, 1938, Schwäbisch-Deutsche Kulturbund, Neusatz.

54. *Ost Dok. 16 Jug.*/4 fol. 1, transcript of Awender's statement, September 29, 1958, p. 7.

55. *Berliner Tageblatt*, February 19, 1936.

56. *R 57 neu*/1070-71.

57. German-Hungarian trade relations had already been strengthened in 1933. *Wilhelmstrasse*, Gömbös-Hitler correspondence, April 1933, Doc. No. 3, 4.

58. *DGFP*, C, II, Ritter (AA) to embassy in Italy, March 12, 1934, Doc. No. 318.

59. Komjathy, *Crises*, pp. 59–61.

60. *DGFP*, C, III, Ulrich to the embassy in Italy, Berlin, June 21, 1934, Doc. No. 23.

61. John F. Montgomery, *Hungary, the Unwilling Satellite* (New York: Devin Adair, 1947), p. 66.

62. *DGFP*, C, III, Heeren to AA, Belgrade, October 22, 1934, Doc. No. 263.

63. *Ibid*., circular by Köpke, Berlin, October 25, 1934, Doc. No. 268.

64. *DGFP*, C, IV, Heeren to AA, Belgrade, July 3, 1935, Doc. No. 191.

65. Wüscht, *Beitrag*, p. 22.

66. *Ibid*., p. 42.

67. *Wilhelmstrasse*, Neurath memorandum, Berlin, November 17, 1934, Doc. No. 28, and Doc. Nos. 43, 56, 62, *passim*.

68. Wüscht, *Beitrag*, p. 28.

69. *DGFP*, D, IV, unsigned memorandum, Berlin, December 31, 1937, Doc. No. 156.

70. Wüscht, *Beitrag*, p. 22.

71. *DGFP*, D, IV, Doc. No. 156. Slovenia is called Slavonia in German.

72. *Ibid.*, conversation of Stojadinović and Hitler, Berlin, January 16, 1938, Doc. No. 163.

73. *DGFP*, D, V, memorandum of Political Division IV, Berlin, January 3, 1938, Doc. No. 158.

74. *R 57 neu*/1072-31, Jugoslaw-Deutsche Klub, Sarajevo, report of activities 1938–39, November 15, 1939, p. 5.

75. *Rundschreiben* No. 5, Schwäbisch-Deutsche Kulturbund, Neusatz, April 5, 1938.

76. *Pressebericht*, Schwäbisch-Deutsche Kulturbund, Neusatz, November 21, 1938.

77. Wüscht, *Beitrag*, p. 152.

78. *Ibid.*, p. 153.

79. *Ibid.*, pp. 155–156. Josef Beer, former assistant *Volksgruppenführer* in the Banat, in his statement to the Bundesarchiv (*Ost Dok. 16 Jug*/13, p. 38), says that Jankó and Altgayer were not appointed to their positions by VoMi or any other Reich authority. Rather, they were "entrusted with the leadership by a responsible election process." In light of the negotiations held in Graz, his statement seems to have been based on insufficient information.

80. *Ibid.*, pp. 22, 23.

81. *Deutsches Volksblatt*, November 30, 1940.

82. *R 57 neu*/1070-71.

83. Wüscht, *Beitrag*, p. 24.

84. *Ibid.*, pp. 154–155.

85. Macartney, *Eastern Europe*, p. 394.

86. Signed by Italy, Germany, and Japan on September 27, 1940, the Tripartite Pact was a mutual assistance treaty.

87. This information does not appear in the published documents. However, Macartney, *Eastern Europe*, p. 394, 2n, authenticates it.

88. *DGFP*, D, V, memorandum by Wiehl, director of the economic policy department, Berlin, February 9, 1939, Doc. No. 288.

89. Macartney, *Eastern Europe*, p. 394.

90. *DGFP*, D, VI, Wiehl memorandum, Berlin, June 29, 1939, Doc. No. 586.

91. *DGFP*, D, VII, memorandum by Kalisch, economic policy department, Berlin, August 17, 1939, Doc. No. 102.

92. *DGFP*, D, VI, Heeren to Ribbentrop, Belgrade, April 13, 1939, Doc. No. 192.

93. *DGFP*, D, IX, Heeren to Ribbentrop, Belgrade, April 27, 1940, Doc. No. 176.

94. *Ibid.*, conversation of Hitler with Cincar-Marković, Berghof, November 28, 1940, Doc. No. 417.

95. *DGFP*, D, XII, conversation between Hitler and Cvetković, Berghof, February 14, 1941, Doc. No. 48.

96. *Ibid.*, Führer's directive, headquarters, March 27, 1941, Doc. No. 223.

97. Wüscht, *Beitrag*, p. 155.

98. *Ibid.*, pp. 173, 180.

99. *Ibid.*, p. 181.

100. *Inland I* Ref. Partei: Politik Jugoslawien 1939–1940, Vol. II, report of Südostdeutsches Institut, Graz, June 10, 1940.

101. *Ibid.*, It was difficult in any case for ethnic Germans to become officers in the Yugoslav army. *Ost Dok. 16 Jug.*/8 fol. 1, report of Oscar Krewetsch, September 1947.

102. *Ibid.*, No. 5365/40, report of Baron's speech in Laibach, April 26, 1940.

103. *Ibid.*, pp. 176–178.

104. *Ost Dok. 16 Jug.*/169, report of Sepp Janko, January 14, 1959, p. 4.

105. Koehl, *RKFDV*, p. 29. For the German-Soviet agreement for the repatriation of *Volksdeutsche* see Schieder, *Documents*, III, 136–146.

106. Koehl, *RKFDV*, p. 50.

107. Quoted by Koehl in *ibid.*, p. 53.

108. *DGFP*, D, VIII, Heeren to Ribbentrop, Belgrade, October 22, 1939, Doc. No. 290.

109. *Inland I* Ref. Partei: Politik Jugoslawien 1939, Vol. I, report of Südostdeutsches Institut, October 27, 1939.

110. *DGFP*, D, VIII, Weizsäcker to Heeren, Berlin, October 28, 1939, Doc. No. 311.

111. *DGFP*, D, IX, Albrecht, deputy director of the legal department, to Heeren, Berlin, May 17, 1940, Doc. No. 258 and 1 n.

112. *Ost Dok. 16 Jug.*/145, essay of Franz Hamm, "journalist and politician," written for the Bundesarchiv.

113. *R 57 neu*/1070, 1–40, December 28, 1940.

114. *Inland I* Ref. Partei: Politik Jugoslawien 1939–1940, Nos. 5365/40, 6409/40, and one unnumbered report.

115. *Ost Dok. 16 Jug.*/2 fol. 1, Franz Hamm, "Politischer Situationsbericht vor 1941," September 2, 1958.

116. *Ost Dok. 16 Jug.*/37 fol. 1, Josef Beer, "Die Haltung der Volksgruppenführung während des Balkanfeldzuges," Stuttgart, January 2, 1958, pp. 2–3.

117. *Inland II g* 99, p. 27–28.

118. *Ost Dok. 16 Jug.*/147, statement of Hans Bock.

119. *Inland II g* 99, p. 67.

120. Dragisa N. Ristić, *Yugoslavia's Revolution of 1941* (Stanford, Cal.: Hoover Institution, 1966), p. 126.

121. Wüscht, *Beitrag*, p. 65.

122. *Ost Dok. 17*/8, p. 8.

123. *Ost Dok. 16 Jug.*/37 fol. 1, p. 7.

124. Wüscht, *Beitrag*, pp. 64–65.

125. *Ibid.*, p. 6.

126. De Jong, *Fifth Column*, pp. 229–230.

127. *Ibid.*, p. 232; Mader, *Spionage Generale*, p. 346.

128. *Ost Dok. 16 Jug.*/37 fol. 1, pp. 2–3, 7; Wüscht, *Beitrag*, p. 189.

129. Wüscht, *Beitrag*, pp. 193–196, referring to the "standard work of the communist military historian, Velimir Terzić," states that there were no sabotage actions at all. Wüscht failed to identify the book. He probably referred to Velimir Terrzić, *Jugoslavija u aprilskom ratu 1941* (Titograd, 1963).

130. Quoted in Wüscht, *Beitrag*, p. 191.

131. *DGFP*, D, XII, minutes of a conference regarding the situation in Yugoslavia, Berlin, March 27, 1941, Doc. No. 217.

132. Italian intelligence successfully imitated retreat orders of the Yugoslavian high command and caused the retreat of certain divisions without engagement. David Kahn, *The Codebreakers: The Story of Secret Writing* (London: Weidenfeld & Nicolson, 1967), p. 470.

133. Ruth Mitchell, *The Serbs Chose War* (Garden City, N.Y.: Doubleday, 1943), pp. 247–250.

134. *DGFP*, D, XII, Ribbentrop to consulate general at Zagreb, Berlin, March 31, 1941, Doc. No. 239.

135. *Ibid.*, Veesenmayer to Ribbentrop, Zagreb, April 11, 1941, Doc. No. 311.

136. *Ibid.*, circular of the foreign ministry, Berlin, May 17, 1941, Doc. No. 534.

137. *R 57 neu*/1072-12, *Stuttgarter Nationalsozialistische Kurier*, May 22, 1941.

138. For a description of conditions in the Batschka, see Chapter VII.

139. *R 57 neu*/1070-1, 42, *Volksdeutscher Ruf*, Vol. II, 1941.

140. *Ost Dok. 16 Jug.*/8, fol. 1, Oskar Krewetsch, "Die Donauschwaben," p. 36.

141. *Informative Handbook over Yugoslavia*, 1952, quoted in Wüscht, *Beitrag*, p. 158.

142. *Ost Dok. 17*/10, p. 18, 43.

143. *DGFP*, D, XIII, memorandum of Luther, director of department of internal affairs, Berlin, July 24, 1941, Doc. No. 149.

144. *Ibid.*, Grosskopp memorandum, Berlin, August 7, 1941, Doc. No. 187, enclosure.

145. *Ost Dok. 16 Jug.*/169, Sepp Janko's letter to Wüscht, January 14, 1959, pp. 3, 4,.

146. *Ost Dok. 16 Jug.*/8, fol. 1, p. 37.

147. *Inland II g* 99, Annex to D, II, 1331 g, Berlin, September 20, 1942.

148. *R 57 neu*/1072-14, 68.

149. *R 57 neu*/1071-27.

150. George H. Stein, *The Waffen SS: Hitler's Elite Guard at War, 1939–1945* (Ithaca, N.Y.: Cornell University, 1966), p. 197.

151. *Ibid.*, p. 169–170.

152. *Ost Dok. 16*/166 fol. 1, "Die Entstehungsgeschichte der Division Prinz Eugen," pp. 12–13.

153. Stein, *Waffen SS*, p. 170. How ineffective this recruitment was is demonstrated by the fact that in Belgrade by September 14, 1942, only thirty-seven *Volksdeutsche* had volunteered, and then only to the auxiliary police and not to the Waffen SS. *Inland II g* 99, report of SS Hauptsturmführer Hoselbarth, Athens, September 14, 1942.

154. *Inland II D*, VIII 354/42 g.

155. *Ost Dok. 16*/153, report of Wilhelmine Slavik, secretary of Keks, p. 10.

156. *Ost Dok. 16 Jug.*/8 fol. 1, p. 40.

157. Wüscht, *Beitrag*, pp. 102, 103.

158. Stein, *Waffen SS*, p. 173.

159. *Ost Dok. 17*/1, p. 135.

Chapter VII: Ethnic Germans in Hungary after 1938

1. *Inland II g*, *Volksdeutsche*, Ungarn, Appendix to Kult A 3270/II.

2. *Ibid.*

3. Lóránt Tilkovszky, "A Volksbund szerepe Magyarország második világháborús történetében" [The Role of the Volksbund in the History of Hungary during the Second World War], *Történelmi Szemle* [Historical Review], Budapest, XI (1968), No. 3, 296.

4. *Pester Lloyd*, Budapest, December 25, 1938.

5. Miklóklos Lackó, *Nyilasok Nemzetiszocialisták 1935–1944* [Arrow Cross Members and National Socialists] (Budapest: Kossuth Könyvkiadó, 1966), p. 165.

6. Tilkovszky, "Role of the Volksbund," p. 299.

7. *DGFP*, D, X, documents on the Second Vienna Award, Vienna, August 30, 1940, Doc. No. 413, pp. 584–587.

8. For an analysis of the German-Romanian protocol see p. 122.

9. *Inland II D* 4./2, 62–17, Pol. IV 2661g.

10. *Ibid.*

11. Schieder, *Documents*, II, 25, 55n.

12. This and the following calculations are based on Bohmann, *Menschen und Grenzen*, II, 29–30.

13. Experts on the *Volksdeutsche* question in the Reich estimated the number of Germans in Hungary as early as 1939 to be 700,000 if one disregarded the effects of magyarization. Walter Schneefuss, *Deutschtum in Süd-Ost-Europa* (Leipzig: Wilhelm Goldman Verlag, 1939), p. 142.

14. *R 57 neu*/1014-1, 1942.

15. Tilkovszky, "Role of the Volksbund," p. 301.

16. Quoted in *ibid.*, p. 302.

17. Testimony during the Basch trial before the Hungarian People's Court. *Magyar Nemzet*, Budapest, January 17, 1946.

18. *DGFP*, D, VI, conversation of Hitler and Gafencu, Berlin, April 19, 1939, Doc. No. 234.

19. *Ost Dok. 17*/22 fol. 1, Johann Wüscht, "Zusammenfassende Darstellung der Gemeindeschicksalsberichte aus Nord Siebenbürgen," p. 15.

20. *Ost Dok. 17*/23, No. 4, from Nord Siebenbürgen, pp. 7, 17.

21. *Ibid.*, p. 19.

22. *Ibid.*, p. 5. For a slightly different interpretation see *ibid.*, No. 25.

23. *Ost Dok. 16 Rum.*/17 fol. 1, report of Dr. Eduard Keintzel.

24. *Ost Dok. 17*/22 fol. 1, p. 37.

25. *Ost Dok. 16 Rum.*/17, interview by Johann Wüscht of Dr. Eduard Keintzel, Koblenz, February 11, 1960, p. 13.

26. Wüscht, *Beitrag*, p. 191.

27. *Ost Dok. 17*/13, Batschka, p. 5.

28. *Ost Dok. 17*/14, pp. 15, 104.

29. *Ost Dok. 16 Jug.*/37 fol. 1, Josef Beer, "Die Haltung der Volksgruppenführung während des Balkanfeldzuges," Stuttgart, January 2, 1958, p. 20.

30. *Inland II D* 6/2, 62–41, Heller of VoMi to Grosskopf in AA, Berlin, July 26, 1941. The following description is based on the VoMi proposal.

31. Tilkovszky, "Role of the Volksbund," p. 305.

32. The *Levente* organization provided premilitary training for the youth in Hungary.

33. *Inland D* VIII 142g, Jagow to Ribbentrop, Budapest, October 31, 1941, p. E227037.

34. *Inland D* VIII 144g, Weizsacker to Luther, Berlin, November 6, 1941.

35. *Ibid.*, pp. 6–7.

36. *Inland D* VIII 213g, Vorberg, officer of NSDAP in the Fuhrer's chancellory, Berlin, December 11, 1941.

37. *Ibid.*, Appendices 1, 2.

38. *Inland D* VIII 217g.

39. *Inland II D*, VIII 159g, Budapest, April 23, 1942, pp. E313886–88.

40. *Ost Dok. 17*/22 fol. 1, p. 26.

41. *Ost Dok. 17*/1, Johann Wüscht, "Zusammenfassende Darstellung der Gemeindeschicksalsberichte aus Jugoslawien," p. 135; *Ost Dok. 17*/13, Batschka, p. 13. There were no units in the Hungarian army organized on the basis of nationality.

42. Tilkovszky, "Role of the Volksbund," p. 305.

43. L. Tilkovszky, "Volksdeutsche Bewegung und ungarische Nationalitatenpolitik (1938–1941)," *Acta Historica*, Budapest, XII, Part II, 329.

44. Paikert, *Danube Swabians*, p. 128; Tilkovszky, "Role of the Volksbund," p. 306.

45. In two counties alone, Tolna and Baranya, the Fidelity Movement gained over 10,000 members. *Ibid.*, p. 128, 4n. Also see report of Basch to AA in *Inland II g* 327, Vol. 3/4, Waffen SS Ungarn, p. 3.

46. *Inland II D*, conversation between Ribbentrop and Himmler, Berlin, September 23, 1942, pp. E31856–57.

47. *Inland D* VIII 481, Appendix, pp. 1–7.

48. Wüscht, *Beitrag*, p. 106.

49. *Inland II g* 327, Vol. 3/4, p. 1.

50. Schieder, *Documents*, II, 33.

51. *Inland II D*, conversation of Ribbentrop and Himmler, p. E313856.

52. Schieder, *Documents*, II, 35, interprets the 20,000 men as volunteers but estimates those actually enrolled as much lower.

53. Paikert, *Danube Swabians*, p. 127.

54. This and the following figures are from *Inland II D* VIII 62-21/2, "Voranschlag 1942–43, Der Deutschen Volksgruppe in Ungarn."

55. *Wilhelmstrasse*, Kaltenbrunner to Himmler, Berlin, October 26, 1943, Doc. No. 559.

56. *Ibid.*, memorandum for the Hitler-Horthy negotiations, Berlin, March 1944, Doc. No. 578, 6n.

57. *Kis Ujság* Budapest, January 17, 1946.

58. For example, Feketehalmy Czeydner, Hungarian army corps commander, informed the German consul at Szeged about the secret punitive procedures the Hungarians wanted to use against those *Volksdeutsche* who volunteered for the Wehrmacht and the SS. He reported that "since he is also a *Volksdeutsche*." *Inland D* VIII 175, German consulate in Szeged to embassy in Budapest, November 17, 1941.

59. Feketehalmy Czeydner and his responsible staff members, for example, were given asylum when they fled before the upcoming military trial. Furthermore, Feketehalmy Czeydner was instantly promoted to SS *Obergruppenführer*. Paikert, *Danube Swabians*, p. 157, 1n. In light of this fact, Johann Wüscht's pamphlet, which tries to prove that the German authorities disapproved and condemned the massacre, seems unsupported. Johann Wüscht, *Die magyarische Okkupation der Batschka, 1941–1944* (Kehl: author's ed., 1975).

60. These alternatives are quoted in Lóránt Tilkovszky, "A Volksbund utolsó éve és a magyar nemzetiségpolitika" [The Last Year of the Volksbund and Hungarian Nationality Policy], *Századok*, Budapest, I (1973), 25–26.

61. *Ibid.*, p. 29.

62. *Inland II D* 677g, Veesenmayer, German ambassador to Hungary, to Ribbentrop, Budapest, April 14, 1944.

63. Tilkovszky, "Role of the Volksbund," p. 309.

Conclusion

1. *Die Bewegung*, Munich, February 8, 1938. The paper called these statistics "tragic fact" and described the "tremendous work" awaiting the Germans in *volkish* "matters" in order to stop this trend.

2. *R 57 neu*/1009-2, No. 12855.

3. Luža, *Transfer*, p. 68, 25n.

4. *R 142*/3, fol. 1.

5. Mader, *Spionage Generale*, p. 210.

6. *Ibid.*

7. *DGFP*, D, VII, Appendix F, "German Financial Support for Racial Germans Abroad," p. 611.

8. *Ibid.*

9. For example, supporting the Iron Guard press.

10. *Ost Dok. 16 Rum.*/9 fol. 1, p. 2.

11. *Ost Dok. 16 Rum.*/90, pp. 11, 13.

12. *Ost Dok. 16 Rum.*/90, p. 12.

13. *Ibid.*, p. 13.

14. *DGFP*, D, IX, Killinger to Ribbentrop, Bucharest, April 14, 1940, Doc. No. 116.

15. Schieder, *Documents*, III, 63.

16. *Ost Dok. 16 Jug.*/13, statement of Josef Beer, p. 39.

17. Stojković-Martić, *National Minorities*, p. 54.

18. Dr. Franz Anton Basch, "Der Deutsche in Ungarn," *Der Deutsche im Ausland*, Ser. No. 21 (Berlin: Auslandsabteilung des Zentralinstituts für Erziehung und Unterricht, 1934), p. 1.

19. For a description of the trial see the following daily papers: *Kis Ujság, Kossuth, Népe, Magyar Nemzet, Szabad Nép*, Budapest, January 17, 1946, *passim*.

20. Paikert, *Danube Swabians*, p. 128, 4n. Bohmann, *Menschen und Grenzen*, II, 49.

21. Stephen Kertesz, "The Expulsion of the Germans from Hungary: A Study in Postwar Diplomacy," *Review of Politics*, XV, No. 2, 179–208. For comparison it is interesting to note that American authorities considered 110,000 Japanese as security risks out of a total 138,834. William Petersen, *Japanese Americans* (New York: Random House, 1971), pp. 20, 67. It suggests that the war hysteria in the U.S. was, at least at the beginning of the war, greater than in postwar Hungary.

22. Annabring, *Das Ungarlandische Deutschtum*, p. 61.

23. Calculated on the basis of 1938 Hungarian census.

SELECTED BIBLIOGRAPHY

Primary Sources

Unpublished Documents

Bundesarchiv, Koblenz

R 2
R 57 neu
R 59
R 142

Ost Dok. 2
Ost Dok. 7
Ost Dok. 16 Rum.
Ost Dok. 16 Ung.
Ost Dok. 20

Archiv des Auswärtigen Amtes, Bonn

Inland II A/B
Inland II D
Inland II g

Staatsarchiv, Vienna

RAA

Published Documents

Annuaire statistique, Yugoslavia, 1936. Belgrade, 1937.
Board of Governors of the Federal Reserve System. *Banking and Monetary Statistics.* Washington, D.C., 1943.
Chief Bureau of Statistics of the Republic of Poland. *Concise Statistical Year-Book of Poland,* 1937. Warsaw: Chief Bureau of Statistics, 1937.
Czechoslovak Ministry of Information. *Statistical Yearbook of the Czechoslovak Republic, 1929.* Prague, 1930.
Documents on International Affairs, 1938. 3 vols. London: Oxford University, 1951.

German Foreign Office. *Documents on the Events Preceding the Outbreak of the War (German White Book)*. Berlin, 1939.

Her Majesty's Stationery Office. *Documents on British Foreign Policy, 1919–1939*. 2nd ser. Oxford: Her Majesty's Stationery Office, 1958.

International Military Tribunal. *Trial of the Major War Criminals before the International Military Tribunal*. 42 vols. Nuremberg, 1945–1949.

Képviselöházi napló [Parliamentary Records]. Budapest, 1933.

L'Office Central Royal Hongrois de Statistique. *Annuaire Statistique Hongrois*. Budapest: Athenaeum, 1933.

Lipski, Josef, *Diplomat in Berlin, 1933–1939*. Edited by Waclav Jedrzejewicz. New York: Columbia University, 1968.

Magyar Tudományos Akadémia Történettudományi Intézete. *A Wilhelmstrasse és Magyarország: Német Diplomáciai Iratok, 1933–1944* [The Wilhelm Street and Hungary: German Diplomatic Documents, 1933–1944]. Budapest: Kossuth, 1968.

Ministère des Affaires Étrangères. *Le Livre Jaune Français (French Yellow Book)*. Paris: Imprimerie Nationale, 1939.

Ministerstwo Spraw Zagranicznych. *Official Documents Concerning Polish-German and Polish-Soviet Relations, 1933–1939 (Polish White Book)*. London, 1940.

Morini-Comby, Jean. *Les Échanges Commerciaux Entre la France et les États Successeurs de l'Empire Austro-Hongrois*. Paris: Centre d'Études de Politique Étrangère, 1936.

Office of the United States Chief Counsel for Prosecution of Axis Criminality. *Nazi Conspiracy and Aggression*. 11 vols. Washington, D.C.: U.S. Government Printing Office, 1948.

Polish Ministry of Information. *Concise Statistical Year-Book of Poland, September 1939–June 1941*. Glasgow: University Press, 1941.

Polish Ministry of Information. *The German Fifth Column in Poland*. London: Hutchinson, 1940.

United States Department of State. *Documents on German Foreign Policy, 1918–1945*, Ser. C, D. Washington, D.C.: U.S. Government Printing Office, 1957.

United States Department of State. *Foreign Relations of the United States*. Washington, D.C.: U. S. Government Printing Office, 1935–1957.

Diaries, Memoirs, Eyewitness Accounts

Burckhardt, Carl J. *Meine Danziger Mission, 1937–1939*. Munich: George D. W. Callweg, 1960.

Gamelin, General Maurice. *Servir*. 2 vols. Paris: Plon, 1946.

Henderson, Sir Nevile. *Failure of a Mission*. New York: Putnam, 1940.

Sturdza, Prince Michel. *The Suicide of Europe*. Boston: Western Islands, 1968.

Weizsäcker, Ernst von. *Memoirs*. London: Gollancz, 1951.

General Works

Albrecht-Carrié, René. *A Diplomatic History of Europe since the Congress of Vienna*. New York: Harper & Row, 1958.

Basch, Antonin. *The Danube Basin and the German Economic Sphere*. New York: Columbia University Press, 1943.

Bohmann, Alfred. *Menschen und Grenzen*. 4 vols. Köln: Verlag Wissenschaft und Politik, 1969–1975.

Bonnefous, Edouard. *Histoire Politique de la Troisième République*. 6 vols. Paris: Presses Universitaires de France, 1962.

Bretton, Henry L. *Stresemann and the Revision of Versailles*. Stanford, Cal.: Stanford University, 1953.

Bullock, Alan. *Hitler: A Study in Tyranny*. New York: Harper Torch, 1964.

Carnegie Endowment for International Peace. *International Conciliation*. New York, 1926.

Deutsch, Harold C. *Hitler and His Generals*. Minneapolis: University of Minnesota, 1974.

De Jong, Louis. *The German Fifth Column in the Second World War*. Chicago: University of Chicago, 1956.

Endiger, Lewis J. *German Exile Politics*. Berkeley, Cal.: University of California, 1956.

Farago, Ladislas. *The Game of the Foxes*. New York: McKay, 1971.

Gatzke, Hans W. *Stresemann and the Rearmament of Germany, 1924–1928*. New York: Bookman, 1963.

Grentrup, Dr. Theodor. *Das Deutschtum an der Mittleren Donau in Rumänien und Jugoslawien*. Münster: Aschendorfsche Verlag, 1930.

Habsburg, Otto. *Döntés Európáról*]Decision about Europe]. Munich: Amerikai Magyar Kiadó, 1955.

Hale, Oron F. *The Captive Press in the Third Reich*. Princeton, N.J.: University Press, 1964.

Herrschaft, Hans. *Das Banat*. Berlin: Verlag Grenze und Ausland, 1942.

Hitler, Adolf. *Mein Kampf*. Boston: Houghton Mifflin, 1943.

Jacobsen, Hans-Adolf. *Nationalsozialistische Aussenpolitik, 1933–1938*. Frankfurt: Alfred Metzner, 1968.

Jacobsen, Hans-Adolf, ed. *Hans Steinacher, Bundesleiter des VDA, 1933–1937: Erinnerungen und Dokumente*. Boppard: Harald Boldt Verlag, 1970.

Jászi, Oscar. *The Dissolution of the Habsburg Monarchy*. Chicago: University of Chicago, 1961.

Kahn, David. *The Codebreakers: The Story of Secret Writing*. London: Weidenfeld & Nicolson, 1967.

Komjáthy, Anthony Tihamér. *The Crises of France's East Central European Diplomacy, 1933–1938*. Boulder, Col.: East European Quarterly, 1976.

Koehl, Robert L. *RKFDV: German Resettlement and Population Policy, 1939–1945.* Cambridge, Mass.: Harvard University, 1957.

Kruck, Alfred. *Geschichte des Alldeutsche Verbandes, 1890–1939.* Wiesbaden: Franz Steiner, 1954.

League of Nations. *The League of Nations and Minorities.* Geneva: Secretariat of the League of Nations, 1923.

League of Nations. *Ten Years of World Cooperation.* Geneva: Secretariat of the League of Nations, 1930.

Leverkuehn, Paul. *German Military Intelligence.* London: Weidenfeld & Nicolson, 1954.

Levin, N. Gordon, ed. *The Zionist Movement in Palestine and World Politics, 1880–1918,* Lexington, Mass.: Heath, 1974.

Mader, Julius. *Hitler's Spionage Generale Sagen Aus.* Berlin: Verlag der Nation, 1971.

Mallory, Walter H., ed. *Political Handbook of the World: Parliaments, Parties, and Press, 1936.* New York: Harper, for Council on Foreign Relations, 1936.

Mann, Golo. *The History of Germany since 1789.* New York: Praeger, 1968.

Meier, Peter, and B.D. Weinryb, E. Duschinsky, N. Sylvrain. *The Jews in the Soviet Satellites.* Syracuse, N.Y.: University Press, 1953.

Moore, W. E. *Economic Demography of Eastern and Southern Europe.* Geneva: Secretariat of the League of Nations, 1945.

Mosse, George L. *The Crisis of German Ideology.* New York: Grosset & Dunlap, 1964.

Paikert, G. C. *The Danube Swabians.* The Hague: Martinus Nijhoff, 1976.

Rothschild, Joseph. *East Central Europe between the Two World Wars.* Seattle & London: University of Washington, 1974.

Royal Institute of International Affairs. *Survey of International Affairs, 1933–1938.* Edited by Arnold Toynbee. London: Oxford University, 1934–1951.

Schechtman, Joseph B. *Postwar Population Transfers in Europe, 1945–1955.* Philadephia: University of Pennsylvania, 1962.

Schieder, Theodor, ed. *Dokumentation der Vertreibung der Deutschen aus Ost-Mitteleuropa.* 5 vols. Bonn: Bundesministerium fur Vertriebene, Fluchtlinge und Kriegsgeschadigte, 1956–61.

————— *Documents on the Expulsion of the Germans from Eastern-Central Europe* (Abridged English translation of the above collection) 4 vols. Bonn, 1961.

Schlabrendorf, Fabian von. *The Secret War against Hitler.* New York: Pitman, 1965.

Schneefuss, Walter. *Deutschtum in Sud-Ost Europa.* Leipzig: Wilhelm Goldmann Verlag, 1939.

Seton-Watson, Hugh. *Eastern Europe between the Wars, 1918–1941.* New York: Harper Torch, 1967.

Stavrianos, L. Y. *The Balkans since 1453*. New York: Holt, Rinehart & Winston, 1966.
Stein, George H. *The Waffen SS: Hitler's Elite Guard at War, 1939–1945*. Ithaca, N.Y.: Cornell University, 1966.
Sugar, Peter F., ed. *Native Fascism in the Successor States, 1918–1945*. Santa Barbara, Cal.: ABC-Clio, 1971.
Thimme, Annelise. *Gustav Stresemann*. Hanover, 1957.
Thurner, Eugen. *Handbuch der Kulturgeschichte*. Konstanz, 1963.
Turner, Henry Ashby, Jr. *Stresemann and the Politics of the Weimar Republic*. Princeton, N. J.: Princeton University, 1963.
Vajna, Viktor, and István Nádai. *Hadtörténelem*. Budapest: Stádium, 1935.
Wandycz, Piotr S. *France and Her Eastern Allies, 1919–1925*. Minneapolis: University of Minnesota, 1962.
Weinberg, Gerhard L. *The Foreign Policy of Hitler's Germany*. Chicago: University of Chicago, 1970.
Ziemer, Gerhard, and Hans Wolf. *Wandervögel und Freideutsche Jugend*. Bad Godesberg: Voggenreiter, 1962.

Czechoslovakia

Beneš, Eduard. *Munich*. Paris: Éditions Stock, 1969.
Bilek, Bohumil. *Fifth Column at Work*. London: Trinity Press, 1945.
Bruegel, J. W. *Czechoslovakia before Munich: The German Minority Problem and British Appeasement Policy*. Cambridge: University Press, 1973.
Luža, Radomír. *The Transfer of the Sudeten Germans*. New York: New York University, 1964.
Mamatey, Victor S., and Radomír Luža, eds. *A History of the Czechoslovak Republic, 1918–1942*. Princeton, N.J.: Princeton University, 1973.
Rasin, Alois. *Financial Policy of Czechoslovakia during the First Year of Its History*. Oxford, 1923.
Rectors of the Czechoslovak Universities. *Czech School Facilities under the Austrian Government and German School Facilities under the Czech Government*. Prague, 1938.
Starkbaum, Dr. Josef, and Dr. H. C. Emanuel Reichenberger. *Heimat der Sudetendeutschen*. Vienna: Volkstum Verlag, 1967.
Stransky, Dr. R. *The Educational and Cultural System of the Czechoslovak Republic*. Prague: Vladimir Zikes, 1939.
Vorbach, Kurt. *200,000 Sudetendeutsche Zuviel!* Munich: Deutschen Volksverlag, 1936.
Wiskemann, Elizabeth. *Czechs and Germans: A Study of the Struggle in the Historical Province of Bohemia and Moravia*. London: Oxford University, 1938.

Hungary

Annabring, Mathias. *Das Ungarländische Deutschtum.* 2 vols. Stuttgart: Südoststimmen, 1952.

Helle, Ferencz. *A magyar-német müvelödési kapcsolatok története* [The History of the Hungarian-German Cultural Relations]. Budapest, 1942.

Hóman, Bálint, and Gyula Szekfü. *Magyar Történet* [Hungarian History]. 5 vols. Budapest: Királyi Magyar Egyetemi Nyomda, 1963.

Kovács, Alajos. *A németek helyzete Csonka-Magyarországon a statisztika megvilágitásában* [The Situation of Germans in Mutilated Hungary in Light of Statistics]. Budapest, 1936.

Lackó, Miklós. *Nyilasok Nemzetiszocialistak 1935-1944* [The Arrow Cross and National Socialists]. Budapest: Kossuth Könyvkiadó, 1966.

Macartney, C. A. *Hungary and Her Successors.* Oxford: Oxford University, 1937.

Macartney, C. A. *Hungary: A Short History.* Chicago: Aldine, 1962.

Macartney, C. A. *October Fifteenth.* 2 vols. Edinburgh: University Press, 1961.

Málnási, Ödön. *A Magyar Nemzet Öszinte Története* [The Honest History of the Hungarian Nation]. Munich: Mikes Kelemen Kor, 1959.

Montgomery, John F. *Hungary, The Unwilling Satellite.* New York: Devin Adair, 1947.

Pukánszky, Béla. *Német polgárság magyar földön* [German Petty Bourgeoisie in Hungary]. Budapest, 1940.

Sulyok, Dezsö. *A Magyar Tragédia* [Hungarian Tragedy]. Newark, N.J.: author's ed., 1954.

Wüscht, Johann. *Die magyarische Okkupation der Batschka, 1941-1944.* Kehl: author's ed., 1975.

Poland

Aurich, Peter. *Der Deutsch-Polnische September 1939: Eine Volksgruppe zwischen den Fronten.* Munich, 1969.

Bierschenk, Theodor. *Die deutsche Volksgruppe in Polen, 1934-1939.* Würzburg: Holzner Verlag, 1954.

Breyer, Richard. *Das Deutsche Reich und Polen, 1932-1937: Aussenpolitik und Volksgruppenfragen.* Würzburg: Holzner Verlag, 1955.

Cienciala, Anna M. *Poland and the Western Powers, 1938-1939.* London: Routledge & Kegan Paul, 1968.

Denne, Ludwig. *Das Danzig Problem in der Deutschen Aussenpolitik, 1934-1939.* Bonn: Ludwig Rohrscheid Verlag, 1959.

Fechner, Helmuth. *Deutschland und Polen, 1772-1945.* Würzburg: Holzner Verlag, 1964.

Marsch der Deutschen in Polen: Deutsche Volksgenossen im ehemaligen Polen, Berichten uber Erlebnisse in den Septembertagen 1939. Berlin, 1940.

Polonsky, Anthony. *Politics in Independent Poland, 1921-1939*. Oxford: Clarendon, 1972.

Rauschning, Hermann. *The Conservative Revolution*. New York: Putnam, 1941.

Rose, William John. *The Drama of Upper Silesia*. Brattleboro, Vt: Stephen Daye, 1935.

Wojciechowski, Marian, and R. Breyer. *Das Deutsche Reich und Polen 1932-1937: Aussenpolitik und Volksgruppenfragen*. Würzburg, 1955.

Romania

American Committee on the Rights of Religious Minorities. *Roumania Ten Years After*. Boston: Beacon Press, 1929.

Clark, Charles Upson. *United Roumania*. New York: Dodd, Mead, 1932.

Fischer-Galati, Stephen, ed. *Romania*. New York: Praeger, 1957.

Herrschaft, Hans. *Das Banat*. Berlin: Verlag Grenze und Ausland, 1942.

Lang, Franz, ed. *Buchenland: Hundertfünfzig Jahre Deutschtum in der Bukowina*. Munich: Verlag des Südostdeutschen Kulturwerks, 1961.

Oprea, I. M. "Nicolae Titulescu's Diplomatic Activity," in *Bibliotheca Historica Romaniae*, XXII, Bucharest (1968).

Seton-Watson, R. W. *A History of the Romanians from Roman Times to the Completion of Unity*. Cambridge: University Press, 1934.

Valentin, Anton. *Die Banater Schwaben*. Munich: Südostdeutscher Kulturbund, 1959.

Yugoslavia

Mitchell, Ruth. *The Serbs Choose War*. Garden City, N.Y.: Doubleday, Doran, 1943.

Ristic, Dragisa N. *Yugoslavia's Revolution of 1941*. Stanford, Cal.: Hoover Institution, 1966.

Stojković, Ljubisa, and Milos Martić. *National Minorities in Yugoslavia*. Beograd: Publishing and Editing Enterprise "Jugoslavija," 1952.

Wüscht, Johann. *Beitrag zur Geschichte der Deutschen in Jugoslawien*. Kehl: author's ed., 1966.

Wüscht, Johann. *Slowenen und Deutsche*. Kehl: author's ed., 1975.

Wüscht, Johann. *Ursachen und Hintergründe des Schicksals der Deutschen in Jugoslawien*. Kehl: author's ed., 1966.

Periodicals and Newspapers

Arató, Endre, "A Volksbund és a Harmadik Birodalom" [The Volksbund and the Third Reich], *Valóság*, IV, No. 1 (1961), 88–90.

Cesar, Gardslaw, and Bohenrich Cerny. "Die Deutsche Irredenta und die Henleinleute in der CSR in den Jahren 1930–1938," *Ceskoslovensky Capis Historicky*, No. 1 (1962), pp. 1–17.

Jedrzejewicz, Waclaw, "The Polish Plan for a 'Preventive War' against Germany in 1933," *The Polish Review*, XI, No. 1 (Winter 1966), pp. 62–91.

Kertész, Stephen. "The Expulsion of the Germans from Hungary: A Study in Postwar Diplomacy," *Review of Politics*, XV, No. 2, 179–208.

Király, Béla K. "Renaissance and Reformation in Hungary," lecture at the annual meeting of American Historical Association, San Francisco, 1973.

Kohnert, Hans. "Agrarreformstatistik aus Polen," *Nation und Staat*, XII (1939), 618–619.

Tilkovszky, Lóránt. "A Volksbund utolsó éve és a magyar- nemzetiség-politika" [The Last Year of the Volksbund and Hungarian Nationality Policy], *Századok*, I (1973), 25–26.

Tilkovszky, Lóránt. "Volksdeutsche Bewegung und ungarische Nationalitätenpolitik (1938–1941)," *Acta Historica*, XII, Part II, 329.

Tilkovszky, Lóránt. "A Volksbund szerepe Magyarország második világháborus történeteben" [The Role of the Volksbund in the History of Hungary during the Second World War], *Történelmi Szemle* [Historical Review], XI (1968), No. 3, 296.

Weinberg, Gerhard L., "The May Crisis, 1938," *The Journal of Modern History*, XXIX (September, 1957).

Budapesti Hirlap, Budapest.

Die Bewegung, Munich.

Dresdener Anzeiger.

Heidelberge Tageblatt.

Kis Ujság, Budapest.

Kossuth Népe, Budapest.

Magyar Nemzet, Budapest.

Münchner Nachricht.

Index

Yugoslavia: agriculture, trade, and commerce, 128 *passim*; associations, religions, and culture, 126 *passim*; cooperation with Reich, 136 *passim*; effect of Reich policy on ethnic Germans, 161; events to 1934, 125; move to right, 133 *passim*; Prinz Eugen Division, SS, 144, 145; reorganization of *Volksgruppe*, 143, 144; *Schwabisch-Deutsche Kulturbund*, 68, 126, 127, 130 *passim*; *Volksdeutsche* participation in war, 140 *passim*